SOROS ON SOROS

Staying Ahead of the Curve

GEORGE SOROS

with
Byron Wien and Krisztina Koenen

John Wiley & Sons, Inc.
New York • Chichester • Brisbane • Toronto • Singapore

Copyright © 1995 by George Soros
Published by John Wiley & Sons, Inc.

Library of Congress Cataloging-in-Publication Data:

Soros, George.
    Soros on Soros : staying ahead of the curve / George Soros.
        p.   cm.
    ISBN 0-471-12014-6 (cloth : alk. paper) ISBN 0-471-11977-6
(pbk. : alk. paper)
    1. Soros, George—Interviews.   2. Soros, George—Political and
social views.   3. Capitalists and financiers—Interviews.
4. Investments.   I. Title.
HG172.S63A5   1995
332.6′9092—dc20
[B]   95-12861

To all the people, in and out of my foundation network,
who are working to create an open society.

PREFACE

This book has its origin in an extended interview conducted by Krisztina Koenen, a journalist working for the *Frankfurter Allgemeine Zeitung* and published in German. Originally John Wiley & Sons wanted to publish an English translation but I decided to embark on an entirely new version. I found the interview format congenial and the project grew into a major undertaking.

The outcome is a summing up of my life's work: The first part deals with my personal background and my career as a fund manager, in interviews conducted by Byron Wien, an old friend who is the investment strategist for Morgan Stanley. The second part deals with my political views and my career as a philanthropist in interviews with Krisztina Koenen; and the concluding part with the philosophy which guided me both in making and spending money, again with Byron Wien. I reworked the material until it became like a Socratic dialogue. I tried to explain who I am and what I stand for.

The philosophy is not about money, it is about the human condition. I have used financial markets as a laboratory for testing my theories. I also got an opportunity to put my ideas to the test in connection with the collapse of the Soviet empire. I believe I have something important to say. It is also important that I should be able to communicate it because my belief in what I call "open society" does not make sense unless it is widely shared. As I finish the book, I feel I have succeeded.

My editor, Myles Thompson, wanted to steer me towards an audience interested in financial markets and I did not resist him unduly because I am very interested in financial markets myself—especially at the present juncture when dynamic disequilibria abound. But I am aiming at a wider audience. I very much hope that those not interested in the financial markets will also find the book worth reading.

I have shown the manuscript to the following people: Ken Anderson, Stan Druckenmiller, Dan Eule, Arminio Fraga, Sue Frunzi, Gary Gladstein, Karen Greenberg, Bohdan Hawrylyshyn, Julia Jurys, Ari Korpivaara, Annette Laborey, Aryeh Neier, Bill Newton Smith, Istvan Rev, Nick Roditi, Susan Soros, Paul Soros, Jonathan Soros, Miklos Vasarhelyi, Bill Zabel, John Zwaanstra.

I want to thank them for their comments but I take sole responsibility for the contents of the book. I would like to thank Emily Loose for her editorial assistance, as well as Frances Abouzeid, Sheila Otner, and Shawn Pattison for their help.

GEORGE SOROS

July 1995

Contents

Contents

weak dollar • Excessive volatility with no constituency to
deal with it • Regulating derivatives

Giving away millions in Europe • The motivation behind
the philanthropy • The Open Society Fund •
Philanthropy with a policy purpose • A commitment to
South Africa • Supporting Eastern European dissidents •
Foundation reach into Hungary • Balancing Foundation
efforts and Quantum Fund activity • Foundations in 25
countries • Notable successes and huge failures •
Adapting to the changing political climate • The danger of
becoming too strong • The Soros Foundation of today •
Central European University • Conflicts of interest in
Eastern Europe • Redefining Foundation purpose

The economic future of Eastern Europe • Optimism for
Central Europe • The Soviet demise • The future of Russia
• Ukraine and Macedonia • Poland as a model for economic
growth and social reform • Observing the process of change
• The fate of Romania • Redesigning Western assistance
programs • Changing the course of history in Eastern
Europe—marginally

Switching focus • Adjusting to the new world order • A
disappointing response to the crisis in Bosnia • An amended
version of freedom • Open society versus laissez faire • The

coming disintegration of Europe • An identity crisis for the U.S. • The failure of the United Nations and NATO • The role of the U.N. in today's conflicts • A looming crisis • The collapse of international financial markets • The meaning of money • Exploring the drug debate • Project on death • Having too much power

Part One

Investing and Global Finance

with
Byron Wien

1

THE INVESTOR

There's a story going around Wall Street these days that opposite Mount Rushmore, there's another mountain, and it's devoted to the world's greatest money managers. Two figures have been chiseled into the face of the mountain, Warren Buffett and your own.

You couldn't find two more dissimilar figures.

Do you think you deserve to be considered one of the world's greatest money managers?

That's a good question. I have to recognize that I am, in fact, up there. How long I will stay up there is another question.

You're not as active in money management today as you have been in the past.

That's why I have a chance to stay up there.

The Quantum Fund has been one of the most successful investment entities since the beginning of time. One thousand dollars invested in 1969 would be worth well over two million dollars today if dividends could have been reinvested. What is so special about Quantum Fund? Is there more to it than your investment

skills? Is there something special about the structure that has made it so successful?

Yes. It is a rather unusual structure, because we use leverage. We position the fund to take advantage of larger trends—we call this macro-investing—and then, within those larger trends we also pick stocks and stock groups. So we operate on many different levels. I think it is easiest if you think of a normal portfolio as something flat or two-dimensional, as its name implies. Our portfolio is more like a building. It has a structure; it has leverage. Using our equity capital as the base, we construct a three-dimensional structure that is supported by the collateral value of the underlying securities. I am not sure whether I am making myself clear. Let's say we use our money to buy stocks. We pay 50 percent in cash and we borrow the other 50 percent. Against bonds we can borrow a lot more. For $1,000 we can buy at least $50,000 worth of long-term bonds. We may also sell stocks or bonds short: we borrow the securities and sell them without owning them in the hope of buying them back later cheaper. Or we take positions—long or short—in currencies or index futures. The various positions reinforce each other to create this three-dimensional structure of risks and profit opportunities. Usually two days—one up day and one down day—are sufficient to tell us how the fund is positioned.

So there are several differences between your fund and an ordinary portfolio. One is that you use leverage. Two is that you invest in a lot of different asset classes. You invest in currencies as well as other financial assets. Three, you sell short as well as go long in those different asset classes. Isn't that correct?

Yes.

You believe your various positions give your portfolio a risk profile that reflects what you call your "macro" view.

Right.

4

And also derivatives play a role. Do they not?

Less than people suppose. We do use index futures, sometimes for hedging purposes, sometimes to gain market exposure either on the long or the short side. We don't use options very much because we don't know how to fit them into the risk exposure we are willing to live with. When you buy options, you're paying the professionals a hefty premium for providing you with a leverage that we can create cheaper ourselves by borrowing against our securities. Admittedly, there is more risk in taking an actual position in a stock and borrowing against it than in buying an option, but we can match our risks better when we are dealing with actual exposure than when we have options. When you sell options, you get paid for assuming risk. That can be a profitable business, but it does not mix well with the risks inherent in a leveraged portfolio, therefore we rarely write options. It just doesn't fit into our three-dimensional structure—it kind of sticks out of the window and threatens to topple the building. That's why we have relatively little use for options.

Are you taking more risk now than you did when the Fund was smaller?

No. I would say we take substantially less risk. In the earlier days, we were leveraging to the hilt.

What does that mean? For a $100 million, how much were you borrowing on average?

That is a meaningless figure because $100 million invested in Treasury bills has a much different risk factor than $100 million invested in 30-year bonds. We try to simplify things. We don't have a real or scientific way to measure risk. People who are in the derivative business have very elaborate risk calculations. We are amateurs. We live in the Stone Age. Deliberately so.

In the last twenty years, there has been a lot of progress made in measuring risk for investment portfolios. Why don't you employ these scientific quantitative methods?

Because we don't believe in them. They're generally constructed on the assumption of efficient market theory. That theory is in conflict with my theory of imperfect understanding and reflexivity. I think that those methods work 99 percent of the time, but they break down 1 percent of the time. I am more concerned with that 1 percent. I see a certain systemic risk that cannot be encapsulated in those assumptions that generally assume a continuous market. I am particularly interested in discontinuities and I find that those measurements are of little use to me.

But we do try to simplify rather than complicate. For instance, when we deal with interest rate exposure, we reduce everything to the equivalence of a 30-year bond. So we convert even a T-bill to a 30-year bond equivalent. And we are willing to invest our capital along three axes: we have a stock exposure, we have an interest rate exposure, and we have a currency exposure. Our exposure varies between plus and minus 100 percent along each axis. But some of these risks reinforce each other; therefore, we are rarely willing to risk 100 percent of our equity along any one of these axes.

Occasionally, there is a fourth axis because we do from time to time take positions in commodities. Recently we have added a fifth dimension. I set up a new fund called "Quantum Industrial Holdings," which makes industrial investments; it establishes actual ownership or part ownership of enterprises. The fund reserves 20 percent of its assets for macro investing of the same kind as we do in Quantum Fund, and actually that 20 percent is sufficient to provide collateral or buying power for a macro structure that covers the entire Fund. The rest is reserved for industrial investments. And then the unused portion of the Fund, that is, monies that are reserved for industrial investment but not actually spent are temporarily invested in Quantum Group shares.

6

This is a new concept that might lead to an even more efficient use of money than the Quantum Fund itself.

Obviously, leverage has been critical to your success. If you hadn't used leverage, how much would the $1,000 have grown to? In other words, how much of the profit of the Quantum Fund over the years has been attributable to leverage?

That's another question I cannot answer. The Fund would have been a totally different animal because many positions we take make sense only because we use leverage. If it couldn't be leveraged, we wouldn't be making that particular investment. Leverage gives us much greater flexibility than if we operated with a two-dimensional portfolio. Managers of bond funds, if they have a positive view of interest rates, can lengthen the maturity of their portfolio to at most, 15 years. When they have a negative view, they can keep the average maturity very short. We have much greater freedom to maneuver. When we are bearish, we can sell short; when we are bullish, we don't have to buy long maturities; we can buy short maturities but use a lot of leverage.

Is that more effective?

It can be. I can give you a recent example: At the beginning of this year, 1995, if you were bullish on interest rates, as we were, that is, if you believed that the Fed may have stopped tightening, you could make a lot more money in short maturities and relatively little in the long maturities because the short end performed much better than the long end.

Because the yield curve changed.

That's right. We do from time to time go into what is called a *yield curve trade,* that is, match long and short maturities against each other. That is done by many professionals who want to limit their risk. But we don't do too many yield curve trades because we usually take a view on the general direction of interest rates; which end of the bond market to play in is just an additional refinement. By contrast, many professionals do nothing but trade one kind of maturity against another.

A lot of work has been done analyzing the success of money managers and it's been determined that asset allocation accounts for at least 80 percent of portfolio results. Stock selection and other factors are only about 20 percent. Do you have a view on asset allocation?

No. I think what you say is probably correct because we make most of our money in "macro" and macro is the three-dimensional equivalent of asset allocation. It is more efficient because in a two-dimensional portfolio you can allocate only a portion of your equity to any particular investment concept, whereas we can sometimes allocate more than 100 percent of our assets to our macro view.

What other aspects of the Quantum Fund make it unique and contribute to its success?

Well, we have a different kind of understanding with our investors than other fund managers. We are a performance fund, that is, we are rewarded mainly in proportion to our profits rather than according to the amount of money we manage. Most fund managers aim to attract as much money as possible, manage it decently enough so that the investors don't get disenchanted and leave them. In other words, they try to maximize the size of their fund because they are rewarded according to the amount of money they manage. We try to maximize the profits of the Fund because we receive a percentage of the profits. Moreover, the profits are measured in absolute terms, not in relation to some index.

And there is another major difference: we have our own money in the Fund. I am an important shareholder in the Fund. Since we have kept the performance fees we have earned invested in the Fund, the longer the Fund exists and the more successful it is, the larger the portion of the Fund that the management owns. That means that we share on the downside as well as the upside: there is an identity of interest between the shareholders and the management. Therefore, the unspoken understanding with our investors is that they are passengers in a car that we drive. Our destination is the same. The nature of the unspoken contract is one of partnership rather than fiduciary responsibility. Naturally, we fulfill our fiduciary responsibilities as well.

What are the characteristics that differentiate Quantum from other funds? There are many funds now that have emulated you, but you are still a pioneer.

There is no fund exactly like ours. There is now a family of funds called hedge funds. But the name "hedge fund" really covers a wide variety of operations. I think it would be a mistake to put all hedge funds into the same basket. First of all, there are many hedge funds that don't use macro investing techniques or use them differently from the ways we do. And there are many hedge funds that use only macro instruments and don't have exposure to particular stocks. With our three-dimensional approach, we make decisions on different levels. There is a macro decision, a certain posture that the Fund adopts. Within that macro posture, there are decisions about stocks to buy or sell and which instruments to use. Generally speaking, if we can implement a macro decision with a macro instrument, we prefer to do that rather than to do it through more specific investments.

What do you mean?

Let me give you an example. Let's say a stock fund is bullish on bonds. It may then buy utilities. We would never do that. We may buy utilities, but only if we are keen on those particular utility stocks. Otherwise, we'll buy bonds because that gives us a more direct exposure.

You mentioned that there's a family of macro hedge funds. What characteristics differentiate Quantum from the other macro funds?

Those are more personal characteristics. That's where the particular attitudes and styles come into play.

How would you describe your particular style of investing?

My peculiarity is that I don't have a particular style of investing or, more exactly, I try to change my style to fit the conditions. If you look at the history of the Fund, it has changed its character many times. For the first ten years, it used practically no macro instruments. Afterwards, macro investing became the dominant theme. But more recently, we started investing in industrial assets. I would put it this way: I do not play according to a given set of rules; I look for changes in the rules of the game.

You have said that intuition is important in your investment success, so let's discuss intuition. What do you mean when you say you use intuition as an investment tool?

I work with hypotheses. I form a thesis about the anticipated sequence of events and then I compare the actual course of events with my thesis; that gives me a criterion by which I can evaluate my hypothesis.

This involves a certain element of intuition. But I'm not sure the role of intuition is so great, because I also have a theoretical framework. In my investing, I tend to select situations that fit into that framework. I look for conditions of disequilibrium. They send out certain signals that activate me. So my decisions are really made using a combination of theory and instinct. If you like, you may call it intuition.

Ordinarily, people think of money managers as having a combination of imagination and analytical ability. If you broke down all the

skills into just those two categories, which one would be your particular strength—imagination or analytical ability?

I think my analytical abilities are rather deficient, but I do have a very strong critical faculty. I am not a professional security analyst. I would rather call myself an insecurity analyst.

That's a provocative statement. What do you mean by that?

I recognize that I may be wrong. This makes me insecure. My sense of insecurity keeps me alert, always ready to correct my errors. I do this on two levels. On the abstract level, I have turned the belief in my own fallibility into the cornerstone of an elaborate philosophy. On a personal level, I am a very critical person who looks for defects in myself as well as in others. But, being so critical, I am also quite forgiving. I couldn't recognize my mistakes if I couldn't forgive myself. To others, being wrong is a source of shame; to me, recognizing my mistakes is a source of pride. Once we realize that imperfect understanding is the human condition, there is no shame in being wrong, only in failing to correct our mistakes.

You have said about yourself that you recognize your mistakes more quickly than others. That sounds like a necessary trait in investing. What do you look for to see if you are wrong?

As I told you before, I work with investment hypotheses. I watch whether the actual course of events corresponds to my expectations. If not, I realize that I am on the wrong track.

But sometimes things get off the track for a short time and then get back on the track. How do you know which is the case? That's what takes talent.

When there is a discrepancy between my expectations and the actual course of events, it doesn't mean that I dump my stock. I reexamine the thesis and try to establish what has gone wrong. I may adjust my thesis or I may find that there is some extraneous influence that has come into the picture. I may end up actually adding to my position rather than dumping it. But I certainly don't stay still and I don't ignore the discrepancy. I start a critical examination. And generally, I'm quite leery of changing my thesis to suit the changed circumstances, although I don't rule it out completely.

You have talked about the "joy of going against the herd." What signs do you look for to determine whether it is time to buck the trend?

Being so critical, I am often considered a contrarian. But I am very cautious about going against the herd; I am liable to be trampled on. According to my theory of initially self-reinforcing, but eventually self-defeating trends, the trend is your friend most of the way; trend followers only get hurt at inflection points, where the trend changes. Most of the time I am a trend follower, but all the time I am aware that I am a member of a herd and I am on the lookout for inflection points.

The prevailing wisdom is that markets are always right. I take the opposite position. I assume that markets are always wrong. Even if my assumption is occasionally wrong, I use it as a working hypothesis. It does not follow that one should always go against the prevailing trend. On the contrary, most of the time the trend prevails; only occasionally are the errors corrected. It is only on those occasions that one should go against the trend. This line of reasoning leads me to look for the flaw in every investment thesis. My sense of insecurity is satisfied when I know what the flaw is. It doesn't make me discard the thesis. Rather, I can play it with greater confidence because I know what is wrong with it while the market does not. I am ahead of the curve. I watch out for telltale signs that a trend may be exhausted. Then I disengage from the herd and look for a different investment thesis. Or, if I think the trend has been carried to excess, I may probe going against it. Most of the time we are punished if we go against the trend. Only at an inflection point are we rewarded.

In addition to going against the herd, you've said one of your techniques is to set yourself outside the process. What do you mean exactly? How do you get outside?

I am outside. I am a thinking participant and thinking means putting yourself outside the subject you think about. Perhaps it comes easier to me than to many others because I have a very abstract mind and I actually enjoy looking at things, including myself, from the outside.

You're renowned for your self-control and detachment. Do you think these are necessary conditions?

Detachment, yes; self-control, no. It hurts me to lose money and it gives me pleasure to win. There is nothing more self-destructive than to deny your feelings. Once you are aware of your feelings you may not feel the need to show them. But sometimes, especially when you are under great strain, the need to hide it may make the strain intolerable. I remember an occasion, early in my career, when I was practically wiped out in my personal account, yet I had to carry on in my job as if there were nothing wrong. The strain was unbearable. I could hardly bring myself to go back to the office after lunch. That is why I encourage my associates to share their problems; I am very supportive, provided that they are willing to recognize that they have problems.

George, in your present mode of operation, identifying good people, both internally and when you pick outside money managers, is very important. Could you comment on the characteristics you look for in identifying people who are likely to be successful in the investment business, both as managers of a fund that you might put money into, and as members of your staff?

Strangely enough, the most important aspect is character. There are certain people whom I can trust, and those are the people whom I want as partners. There are incredible moneymakers whom I don't trust, and whom I wouldn't want to have as partners. When Michael Milken went out of business, it created a vacuum in the junk bond business. I was very tempted and very eager to move into that vacuum because there was a lot of money to be made in it. I interviewed several people who had been working in the Milken machine, as potential outside managers or partners. But I found that they had a certain amoral attitude, which was characteristic of the trading (as distinct from the investment banking) part of that machine. They were clearly very aggressive, capable, intelligent, bright people, but there was this amoral attitude that signaled lender beware, and I didn't want to be in the position of lender. I just didn't feel comfortable.

J. P. Morgan's son was once asked to describe the characteristics that he looked for in a person before he loaned him money, and he said that character is by far the most important thing. "If I didn't trust a man, I wouldn't lend him a penny, even if he put up all the collateral in Christendom."

Well, I'm not as pure as he is. But then, I am not in the lending business.

Investing obviously requires a great deal of risk taking. Let's talk about the difference between this amoral approach and a responsible, aggressive, high risk approach.

What is there to say? Risk taking is painful. Either you are willing to bear the pain yourself or you try to pass it on to others. Anyone who is in a risk taking business but cannot face the consequences is no good.

What do you think makes for a good investor? What about intelligence? What role does it play in the making of a good investor?

People with the same intelligence may differ in character. Some go to the brink but never go over, and others go to the brink and occasionally go over. That is something that is very difficult to identify. But I don't want somebody who works for me going over the brink.

Do you want people going *to* the brink?

I am a person who went to the brink on occasion. But I had all my accumulated wealth riding on the line. I don't want other people going to the brink with my money. Once I had a very talented currency trader who, unbeknownst to me, put on a big currency risk. It was a profitable trade, but I immediately parted company with him because I felt I had been warned: I would have no one to blame but myself if we were hit by an unexpected loss.

There are some people who believe it's possible to be too smart in this business and that the smartest people are rarely the most successful investors.

I hope you are wrong.

That brings me to something that came up in your earlier books and has been referred to obliquely here: your own opinion of yourself. You have said in the past that you have a sort of messianic complex, a feeling that you were really put on the earth to have the kind of success that you have achieved. Is that the reason for your success? Is it the result of a combination of character, intelligence, and something we haven't talked about, a certain fearlessness that relates to the brink concept that you mentioned earlier?

I certainly don't feel messianic about investing. I indulge my messianic fantasies in giving away money that I've already earned. I don't indulge these fantasies in making money. I try to curb my fantasies. And I don't think that there is anything messianic about making money. But going to the brink is something else—it serves a purpose. There is nothing like danger to focus the mind, and I do need the excitement

15

connected with taking risks in order to think clearly. It is an essential part of my thinking ability. Risk taking is, to me, an essential ingredient in thinking clearly.

Do you derive this excitement from your love of the game or from its danger?

The danger. It stimulates me. But don't misunderstand what I am saying: I don't like danger; I like to avoid it. That is what makes my juices flow.

How is it that you stay ahead of the game?

As I have said already, I look for the flaw in every investment thesis. When I find it, I am reassured. As long as I can see only the positive side I worry. Again, don't misunderstand me. I don't reject an investment thesis just because I can't see the negative side; I just remain leery. On the other hand, I am particularly keen on investment theses that the market is reluctant to accept. These are usually the strongest. Remember the saying, "The market climbs on a wall of worry."

Okay, critical thinking is one important factor. What other things do you consider important?

The amazing thing about investing is that there are so many different ways of doing something. We can be described as momentum investors, but there are value investors who do extremely well. Value investors don't do so well in our shop, because they don't have anybody to talk to. I had a very interesting experience with P. C. Chatterjee, one of my investment advisors. His concept was to look at technology companies as asset-rich companies, where the customer was treated as an asset. If a company had a strong customer base, it could be worth a lot even though it had a lousy management and a lack of products.

And he felt that with a little push, these values could be unlocked. It proved to be a valid concept. For instance, he bought a big position in Paradyne. I went to see the company with him and, when I learned about all the problems they had, I came out quite despondent, wondering why the hell we owned the stock, and how we were going to get out. Yet, within a few weeks, AT&T bought the company for double the price we paid. He was right about the value of a strong customer base, but his way of looking at companies didn't fit in with mine.

Let me give you another example: There are periods of choppy markets when my style of investing is worse than useless. I insist on formulating a thesis before I take a position. But it takes time to discover a rationale for a perceived trend in the market; and sometimes the market will reverse the trend just when I manage to formulate a theory justifying it. If it happens repeatedly, it can be devastating. I am good at riding the tide, but not the ripples of a swimming pool. There was a period, in the early 1980s, when there seemed to be no tide, only ripples. I found a commodity fund manager, Victor Niederhoffer, who had a system for riding the ripples. He was well grounded in random walk theory. He looked at markets as a casino where people act as gamblers and where their behavior can be understood by studying gamblers. For instance, gamblers behave differently on Mondays than on Fridays, differently in the morning than in the afternoon, and so on. He regularly made small amounts of money trading on that theory. I gave him money to manage, and he made a good return on it. There was a flaw in his approach, however. It is valid only in a trendless market. If there is a historical trend, a tide, it can overwhelm these little waves that are caused by gambling behavior and he can be very seriously hurt because he doesn't have a proper fail-safe mechanism. I mention him because his approach is diametrically opposed to mine and there are times when his approach is appropriate. I have learned to be very broadminded as to the right approach. I am willing to use different people employing different approaches as long as I can rely on their integrity.

What happened to Victor Niederhoffer?

He made good money while the markets were sloshing around aimlessly. Then he started losing money, and he had the integrity to close out the account. We came out ahead. Very few commodity traders would have done that.

How is he doing lately?

He's doing very well.

Do you have money with him now?

No.

Do you look for any other characteristics when you interview someone?

I'm a very bad judge of character. I'm a good judge of stocks, and I have a reasonably good perspective on history. But I am, really, quite awful in judging character, and so I've made many mistakes. It took me five years and a lot of painful experiences to find the right management team. I am pleased that finally I found it, but I cannot claim to be as successful in picking a team as I have been in actually managing money.

I think that I'm very good as a senior partner, or boss, because I have a lot of sympathy for the difficulties that fund managers face. When they are in trouble, I can give them a lot of support, and that, I think, has contributed toward creating a good atmosphere in the firm. But I'm not so good at choosing them.

How much of your ability derives from choosing the markets rather than the investment?

It varies. There have been times when I focused on particular stocks and other times when I selected markets or market segments. As I said before, I don't play the game by a particular set of rules; I look for changes in the rules of the game.

If you are looking for changes in the rules of the game, there must be days in the course of a career that are critical. If you work with great intensity on a consistent basis, you don't recognize those days. One of the differences between you and me is that you seem to recognize those special days.

Very early in my career, when I was an assistant in the trading box opposite the stock exchange in London, I had a boss, Colonel Pougatsch, who was a very meticulous person. He came in every morning and sharpened his pencil to a very sharp point. He said to me that if there is no business to be done, then the point of the pencil should be as sharp when you leave as it was when you came in. I have never forgotten his advice.

More generally, running an investment portfolio is not work in the ordinary sense of the word. It is something else. It is risk taking. The amount of work you need to do is inversely related to your success. That is to say, if you are working at what is normally considered work, if you are a salesman or a craftsman, your success is directly related to the amount of work you put in. The more you hammer away, the more goods you produce; the more customers you visit, the more orders you are likely to take. There is a direct relationship. When you are taking risks, if you make the right judgment, if you have the right insight, then you don't need to work very hard. But if you make a mistake, and there is a divergence between your hypothesis and the actual course of events, you need to do some really serious research to find out what's wrong. The less successful you are, the more you're going to have to work to correct the situation. If the portfolio is doing well, you'll have to work less. There is an inverse relationship.

But, is that so? Aren't you kidding yourself? Sometimes, when everything's going right, it's just about to go disastrously. Don't you

sometimes have to do a lot of anticipatory work when everything's going right, just to get ready for the time when everything's going to go wrong?

Of course, that's how it should be. But I don't like working. I do the absolute minimum that is necessary to reach a decision. There are many people who love working. They amass an inordinate amount of information, much more than is necessary to reach a conclusion. And they become attached to certain investments because they know them intimately. I am different. I concentrate on the essentials. When I have to, I work furiously because I am furious that I have to work. When I don't have to, I don't work. This has been an essential element in my approach. If I knew what was going to go wrong, I'd do something to prevent it. But that is not how things work. Let's face it, there is a boom/bust sequence in the performance of individual portfolio managers also. They get it right, and they do very well, and then they get too cocky, and eventually it catches up with them. I'm not exempt from that. It often happens that when things go well, I relax, and then they start going wrong. The situation can change very rapidly. Either I'm on top of the situation, or the situation is on top of me. That is why one should never lose one's sense of insecurity. Experience has taught me that usually I can contain the damage within a 20 percent limit. If I look back on my performance, there are many instances where I lost up to 20 percent in the course of a year from the top to the bottom of that particular move, and then corrected it, and finished the year with a positive result.

Do you employ a formal procedure to cut your losses?

Not at all. In fact, if something goes wrong and I know what it is, but I think that the original thesis is valid, and that the damage is coming from an extraneous source, I am more likely to increase my position than to sell out. I need to know why I'm losing money.

How do you find out when things are going wrong?

I feel the pain. I rely a great deal on animal instincts. When I was actively running the Fund, I suffered from backache. I used the onset of acute pain as a signal that there was something wrong in my portfolio. The backache didn't tell me what was wrong—you know, lower back for short positions, left shoulder for currencies—but it did prompt me to look for something amiss when I might not have done so otherwise. That is not the most scientific way to run a portfolio.

But you are no longer engaged in the management of the Fund.

If I were, I would not be talking to you now. For a long period, I was effectively managing the Fund all by myself. I was the captain of the ship and I was also the stoker who was putting the coal on the fire. When I was on the bridge, I rang the bell and said "Hard left," and then I would run down into the engine room and actually execute the orders. And in-between I would stop and do some analysis as to what stocks to buy and so on. Those days are over. Now I have an organization. I've even handed over the captaincy of the boat to someone else. I act only as chairman of the board dealing with strategic issues.

Are you telling me you are only a passenger on the boat?

Well, I would say that I am a little bit more than that. I'm more like the owner of the boat.

Do you ever wander into the pilot house and take the controls?

I visit the captain, but I never take control because it is a very responsible job and it would be very harmful if I interfered with that responsibility.

21

At what point did you begin to disengage from active money management?

In 1989, when I became so involved in the revolution that was taking place in Eastern Europe, I couldn't continue running the business on a day-to-day basis. I couldn't keep on being on the line. I handed over the reigns to a team of younger people headed by Stanley Druckenmiller.

But you're generally held responsible for making $1 billion on sterling in 1992—and that was after you turned over the reins to Stanley. Should he be given the credit for that?

Yes. I never claimed credit for it. I was involved in the process. As coach, I said to him that this is a once-in-a-lifetime opportunity, the risk-reward relationship is extremely favorable, and therefore we should play it on a larger scale than normal. And he took my advice.

So you're responsible for the degree of leverage that the Quantum Group of Funds had then, but the original idea to go short on sterling was his?

Yes. He consulted me, but it was his decision.

Isn't it fair to say that without your encouragement he would never have leveraged up to the extent that Quantum did? Didn't you press him to go as far as he went?

I advised him to go for the jugular. He might have done it without me. Actually the leverage that we employed was not all that great, because we had only our equity at risk, or maybe a little more than that. In that kind of situation, we could have risked our equity several times over.

That was one of your great successes. Over the past years the Fund also made some judgments on the direction of currencies that haven't worked out so well. What role have you played in those?

Exactly the same role as in sterling. We were wrong on the yen in 1994, although the extent of our losses has been greatly exaggerated. It has been said that we lost $1 billion, but that's incorrect. We lost $600 million in February 1994, but made it up by the end of the year. There's no question that we were on the wrong foot for most of the year. I was part of the thinking process and therefore I have to take exactly the same responsibility as I do on sterling. I also played a role in establishing where we were making a mistake. We were focusing on the unfolding drama between the United States and Japan on the issue of trade; at the same time, there was a more fundamental cause for the strength of the yen that we failed to recognize.

You don't spend as much time in New York as you used to. You are mainly in Eastern Europe working on your Foundation activities.

Not any more. I am spending less time in Eastern Europe than in the last five years.

How often are you in contact with the office in New York about business affairs while you're away?

Whenever the telephone connections are good enough, I talk to the office daily.

And you talk to Stan?

Yes, and to some of the others.

Does Stan seek your advice? Do you channel him in certain directions or are most of your conversations respondent to questions?

He is in charge of running the Fund, and I don't impose anything on him. Stan is in many ways better at age 40 than I was at his age.

Is that the reason for the continued success of the Quantum Fund?

Only partially. Stan is a very fair and open-minded person, so he's been able to attract high quality people to the firm. The reputation of the Fund has also grown, especially after the sterling crisis. We have been able to get the best young people to join the firm, so we now have a great depth of management, something we never had before.

THE GURU IN TRAINING

A person is a product of the people who influenced him. Let's talk about the people who influenced you. Your father has had a profound influence on you and your ideas. Tell me what kind of impact he made and what aspects of his life were particularly important to you.

I think the impact was really from both my father and my mother, and they influenced me in different ways. I loved both of them dearly, but they were very different people and there was a lot of tension between them. Since I loved them dearly, I internalized both of them and I also internalized the tension. That tension has been a driving force in my life. I have been acting out the drama of two different people inside me. It has enabled me always to see the other point of view. I agreed with my father on practically everything except the way he treated my mother. My father taught me how to deal with the world, my mother taught me how to be introspective. I adopted my father's point of view, but I was much closer to my mother in my nature. My father was outgoing, gregarious, genuinely interested in other people's fate. He liked to draw them out but did not like to share his own inner feelings. Probably he did not like to deal with his own feelings at all; that is why he took so much interest in others. My father liked to stay on the surface; my mother was inclined to delve deeply. She was self-critical to the point of being self-flagellating. She had a religious, mystical streak that I didn't share, but I shared her interest in the mysteries of existence. My mother adored my father and accepted his judgment on all matters, even if it meant going against her own nature. This created some inner conflicts. She was conflicted in other ways as well. She was deeply hurt by the anti-Semitism that was endemic in Hungarian society and she developed ulcers in the early years of World War II. She also felt inadequate without a career of her own. In some ways, she was her own worst enemy. Since I had internalized her, I had to fight against this losing streak. Sometimes I felt that I had become such a big winner because I had to subdue a big loser inside me. When I went through a period of inner turmoil, in 1982, it reminded me of the conflict between my parents. That was also the time when I worked out many of the hangups I had inherited from my mother. In bringing them to the surface, they dissolved.

Why were you so close to both your father and your mother?

My mother was inclined to intimacy, and I was a kindred soul. My father was a very unusual person and I idolized him. I know I'm somewhat biased, but, even at this late stage in my life, I still consider him quite an exceptional person. He spent a lot of time with me as a little child. I used to meet him after school, and we would go swimming. After swimming, he would tell me another installment of his life story. It was like a soap opera that I absorbed totally. His life experience became part of my life experience.

What are some of the details of that soap opera?

He started out in life as a very ambitious young man. He volunteered in the First World War and he was promoted to lieutenant. Then he was taken prisoner of war on the Russian front and sent to Siberia. He was still very ambitious. He edited a newspaper called *The Plank*. It was written by hand and nailed to a plank. The authors hid behind the plank and listened to the comments of the readers. I remember seeing the collected copies of *The Plank* as a child; he brought them home from Siberia. Then he was elected prisoners' representative in the camp. Some prisoners escaped in a neighboring camp and the prisoners' representative was shot in retaliation. He decided that it would be better to escape than to be shot for other people's escaping. He selected some 30 people for their skills—carpenter, cook, doctor, and so on, because he had no practical skills—and they broke out of camp.

He had a plan to build a raft and drift down to the ocean. But he made one major mistake because his geography was somewhat deficient: he didn't realize that all the rivers in Siberia empty into the Arctic Ocean. They built this raft and they floated down the river, and it took them quite a few weeks to discover that they were heading for the Arctic Ocean. Finally they realized that they would have to make their way from the wilderness to civilization. That took them several months, and because of the Revolution they were caught up in the turmoil in the region. At that time, a Czech officer ruled Siberia from an armored railroad car. There were Reds and Whites, and they kept on killing each other and killing the population. He went through some horrendous experiences that taught him the value of being alive.

He returned to Hungary a changed man. He had lost his ambition. He didn't want to be prominent anymore. My father wanted to enjoy life and maintain his independence, but he did not want to become wealthy or influential. In fact, he was the only person I know who actually lived on his capital. He married my mother and, partly through that marriage and partly from profits he made on publishing an Esperanto journal, we owned a certain amount of real estate. He was a lawyer, but he didn't like to work more than was absolutely necessary. I remember, as a little child, he would send me over to his main client to borrow some money and then we would go on a skiing holiday. When we returned, he would be in a very bad mood for several weeks while he was trying to make some money to repay the debt. And then, during the war, he started selling property. By the time of the German occupation, we had sold practically all the property we had. This showed very good judgment because we would have lost the property anyhow. As a disinvestment it was extremely well timed. Nevertheless, very few people have the courage to live on their capital. "I carry my capital in my capital," he used to say—capital means "head" in Latin. I really admired his attitude. What a contrast from my career! Yet, in a funny way, I have emulated him because I never became a prisoner of my wealth.

You've mentioned that the way your father responded to the Nazi invasion of Hungary had a profound effect on you. Can you explain that?

The German occupation came in March 1944. I was not yet 14. That was my father's finest hour, because he knew how to act. He understood the situation; he realized that the normal rules did not apply. Obeying the law became a dangerous addiction; flaunting it was the way to survive. Having experienced the Russian Revolution, he knew what to do. He made arrangements for the family to get false identity papers, and he found places for us to live or to hide. He helped not only his immediate family, but a fairly large number of other people around him. I can truthfully say that he saved dozens of lives. He was much busier than he had ever been as a lawyer. At one time, we lived in a rented room that could be reached only through a bathroom and people were lining up in the bathroom to consult him.

This was a period of exciting adventures. I could go on and on about it because it is etched in my memory, although I rarely talk about it. The important and paradoxical point is that 1944 was the happiest year of my life. This is a strange, almost offensive thing to say because 1944 was the year of the Holocaust, but it is true. I was 14 years old. I had a father whom I adored, who was in command of the situation, who knew what to do and who helped others. We were in mortal danger, but I was convinced that I was exempt. When you are 14 years old, you believe that you can't really be hurt. For a 14-year-old, it was the most exciting adventure that one could possibly ask for. It had a formative effect on my life because I learned the art of survival from a grand master. That has had a certain relevance to my investment career.

We all survived, and then the Russians came in. There were still some interesting adventures, but gradually life lost its thrills. As the communist regime laid its dead hand on the country, I felt constricted, narrowed down, shut in. I also felt that my father's sway over me was excessive. "It isn't natural for a 15-year-old to think like a 50-year-old," I told him.

"Why don't you strike out on your own?" he asked me, "Where would you like to go?"

"England," I answered, because we had been listening to the BBC, and I was very much impressed by the British sense of fair play and objective reporting; "or I would like to go to the Soviet Union, because I'd like to find out the nature of this new system that we have to live under."

"Well, I've been to the Soviet Union," my father said. "I can tell you all about it."

That is how I decided to go to England. It took me several years to realize that it was his decision, not mine, and I love him all the more for it. He said he had a relative there who might help me to get into a school. I wrote to him, but nothing happened. So my father said, "Why don't you send him a postcard every week, just to remind him that you exist," which I did, and eventually he came through with an admission to a school. Then I applied for a passport, but at that time, it was very difficult to get one. Every week the waiting time became longer by an additional week, so it seemed to be an endless process. My father said, "You should go and complain; ask to see the officer in charge." Which I did, and that made me a well-hated person in the passport office. My brother, who was 21, that is, four years older, had a schoolmate who was working for the political police, and he asked this friend to walk my file through the various offices. He had considerable difficulty doing this because the head of the office said, "I'm willing to give a passport to anyone, except to that obnoxious young kid who is always complaining." Eventually I got a passport.

I left at the age of 17, and my father didn't have much direct influence on the rest of my life.

Before you left Hungary, you had some harrowing experiences. How did those experiences affect you?

They were not harrowing at all. I was aware of the danger but I felt invulnerable. I was aware of the suffering around us, but we did everything we could to help others. Just to give you a small example, we used to stand in line for cigarettes—they were distributing five cigarettes per person—and then give them to Jews who were restricted to Jewish houses and couldn't line up. Perhaps the only time I was physically affected was immediately after the siege of Budapest when there were lots of corpses lying about. There was one with its skull bashed in. I felt sick for a few days afterward.

Tell the story of when your mother was brought to the police station and managed to fool the authorities? She must have had nerves of steel.

She was living by herself in a weekend cottage and the neighbors became suspicious. They reported her to the police. The police questioned her, but she acted so calmly and naturally that they released her with an apology. During the interrogation, she was so detached she felt she was observing herself from the ceiling, making sure she was making the right impression. After her ordeal was over, the enormity of the danger struck her and she became very shaky. She escaped to Budapest and my father put her in a hotel. I remember telling her rather impatiently to pull herself together.

What lessons did you learn in particular from your mother as opposed to your father?

That's hard to say. I think I inherited my analytical, self-critical nature from her, but most of the lessons are from my father. Generally speaking, during that period, my father was right and my mother, when she differed from him, was usually wrong. That was not just my view, but also my mother's. Perhaps that tells you something.

Did you go back to Hungary often?

No, I couldn't go back at all. We were separated, seemingly, forever. I left in 1947. I got my passport, and then went to Switzerland to attend an Esperanto conference, because my father was an Esperantist. At that time, you also needed a Soviet exit permit, and I didn't have one. It was a group permit for the Esperanto conference and I missed the group because I didn't get my passport in time, so I had to go after them. I just got on the train and, fortunately, I managed to get through without actually having to show the permit. So I met my father there, but he went back to Hungary and I had to stay in Berne, waiting for my English visa. I didn't know how long it would take to get it, and I only had a couple of hundred Swiss Francs that my father gave me. So I spent my time trying to save money. I got the visa in about two weeks and I went to England. That was the end of his influence, although he did manage to send me some money in England. He came out in 1956 with my mother, and the family was reunited here in 1956.

When did he die?

In 1968. He was 75.

And your mother?

She died much later, in 1989. She came into her own after my father's death. She learned to be independent; she went to college when she was 60 and continued to grow until she died at age 86.

Were there other people who had an influence? How did your brother influence you?

My brother gave me my first experience of injustice. He was four years older, and he beat me up and teased me a lot, and my parents didn't protect me. I complained, but never got any satisfaction. We met again when I was 24 and became good friends.

He was never involved in the investment business, right? He made his own career.

He was the real talent in the family. He started an engineering company in his basement at 30, revolutionized the technology of bulk material ports and had the number one company in the world in just 15 years. He got numerous prizes for creative engineering and designed the facilities that handle a third of the world trade in bulk materials.

In the late 1960s, I sold my brother's business to Ogden Corporation during the conglomerate boom. It was a very amusing negotiation. I got double the price his company was worth because Ogden could promote him as their resident genius who made their stock more valuable. I called it a biblical transaction, in which I got two plates of lentils for my brother. Unfortunately, they paid him in stock. I negotiated downside protection down to half the current price, but the stock fell by three quarters. Eventually he bought the company back and became independent again. He sold his business again recently, and we are working together in all sorts of ways.

Are there other people who had an influence on you?

Many people, I'm sure. But I can't say that their effect was in any way comparable to the influence of my parents.

How about Karl Popper? He was one of your teachers and one of the great philosophers of the 20th century. How did he influence you?

He influenced me with his writings and his thinking. I had relatively little to do with him on a personal level. He was not my regular teacher at the London School of Economics. I finished my degree course, which was supposed to take three years, in two. I had to spend an extra year as a registered student to qualify for the degree, and I was allowed to select a tutor. I chose him because I was very much taken by his philosophy. I had lived through Nazi persecution and Soviet occupation. Popper's book, *Open Society and Its Enemies,* struck me with the force of revelation—it showed that fascism and communism have a lot in common, and they both stand in opposition to a different principle of social organization, the principle of open society. I was even more influenced by Popper's ideas on scientific method. I wrote some essays for him and he was very encouraging when I met him in his home, but I saw him no more than twice. And then, when I wrote my philosophical treatise, "The Burden of Consciousness," which was very much a regurgitation of his ideas, around 1962, I sent it to him, and I got a very enthusiastic response from him, which encouraged me to go and see him. He gave me a date at the London School of Economics. There were a lot of people waiting for him, and they were very upset when they found out that I had a date to see him, because they were all his students and needed his attention. I felt like an intruder. So I went out of the room and waited in the corridor, in front of the elevator. When he stepped out of the elevator, I introduced myself, and he took one look at me and he said, "But you're not American!" and I said "No." He said, "That is terribly disappointing, and I'll explain to you why. When I got your treatise, I felt that finally an American had understood my teachings about open society and closed society. That meant that I had managed to communicate my ideas. But you lived through it all, so you don't count and that is why I'm disappointed." Still, he was very supportive and encouraged me to carry on. I saw him occasionally after that. The older he got, the more frequent our contacts became. It was during his last ten years that I had a real relationship with him, but by that time, he was no longer at the height of his powers. We had a wonderful, really touching meeting in Prague just before he died, when he came and gave a lecture at the Central European University in June 1994. He enjoyed it so much that he was going to come and open the school year in Budapest in September. But he died before then. That's really the extent of my contact with him. So it's not really the man, but his ideas that influenced me. Even though I refer mainly to Popper, I was also influenced by a number of other thinkers, like Frederick Hayek, Alfred North Whitehead, and others.

How about all the powerful and famous people you meet now? An article described you as having one president for breakfast and another for dinner.

In the past five years or so, I have met many important players on the stage of history. What a difference from my earlier incarnation! I used to live in virtual isolation; now most doors are open. I must confess I like it better this way; my only regret is that I lack the time and energy to follow through. I wish I could spend more time with some of the people I met recently. And I don't mean so much people in power, but people of consequence.

Does anyone particularly stand out in your mind?

Andrei Sakharov, the physicist, above all. He was the most painfully honest man I ever met. He simply could not bear telling a lie. Yet he was a very gentle man, however scathing the opinions he would express. He embodied the ideal of a scientist in pursuit of the truth—that is why he was so widely respected. He took his responsibility terribly seriously. In the first more-or-less free election, he was elected to the Supreme Soviet and became one of the leaders of the Popular Front. It killed him—he died of a heart attack after a gruelling day in

Parliament. I had the feeling that he died of grief because he was unable to do enough.

I love Havel, too, with all his faults. He turned the early days of his presidency into a lighthearted, inspiring theater. I remember visiting him on a public holiday. There was a mysterious announcement that the Castle was open to the public. The people who turned up were treated in the same way as the invited guests. When the crowd overflowed, tables were set up in the courtyard and sausages and beer served. It was the most joyous occasion I ever attended. He explained to me that he made the announcement deliberately vague so the Castle wouldn't be overrun.

I had very good contact with Bronislaw Geremek, Walesa's political adviser during Solidarity days, from the first time we met, which was in 1988. We did not meet often, but each time was memorable and I feel very close to him.

The political personality I feel closest to is Grigory Yavlinsky. He was the main architect of the Shatalin Plan and the leader of the delegation I brought to the World Bank meeting in 1990. The role he played was entirely his own invention; he created it out of nothing. His vision was—and remains—closest to mine. We have had our differences, but as time goes on, my respect for him continues to grow, mainly because he is literally putting his life on the line for his beliefs.

I could go on. One of my rewards is that I do meet interesting people and participate in interesting events.

It occurs to me that your investment philosophy has evolved out of your personal experience. Let's talk about some of that background. When did you first get into business? What was your first job?

It had nothing to do with finance. I became a trainee in a fancy goods manufacturer in England. The company made novelties, souvenirs, costume jewelry, and so on. It was not easy to get a job when I got out of college because I was a foreigner without connections. I got the job through a friend of mine, a part-time fellow student who was working for this firm.

You were a salesman, right?

I was a so-called management trainee, but they didn't have a training program, so I ended up as a salesman. Then I worked for one of my customers who was a wholesaler. I became a traveling salesman selling to retailers in Welsh seaside resorts, and that was a low point in my career. It took me very far away from my concept of myself. Plus, it was a very difficult job. Its main advantage was that it gave me a car, a Ford Anglia, which was the lowest-priced model in the Ford line in Britain. The first job the wholesaler gave me was to try and sell to tobacconists in London, but all these tobacconists were organized into wholesalers' groups, so there was absolutely no chance of selling to them. It was also very difficult to park the car in London, so I felt kind of shut out. The feeling was somewhat relieved when I got the territory on the Welsh seaside, so at least I could make some sales. Nevertheless, I realized that this kind of work was not really what I had studied for, or what my parents expected of me. I decided to make a complete break. I wrote a letter to all the merchant banks in London addressing each one personally to the managing director of the firm, which was not something that was done in those days. You didn't write letters to people you didn't know.

This elicited some rather amusing responses. There was someone called Walter Salomon who called me for an interview, just to point out that I misspelled his name. I also got an interview at Lazard Freres, which was very enlightening because the managing director told me, full of good will, that I was barking up the wrong tree wanting to go into the City. He said, "Here in the City we practice what we call intelligent nepotism. That means that each managing director has a number of nephews, one of whom is intelligent, and he is going to be the next managing director. If you came from the same college as he did, you would have a chance to get a job in the firm. If you came from the same university, you may still be all right. But you're not even from the same country!" He advised me to stay away from the City because, he said, people came into merchant banks mainly to manage their own money, and therefore they expected less in the way of salary than in industry. They got, at the age of 40, what people in industry might already reach at age 30.

You said that when you were in Wales, that was the low point of your life.

A low point.

OK, we'll get to some other low points. One of the low points was that your life wasn't going in the direction that other people had expected it would. But you also had a very high opinion of yourself at that point.

I always had exaggerated expectations of myself, undoubtedly inculcated in me by my parents. When a father you respect takes you seriously, you have got to take yourself seriously. It's only recently that reality has caught up with my expectations.

So, you went ahead and had interviews with financial institutions in London. Did anybody give you a break?

Amusingly, in light of my interview at Lazard Freres, I got a job at Singer & Friedlander, where the managing director was, in fact, Hungarian. So the Lazard Freres thesis was proven right: I came from the same country as the directors, they gave me a chance because of it. That was in 1953.

Did you feel that the fact that you were Jewish played a role in your selection?

Perhaps. But the main factor was that I was a Hungarian, both in being rejected or not considered in other places, and in being accepted at Singer & Friedlander.

What did you do there?

I became a trainee and had a salary of, I think, seven pounds a week.

Was that more or less than you were making as a salesman?

It was a little less, and I was made to do some very boring, humdrum jobs, which I did very badly. The worst of these was when I had to make postings in a double-entry bookkeeping system by hand, because we didn't have machines for recording foreign currencies. There was a big aluminum plate on which I had to put the debit and the credit sheets and a control sheet. At the end of the day, the credits and debits were supposed to balance out to zero on the control sheet, but there was not a single day when they came out correctly. My supervisor had to reconcile the figures, which didn't endear me to him.

Then I had some training in the arbitrage department, working in the "box." It was next to the stock exchange, where the brokers sat around waiting for orders, and my boss was talking to Johannesburg, Brussels, Paris, and New York all the time. He was trading mainly in gold shares. Again, I didn't shine; he was a very meticulous, precise person, and that is not my strong point. So, he sent me back to the main office.

Then came an occasion when I went to Paris for the weekend to meet my brother, and I got fogged in and couldn't get back until Tuesday. When I got to the office on Tuesday, people looked at me as if I weren't there at all, and after a while I was sent in to see the managing director who took me to task. "Why did you miss Monday?" he asked. I used the opportunity to ask what my prospects in the firm

38

were, and he told me that he didn't get terribly encouraging reports about my performance. He told me that the sky was the limit if I managed to bring in some business, but if I expected them to find a niche for me, I would wait forever because they had no specific assignments in mind. They didn't mind having me around because I didn't cost very much, but I was a fifth wheel in whichever department I was placed.

What kind of business did they want you to bring in?

Any clients or deals, or anything that would make money. I asked whether he would mind if I looked for a job elsewhere, and he told me that I would go with his blessing. I came out from this meeting and went to lunch with another trainee, who was there from New York. It was Robert Mayer, whose father owned a small brokerage firm in New York, and I told him what had happened. He told me that his father was looking for someone in New York. He said he would have mentioned it to me earlier, but he felt that, since I was a trainee, it would be inappropriate for him to entice me away from the firm. He asked me if I would be interested in going to New York, and that's how I came to work on Wall Street. The whole process took some time.

When did you arrive in New York?

In September 1956. That is another rather amusing story. When I applied for a visa, the authorities refused me. They said that I was too young, at 26, to be a specialist whose services were urgently required and could not be filled by local talent. F. M. Mayer then got an affidavit from Franz Pick, author of the *Black Market Yearbook*, who testified that arbitrage traders had to be young because they died young. On that basis, I got the visa. But I never forgot his affidavit and I got out of the arbitrage trading business as fast as I could. When I arrived in New York, I started trading in international arbitrage—that is, buying securities in one country and selling them in another.

What kind of stocks were you trading?

At that time, mainly oil stocks. That business declined after the Suez crisis abated. Then I developed a new form of arbitrage, which I called internal arbitrage. A number of new issues came out combining common stocks, warrants, and bonds that were not immediately separable, and I developed a way of trading them separately before they could be officially detached from each other. That turned into a very good business, and we made quite a bit of money in this specialized niche.

So you were actually a global investor almost from the beginning of your career?

I was a trader, which is very different. I was anything but an investor. I bought and sold quickly and I was not allowed to carry positions except within very strict limits. Then came the boom in European stocks. It started with the formation of the Coal and Steel Community, which eventually became the Common Market. There was massive interest in European securities among United States banks and institutional investors who thought they were getting in on the ground floor of a United States of Europe. I was approached by Wertheim & Co. and I joined that firm as a securities analyst in European securities and also as a trader. Later I also became an institutional salesman. At the time, the information available about European companies was extremely rudimentary. I put out memoranda that you would find heartbreaking if you read them today because they were so amateurish.

Were they superficial?

No, they were not superficial, but they were conjectural. Information was not easily available; consequently many of the conclusions had to be imputed from limited data. I became one of the leaders of the

European investment boom. It made me a one-eyed king among the blind. I had institutions like Dreyfus Fund and J. P. Morgan practically eating out of my hands because they needed the information. They were investing very large amounts of money; I was at the center of it. It was the first big breakthrough in my career.

What year was this?

That was 1959 through 1961. I was the first to make a study of the German banks showing that their stock portfolios were worth a great deal more than their total capitalization. Then I turned my interest to Allianz Insurance. Next, I wrote a veritable book on the German insurance industry. I identified a group of insurance companies, the Aachner-Muenchner group, which all had cross-holdings in each other. I added up all those cross-holdings and showed that you could buy some of the stocks at a tremendous discount from their actual values, once the cross-holdings were figured in.

Nobody in the United States was doing this kind of work at the time?

That's right. This was original work. Just before Christmas I went to J. P. Morgan, showed them the chart of these 50 interconnected companies, and told them my conclusion. I said that I was going to write it up during the Christmas holidays. They gave me an order to start buying immediately, before I completed the memo, because they thought that those stocks could double or triple on the basis of my recommendation. That was the peak of the boom in European stocks and also in my career as a foreign securities analyst. Shortly thereafter came the interest equalization tax. President Kennedy introduced a 15 percent surcharge on foreign investments in order to protect the balance of payments. My business was destroyed overnight. I then left Wertheim.

41

Was that a particularly difficult point for you?

A lot of these things are rather poignant. The interest equalization tax hit me personally because, before it was introduced, I had made a very large trade in Tokio Marine and Fire Insurance Company, which was about to issue American Depository Receipts (ADRs). I bought the shares in Tokio and I sold the ADRs on an "if and when issued" basis to some institutional investors. There was an exceptionally good margin of profit in the trade because there was an element of risk in it. The potential danger was that maybe the ADRs would not be issued. This potential danger became actual when the interest equalization tax was imposed. For a few days, the Tokio Marine and Fire deal hung in the balance. This trade had been approved by the partner in charge, but when the other partners questioned him, he denied that he had given permission for me to go ahead. So I was left holding the bag.

These securities were held in the account of the firm?

Yes. We sold the ADRs against them "if and when issued," but if they were not issued, the firm would be left holding the common shares for its own account and we would have to sell them back in Tokyo at a big loss. After a few days, the ADR issue did go through, and the profit was realized. I talked to the other partners of the firm and I explained to them the facts, but I felt that the atmosphere of suspicion could not be totally dispelled because if I was telling the truth the partner was a liar. It would cling to me as long as I was in the firm, so I waited a decent amount of time and then I looked for another job. When I left, the partner in charge said he would never say anything bad about me as long as I didn't say anything bad about him. I went to Arnhold & S. Bleichroeder.

How did you end up there?

I had an open offer, which I accepted. They had been looking for someone for a while. But, when I took the job, I had practically nothing to do because the European securities business had been destroyed by the interest equalization tax. There were still some very profitable transactions to be made, however, in selling back to Europe the shares that the American institutions wanted to unload. Again, there is a rather amusing anecdote in this connection. When I first discovered Allianz, and published my insurance opus, the Allianz management wrote a letter telling Dreyfus that they were making a mistake buying these shares. Allianz said my analysis was false and misleading, and the shares were overvalued. Dreyfus disregarded the letter and continued buying and the shares doubled or tripled. After the interest equalization tax was imposed, they wanted to get out, and so did J. P. Morgan. I went directly to Allianz and offered them the shares. Then they wrote another letter explaining to Dreyfus how it was a mistake to sell the shares, because Allianz was going to have strong earnings, increase the dividend, and do a number of other positive things. But the price was much higher than at the time they had said the shares were overvalued. Eventually, they placed the shares within the controlling syndicate.

What did you do then?

Business became scarcer and scarcer, and I retired to philosophy. From 1963 to 1966, I spent time trying to rewrite my philosophical dissertation.

And you actually gave up your job?

No. I stayed employed, but my mind was on philosophy and not on business.

What became of your philosophical digression?

I had written a philosophical essay under the title of "The Burden of Consciousness," which I completed in 1961 or 1962. I had it run off by the copying department of Wertheim & Co. That was what I was trying to rewrite during this period, but I didn't make much progress. There came a day when I was rereading what I had written the day before and couldn't make sense of it. I realized that I was spinning my wheels. That was when I decided to get back into business.

What did you think you might accomplish with this philosophical work? Did you have a specific objective?

I thought that I had some major new philosophical ideas, which I wanted to express. I now realize that I was mainly regurgitating Karl Popper's ideas. But I haven't given up the illusion that I have something important and original to say.

What would that be?

That our understanding of the world in which we live is inherently imperfect. There is always a discrepancy between the participant's views and expectations and the actual state of affairs. Sometimes the discrepancy is so small that it can be disregarded but, at other times, the gap is so large that it becomes an important factor in determining the course of events. History is made by the participant's errors, biases, and misconceptions.

We'll get to that later; for now, I'm curious about when and how you got back into the business world.

In 1966, since I didn't know much about American securities, I wanted to find a way to educate myself. I set up a model account with $100,000 of the firm's money, divided it into 16 parts, and invested one or two units into any stock that I considered to be especially attractive. I wrote a short memo explaining the reasons why I bought each issue, and I followed up with monthly reports reviewing the portfolio and discussing developments within the portfolio. I also provided a monthly performance record. I used this model account as a sales tool to develop business with institutional investors. This was a very successful format, because it put me in contact with the investment community. During the years when I had been writing my philosophy, I had lived in a vacuum. Now, I was able to test my investment ideas on potential investors. If I got a good response, I realized that I was onto a good idea; if I got a negative response, I had to seriously question whether I was on the right track. I got some very valuable feedback.

That doesn't sound like you. You don't usually let other people tell you whether you've got a good idea or not.

Testing your views is essential in operating in the financial markets. Let me give you one example: there was a company called American SealCap. When I visited management, they had a wonderful story to tell. I bought the story. One of my potential customers called me and said this was a great story, but there was a catch to it: management was notorious for lying. That was useful information. It shows how valuable it is to get this kind of feedback.

One of my first major efforts was in the trucking industry. I put 4 of the model's 16 units into trucking stocks. That worked out very well and it gave the model account a pretty good performance. Then, based on the model portfolio, we established a small investment fund called First Eagle Fund. In the following year, 1969, we established another small fund with a capital of $4 million called the Double Eagle Fund. This was a hedge fund: it was allowed to sell short as well as go long, and it was also allowed to use leverage. Then, as the two funds began to grow, a potential conflict of interest arose. We were recommending stocks to our clients that we were also buying for our own account. Even though we were disclosing all our purchases, it became an impossible situation, especially when it came to selling. I gave up the model portfolio, left Arnhold & S. Bleichroeder, and set up my own hedge fund in 1973.

Was this the beginning of what was to become the Quantum Fund?

Yes, but at the time it was called Soros Fund.

How did you set this up?

The shareholders of Double Eagle could decide whether to come with me or stay with Arnhold & S. Bleichroeder. The parting was amicable, and Arnhold & S. Bleichroeder continues to be a clearing broker and principal custodian for Quantum Fund to this day.

3

THE STORY OF
QUANTUM FUND

ow much capital did Quantum Fund start with?

Its predecessor, Double Eagle Fund started with $4 million in 1969. It became the Soros Fund in 1973 with about $12 million.

How much of that $12 million was your own money?

Very little at that time. The management team was entitled to 20 percent of the profits. I had a junior partner, Jim Rogers. We kept our share of the profits invested in the Fund and we earned the same return on it as all the other shareholders plus we got 20 percent of the profits each year, so our share in the Fund accumulated over time.

Jim Rogers is now well known as the author of *Investment Biker* and is an analyst for CNBC. Where did you meet him?

He had worked as an analyst for a small firm on Wall Street, and then he came to join me at Arnhold & S. Bleichroeder. It was the two of us against the world. Jim Rogers was an outstanding analyst, and extremely hardworking. He did the work of six. At the same time, he understood and shared my intellectual framework and my investment philosophy, so we had a very good give and take. It was a very fruitful partnership. We grew and grew, which created some problems because Jim Rogers did not want to add more staff. He loved our partnership and did not want to admit any outsider into it. I was pressing to enlarge the team to keep pace with our increasing size. Jim resisted it, but we did take on some trainees whom Jim Rogers trained from scratch, because our ethos at the time was to have nothing to do with Wall Street and we thought that anybody who had a Wall Street brokerage background had been irremediably spoiled.

What did you think was so wrong with Wall Street?

We both started with the postulate that the markets are always wrong. Actually the big difference between Jim Rogers and me was that Jim thought that the prevailing view was always wrong, whereas I thought that we may be wrong also. Wall Street wisdom was, by definition, conventional wisdom, and since we not only wanted to be different but *were*, in fact, different, somebody coming in with conventional wisdom would not fit in into our operation. Jim Rogers felt very strongly about this. I was less intransigent; I would have been willing to take someone from Wall Street, but this was his point of view and, since he did all the work, I yielded to him.

If he did all the work, what did you do?

I made all the decisions.

He only did analysis? He didn't pull the trigger?

He never pulled the trigger. He was not allowed to pull the trigger.

Why? Wasn't he any good at pulling the trigger?

That's right. He was very good at analysis. That was the division of labor between us.

So, he would bring you ideas, and he would say, "What do you want to do?"

Sometimes. At other times, I generated the ideas and he would do the research. I also did some research, particularly if we were entering a new area or if something went wrong. Generally, we followed the principle of investing first and investigating later. I did the investing and he did the investigating.

Were there times when you'd do the investing and he'd do the investigating, and he would find something wrong with the idea, but you would still keep the stock?

That's right. Those were, in fact, the very best situations because we also knew the flaws; we knew where to look for trouble, when to get out. We were ahead of the game and were very comfortable holding the stock. We were always looking for the flaws. Occasionally, we would realize that the idea was totally false and then we would get out as fast as possible.

But I remember, George, being involved in a few stocks that you were interested in at the time. You would call me and talk to me much as an analyst. So you must have done some analytical work yourself.

Oh, absolutely. I was working quite hard in those days, and became quite an expert in some industries. Usually I had to become an instant expert because, if I had a new idea, I would have only a few days to become familiar with a new industry. But I recall a couple of instances where I delved quite deeply.

The one I'm thinking of was an oil service company.

It was called Tom Brown. Oil service was actually Jim Rogers' idea. We made a lot of money on the long side and then we lost a lot of money on the short side. You can't fight a promoter when he strikes oil. He boasted that he would name his gushers "Soros Number One," "Soros Number Two," . . . in honor of our large short position. He had a great sense of humor, but we were not amused.

Can you give some examples of other prospects you analyzed then?

One is the Mortgage Guaranty Insurance Company, or MAGIC, as we called it. When the California residential home market collapsed, the market thought the company might go broke, but it survived the test and we made a fortune. That is when I made the rule that one should own stocks when they have successfully passed a difficult test, but one should avoid them during the test—something that is easier said than done.

Then there was the Real Estate Investment Trust industry (REITs), which I put on the map. We got it right coming and going. I issued a study in which I described it as an initially self-reinforcing, but eventually self-defeating, process that would end badly with most REITs going bust. But the end was at least three years away, therefore the stocks should be bought now. We did well on the long side and sold out well before they reached their peak. Then, several years later, they started falling. I felt it was too late to go short, but then I re-read my memo that predicted that they would go bust and I realized that it could never be too late. It was the only time I made more than 100 percent on my money on the short side because, as the stocks went down,

I kept topping up my short positions. I did that with about $1 million, but that was a lot of money for my hedge fund at the time.

And what great ideas did Jim Rogers contribute?

Probably his most important idea was the defense industry, which was totally neglected at the time. There were only one or two analysts surviving from the previous defense boom who still followed it. Jim Rogers discovered stocks like E Systems and Sanders Associates.

Was there any research project you were particularly proud of during this period?

I got technology right around 1978 or 1979, for the first and only time in my life. Jim had this idea that the world was switching from analog to digital. He wanted to sell the analog companies short, but I was more interested in the long side. This was a time when technology stocks were in the doghouse. Distributed data processing was spreading like wildfire, but the shares were selling at low price/earnings ratios because the market was growing too rapidly for the existing suppliers to maintain their market share. Investors feared that the giants would come in and make mincemeat out of these fledgling companies. Due to these fears, the companies concerned could not raise any capital from outside sources and had to rely on internally generated cash for growth. They could not meet the demand, and there was indeed an opening for the existing computer giants to enter the market. Here was a self-fulfilling prophecy of the worst kind. It provided a wonderful profit opportunity when investor psychology reversed.

Jim and I went out to the AEA (American Electronics Association) conference in Monterey—it was called WEMA then—and we met with eight or ten managements a day for the entire week. We got our arms around this whole difficult field of technology. We selected the five most promising areas of growth and picked one or more stocks in each area. This was our finest hour as a team. We lived off the fruits of our labor for the next year or two. The Fund performed better than ever before and the strain on our relationship became intolerable, because the Fund was growing rapidly but the management team was not.

But you had hired some people by then.

Right. We had brought on some very talented people. They were either totally new to the business or had a limited amount of experience. When they began to learn and started to take issue with Jim, Jim couldn't stand the criticism coming from below. He was very, very receptive to criticism coming from me. He never had a problem with that, but he couldn't stand his disciples criticizing him or disagreeing with him, so as soon as they became really productive, he would go out of his way to destroy them, which created a very unpleasant atmosphere. It also deprived us of these people just when they were coming into their own. And so, a vacuum developed around us. We were getting bigger and bigger, but we had to do all the work ourselves. Our success was punished by ever-growing work and responsibility. It eventually came to the point where it broke up our partnership.

Did you go to Jim to explain what you've just described to me?

Yes. I believe it was in Monterey that I spelled out a three-step strategy to Jim. The first step was to try and build a team together. If we didn't succeed, the second step was to build one without him; and, if that didn't work, the third step was to do it without me. And that is what happened. To prepare, I changed the name from Soros Fund to Quantum Fund. I said it was to celebrate the quantum jump in the size of the Fund and of course I was intrigued by the uncertainty principle of quantum mechanics, but the real reason was to get my name off the line.

And what happened then?

We started Phase One in 1978 and recognized that it wasn't working at the beginning of 1980. We parted company, but the Fund continued growing at a breakneck pace throughout 1980 and the beginning of 1981. I was running the Fund all by myself, with a very small staff, and the strain became unbearable. This was Phase Two. It led to a crisis in 1981. In September of that year, I retired from active management and farmed out the capital of Quantum Fund to other managers. That was Phase Three.

Tell us about the crisis of 1981.

It started much earlier, around the time I spelled out my three-stage strategy. Here I was, extremely successful, but I made a point of denying my success. I worked like a dog. I felt that it would endanger my success if I abandoned my sense of insecurity. And what was my reward? More money, more responsibility, more work—and more pain—because I relied on pain, as a decision-making tool. The Fund reached $100 million in size; my personal wealth must have been around $25 million, and I was close to the breaking point. It did not make sense. I decided to come to terms with my success by accepting the fact that I was successful even if it meant that I ceased to be successful, because my success was dependent on my self-denying, self-critical, self-torturing attitude. Perhaps I was about to kill the goose that laid the golden eggs, but what was the point of laying those golden eggs if my life kept getting more miserable? I had to start enjoying the fruits of my success; otherwise the whole endeavor did not make sense.

Your definition of success didn't have anything to do with your lifestyle?

It had to do with my work, not with my lifestyle. Generally, a benefit of being successful was that I could afford the things that I wanted, but I

53

did not have any extravagant tastes. I always lived on a scale that was more modest than my financial resources. But that was not the issue. The issue was the degree of pain, tension, and insecurity I was willing to live with.

Then what did it mean to "come to terms with" your success?

Exactly as I said: I changed my attitude. I accepted the fact that I was successful. I abandoned my insecurity, fully recognizing the dangers involved. Then came a rather wild period. I separated not only from Jim Rogers, but also from my first wife.

Why did your marriage break up?

It was part of this psychological turmoil that I went through. It was not directly related, because my wife had been very supportive, very tolerant of my involvement in business. Still, this change in my attitude unsettled our relationship. And so, there came a rather wild period when I parted company with my partner, with my wife, and I was left alone running a $100 million fund. I deliberately loosened the constraints under which I had been operating up to that time. The result was, ironically, a period of absolutely fantastic performance. We practically doubled our money in each of the next two years. The Fund jumped from $100 million to almost $400 million.

What do you mean when you say "you loosened the constraints"?

It turned out that I had been far too self-critical and self-controlled. I had insisted on knowing far too much about every situation before I made an investment, and often I ended up selling that investment far too soon because I thought that it was not as sound as it ought to be. Part of the reason for this was that I always had a reservoir of new ideas that were pushing their way into the portfolio, and pushing a lot of existing investments out of the portfolio.

Prematurely?

Prematurely. My style of management was too tight and too cramped. And so, now, I let it rip. I did not insist on knowing quite so much about every situation.

More intuitive?

Yes, in the sense that I wasn't doing so much ground work, and I allowed my reservoir of information to become depleted. I entered this wild period with a store of knowledge that I could apply to practically any new opportunity that might surface. I remember looking at myself with awe, amazed at the speed with which I could react, the wealth of information I could draw on, and the analogies I could apply. I was on top of every situation, I was able to establish connections that were not readily visible to others, but I also felt that I was a depleting asset. The machine that I was, was running down. While the Fund grew from $100 million to $400 million, I felt that the controls were slipping from my hands. I knew less about the situations that I entered than about the ones I exited. I realized I could not keep it up much longer because I would need a lot more ideas to feed a $400 million fund than I had needed at the beginning of this wild ride. The pressure became really almost too much to bear. Even though I was much looser, I was not irresponsible; I felt the responsibility, even if I was acting with much less caution than previously. And it really turned into an internal conflict where I felt the Fund was an organism, a parasite, sucking my blood and draining my energy. I asked myself, who is more important, the Fund or me? Is the Fund a vehicle for my success, or am I the slave of my Fund? That's what prompted me to implement the third step of the strategic plan I had outlined to Jim Rogers in Monterey in 1978. I wanted to get off the firing line.

This is when you were trying to move the Fund into a new phase. But you had some trouble doing this, right?

I was looking for people to share responsibility for the management of the Fund and, when I could not find anyone, I started looking for people to whom I could delegate full responsibility. This had the unfortunate result of turning my inner turmoil into public knowledge. The more people I talked to, the more people became aware of my state of mind, and the worse my state of mind became.

Word got around that I was in some kind of crisis. And I made a fatal mistake: I did not stop running the Fund while I was looking to find people to manage the Fund. I should have really put the Fund on ice, and then reorganized the management. But I kept on making investment decisions at the same time that I was interviewing people.

And what was the effect of all that turmoil on the Fund?

It resulted in the Fund losing money for the first time in its history. I informed my shareholders of my problems, and gave them the option to withdraw from the Fund. In September 1981, when we were down some 26 percent, we also had some fairly large redemptions. The Fund was cut from $400 million to $200 million. It was the result of an internal conflict between me and my Fund, which the Fund lost, being down 22 percent for the year, and I won, because I came out on top.

In what sense? How would you define coming out on top?

I refused to remain the slave of my business. I established that I am the master and not the slave. It was a big change in many ways, because I began to accept myself as someone who is successful; I overcame fear of the misfortune that might befall me if I admitted my success.

Was that a guilt thing? Did you think that if you admitted your success you would jinx it?

No, it was a little more than that and I think the fear was well founded. When you are a serious risk taker, you need to be disciplined. The discipline that I used was a profound sense of insecurity, which helped to alert me to problems before they got out of hand. If I gave up that discipline, I would have to fall back on due diligence and other forms of routine and routine is not my strong point. I was afraid to admit my success because it might undermine my sense of insecurity. Once you take your success for granted, you let down your guard. When you are in trouble, you just sit back; you know you are successful and you will always get out of trouble somehow. That's when you have lost your ability to get out of trouble.

You had a fear of complacency.

That's right. But I think that I underwent a serious change in my personality during that period. There was a large element of guilt and shame in my emotional makeup, but I worked through it. I had some sessions with a psychoanalyst. It was rather superficial in the sense that I was never on a couch and it was only once or twice a week. Nevertheless, it was a very important process. I revealed my biases, and by bringing them into the open, I recognized that they made no sense and therefore I could dismiss them.

Once I had a stone in the salivary gland in my mouth, which was extremely painful. The doctor took it out in an operation, which was also very painful. The stone was a round, hard ball. I wanted to preserve it because of all the pain that it had caused me. In a few days, I looked at it and it had turned into dust. It was pure calcium, which becomes powder when it dries. That is what happened to my hang-ups. Somehow, they dissolved when they were brought to light.

You became generally more positive about life at that point, right?

Yes. I felt I had accomplished something. I certainly became a pleasanter person to live with. I'm sure that my first and second wives have totally different perceptions of who I am. I tell my present wife, Susan, what kind of person I used to be, and I don't think she can quite believe me.

And what happened to the Fund?

By September 1981, I had liquefied the Fund and turned it into a fund of funds. My plan was that I would give out portions to other fund managers, and I would become the supervisor rather than the active manager. And then 1982 to 1984 were rather lackluster years and this arrangement didn't work too well.

Farming out portions of the Fund management was unsuccessful at that time?

I took on some outside managers. Some of them did well and continued to manage money for many years; others did less well. I also engaged a resident money manager, Jim Marquez. The overall performance was mediocre, and I became dissatisfied with the arrangement, so I decided to come back and become more active. Jim Marquez couldn't put up with that, so he left.

In 1984, you decided that you weren't going to farm out all the money to other fund managers. You decided to get back into the investment business and to build a team. It was just a question of identifying the good players.

That came a little later. At first I did not have a team and I had to reenter the fray on my own.

That was the time you began your real-time experiment. Explain what that was.

In order to get myself intellectually engaged again in investing, I decided to try to write a book about my approach to investments. I started what I called a real-time experiment. The idea was to record the decision-making process as it unfolded. Since I regard investing as an historical process, it seemed to me the right kind of experiment to conduct. Not a scientific experiment, but an alchemical experiment, because I expected the fact that I was conducting an experiment to influence the results. I hoped that the influence would be positive, and my hopes were fulfilled. We had another period of explosive growth. Therefore, although the experiment did not really prove the theory according to scientific standards, it justified itself according to the standards established by the theory. It was one of my contentions that theories and experiments can influence the subject matter to which they refer. So, in 1985, I started the real-time experiment.

You described this in *The Alchemy of Finance.*

Yes, it's in the book. The real-time experiment turned out to be a very good idea because it stimulated my thinking. Having to explain my reasons for making decisions forced me to become more coherent; it imposed a certain discipline on me, which was very helpful. The real-time experiment covered the Plaza Accord in September 1985, which was a major coup for me and for the Fund. We made approximately 114 percent in the 15 months of the real-time experiment. It was probably the highest honorarium ever received by an author for writing a book.

Let's talk about the Plaza Accord and explain how that fits into the real-time experiment. On Sunday, September 22, the Group of Five met at the Plaza Hotel, and decided that the dollar, which was

extremely strong during the early 1980s, had gotten to a point where it was just too high. They entered into an agreement to depreciate the dollar. Can you tell me how you recognized the importance of that, and what you did about it?

As I described in *The Alchemy of Finance,* the Plaza Accord meant that the regime of freely floating exchange rates had come to an end and it was replaced by what is called a dirty float. The mold was broken and this was a new game. I thought that it was a necessary step for them to take, and I recognized the significance of this new departure. Even though I already had a long position in the yen and the mark, I moved in and heavily increased those positions. I don't recall now whether I did it right away. I probably did, and then I stopped, and then I bought some more. But, at any rate, that was a case where I felt that I was ahead of the curve. I already had a position, and could afford to increase it and go for the jugular. I took on a very large position, which paid off handsomely.

Your strategy worked well with the Plaza Accord, but you had a different experience shortly thereafter. Can you describe what happened with Black Monday?

My book was published in 1987 and I went around talking about it. I went to the John F. Kennedy School of Government at Harvard to discuss my boom/bust theory, and I came out of the meeting to find that the market had sold off sharply. This was, I think, the Wednesday before Black Monday. That's when I should have been in the office and getting the hell out of the market, but I missed it. I could see trouble coming, but I thought it would come first in Japan, where a financial bubble was developing, so I was short Japan and long the United States. In any event, the hit came in the United States. The Japanese market did not crack, because it was supported by the authorities. My short positions in Japan actually became a burden and forced me to liquidate my long positions, in order to avoid the possibility of a margin call. I had to pull back, which I did with alacrity because my principle is to survive first and make money afterwards. We suffered a very serious loss in a matter of a few days. However, we were way ahead for the year, so we actually ended the year, 1987, in the plus column with a profit of, I think, 14 percent.

By 1987, you had built up something of a management team.

Right. I had a team of four senior analysts/managers. If you recall, you were rather skeptical at the time about whether I would be able to work with them and give them enough leeway. But I was only too happy to delegate authority, and I distanced myself from the running of the business. I left it more to them, without actually removing myself from the top spot. During 1987, my book attracted Stanley Druckenmiller, who was, at that time, a fund manager at Dreyfus. He read my book and he sought me out to discuss it because he found it intellectually stimulating. We got to know each other, and I asked him to join my firm. He was very loyal and refused to leave Dreyfus because he felt that he would be highly rewarded for having made a lot of money during a difficult year. He had handled the crash much better than I did. But, at the end of the year, when the reward was not forthcoming, he felt free to join me, which he did in September of 1988. He took charge of what we call the macro investing. I was still the boss, but I was increasingly absent because I was very involved in China and Russia and Eastern Europe. He made the macro decisions and the team that I had engaged at the beginning of 1987 was in charge of stock picking. Stan didn't perform as well during his first year with me as he had expected he would, and he blamed it on my presence, which somehow hemmed him in, made him self-conscious, or cramped his style. He was getting quite frustrated. There was no conflict between us, but he was feeling dissatisfied with himself. He didn't hide it, either. Therefore, when my involvement in Eastern Europe became so great that I was often not around at all, I put him fully in charge. We made it more formal, but it had been my understanding anyhow. Still, it helped him. Before, he probably felt he was in charge as long as he was doing all right, but maybe he wouldn't be in charge if he didn't do so well. When he really took over, we developed a coach-and-player relationship, which has worked very well ever since. In my role as coach, Stan and the other players can come to me for advice, bounce ideas off me, without feeling that I'm going to interfere with their play-calling, or take the ball from them and run with it myself. I think that is a very useful method of operating. I'm also in charge of allocating their profit participation. Half the profit of the management company is reserved for the management team. I divide the pie. And that again is very useful because they know that I am interested in the overall performance of the Fund over the long term. They accept that I am an impartial and fair judge, and that makes for a good team spirit. I am also in charge of the overall firm strategy such as the decision to start new funds or to wind up existing funds or enter new areas of business.

When did you move into this new role?

In the late summer of 1989, when the revolution in Eastern Europe heated up. As I said earlier, I couldn't continue running the Fund on a day-to-day basis; I couldn't stay on the line in terms of decision making. It turned out to be a wonderful move. We had excellent performance for three years running, another boom period in the history of the Fund.

The three years were 1991, 1992, and 1993?

Yes.

But 1994 was not such a good year.

The second worst year in the history of Quantum Fund. Still, we managed to show a modest profit—not bad after a magnificent three-year run. It is normal to give back a portion of one's gains at the end of a major move, and it happened this time too, but it was much smaller than on previous occasions, in 1982 and 1987. 1995 promises to be even more difficult than 1994. We started off nearly 10 percent in the hole, but I am confident that we will come out ahead. The team has its head in the right place, and we have greater depth of management than at any time in the history of the Fund. There is no way one could produce results like ours without ups and downs.

As I listen to the story of the Quantum Fund, what seems from the outside like an unbroken chain of success turns out to be a series of ups and downs. Your record is phenomenal: a nearly 35 percent average annual return to shareholders over 26 years—after the management's participation in profits. $1000 invested in 1969 would have grown to approximately $2,150,000 if dividends could have been reinvested. Yet, if I look closely, I can see several distinct periods. The first ten years, you and Jim Rogers against the world. Then a boom/bust from 1979 to 1981. Then a brief interregnum, when you farmed out portions of the Fund to other managers. Then the real-time experiment followed by the crash of 1987—another boom/bust sequence. Then the reign of Stanley Druckenmiller.

You are absolutely right.

Hasn't the size of the Fund become a problem?

Yes it has. It is an ecological problem. We are too big for our environment. I recognized the problem in 1989 and decided to start distributing our earnings to our shareholders. We also started diversifying. We established a fund for emerging markets, we went into real estate, into industrial participations.

Isn't that terribly dangerous? Look at what happened to great growth companies like Xerox when they diversified.

I recognize the danger, but I regard it as a challenge. It helps to focus my mind. If we didn't try to adjust our modus operandi to our increased size, the danger would be even greater.

Since you have become so famous, people are watching you very closely. Doesn't that inhibit your freedom of movement?

Yes, it does. But there are so many false rumors about our activities that they often obscure what we are really doing. Our reputation has brought us some positive benefits, too, especially in the area of making industrial deals. But the greatest benefit is the management team we have been able to attract. We are not ready for extinction yet. Even so, we must not set the hurdle too high. We cannot possibly repeat the performance of our first quarter century. If we did, we would end up owning all the shares in the world. We cannot afford to grow any bigger. And I would be satisfied if we showed half as good a performance in the coming 25 years as we did in the past 25.

THE THEORY OF INVESTING

Let's talk about the framework you use in your investing. You first wrote about this in *The Alchemy of Finance,* and you've indicated that this book was a breakthrough in your thinking. Why is the book so important to you?

It's my life's work. When the chips are down, philosophy is the most important part of my life.

But it's exactly your philosophy that has everyone confused. Why?

The main idea is that our understanding of the world in which we live is inherently imperfect. The situations we need to understand in order to reach our decisions are actually affected by those decisions. There is an innate divergence between the expectations of the people taking part in events and the actual outcome of those events. Sometimes the divergence is so small that it can be disregarded, but at other times it is so large that it becomes an important factor in determining the course of events. That is not an easy idea to communicate.

I can summarize the main idea in a few words—two words, in fact: imperfect understanding. But these two words are not really enough to convey the full idea because the imperfection relates not only to our understanding, but also to the situation in which we participate, the reality we seek to understand. That reality is a moving target because it is affected by our understanding.

On the one hand, reality is reflected in people's thinking—this is the cognitive function. On the other hand, people make decisions that affect reality and these decisions are based not on reality, but on people's interpretation of reality—I call this the participating function. The two functions work in opposite directions and in certain circumstances they can interfere with each other. The interaction between them takes the form of a two-way reflexive feedback mechanism.

Why do you call it reflexive?

You have heard of reflexive verbs, where the subject and the object is the same, haven't you? It is a feature of the French language. The word reflexive also has to do with reflection. It should not be confused with reflexes.

It is all in *The Alchemy of Finance,* isn't it?

The Alchemy of Finance was an important breakthrough for me because I managed to state the idea of reflexivity, which is crucial to my analysis of market behavior. However, I stated the idea imperfectly. Initially, the book was not terribly successful because very few people understood what I was trying to say. I did not get the kind of intellectual feedback that I was looking for. Still, there were some satisfying exceptions, like my encounter with Stanley Druckenmiller, who sought me out after reading the book; or there was Paul Tudor Jones who insisted that anybody who wanted to work for him first had to read the book and understand it. A small group of people seem to have gotten the idea.

Now that I have become a public figure, the book has begun to be taken seriously. I am beginning to get some worthwhile feedback, which has revealed some weaknesses in the theory as I stated it. I now recognize that I have been quite imprecise in using certain words, even the term "reflexivity." I use it to describe the structure of events that have thinking participants. I also use it to describe specific instances where the two-way feedback mechanism disrupts both the course of events and the participants' perceptions in a way that gives rise to a disequilibrium.

The first is a way of looking at things, a general theory that has universal validity. The second is a phenomenon that occurs only intermittently, but when it does, it makes history.

Let's deal first with your general theory of reflexivity.

Essentially, it has to do with the role of the thinking participant, and the relationship between his thinking and the events in which he participates. I believe that a thinking participant is in a very difficult position, because he is trying to understand a situation in which he is one of the actors. Traditionally, we think of understanding as essentially a passive role, and participating is an active role. In truth, the two roles interfere with each other, which makes it impossible for the participant to base any decisions on pure or perfect knowledge.

Classical economic theory assumes that market participants act on the basis of perfect knowledge. That assumption is false. The participants' perceptions influence the market in which they participate, but the market action also influences the participants' perceptions. They cannot obtain perfect knowledge of the market because their thinking is always affecting the market and the market is affecting their thinking. This makes analysis of market behavior much harder than it would be if the assumption of perfect knowledge were valid.

Economic theory needs to be fundamentally reconsidered. There is an element of uncertainty in economic processes that has been largely left unaccounted for. None of the social sciences can be expected to yield firm results comparable to the natural sciences, and economics is no exception. We must take a radically different view of the role that thinking plays in shaping events.

We are accustomed to think of events as a sequence of facts: one set of facts follows another in a never-ending chain. When a situation has thinking participants, the chain does not lead directly from fact to fact. It links a fact to the participants' thinking and then connects the participants' thinking to the next set of facts.

In trying to understand the thinking participants' role, what is it we must understand?

The first thing we must understand is that participants cannot confine their thinking to facts. They must take into account the thinking of all participants including themselves. That introduces an element of uncertainty in the sense that the participants' thinking does not correspond to the facts—yet it plays a role in shaping the facts. Instead of correspondence, there is almost always a discrepancy between the participants' perceptions and the actual state of affairs and a divergence between the participants' intentions and the actual outcome. This divergence is the key to understanding historical processes in general and the dynamics of financial markets in particular. In my opinion, misconceptions and mistakes play the same role in human affairs as mutation does in biology.

That is my core idea. It has, of course, a great number of ramifications. It may not be important to others, but it is terribly important to me. Everything else follows from it. And I have noticed that my view of the world is, in many ways, very different from the prevailing view.

The prevailing wisdom is that financial markets are in equilibrium. There are divergences, of course, because markets are not perfect, but they are in the nature of random walks and they tend to be corrected by other random events. This view is based on a false analogy with Newtonian physics.

I take a radically different position. In my view, the divergences are inherent in our imperfect understanding. Financial markets are characterized by a discrepancy between the participants' perceptions and the actual state of affairs. At times it is negligible; at other times the course of events cannot be understood without taking it into account.

Can you give some examples in the financial markets?

Usually, they take the form of boom/bust sequences. But not always. The boom/bust sequence is asymmetrical—slowly accelerating and then culminating in a catastrophic reversal. I discussed several cases in *The Alchemy of Finance:* the conglomerate boom of the 1960s, the classic case of the Real Estate Investment Trusts, the great international lending boom of the 1970s that culminated in the Mexican crisis of 1982, and so on. I developed a theory about freely fluctuating exchange rates, which also have a tendency to go to extremes, but the extremes tend to be more symmetrical. I discussed some impure cases, like the leveraged buyout and takeover boom of the 1980s. In all these cases, there is a reflexive interaction between a prevailing bias and a prevailing trend. The point is that these cases are in some sense exceptional. There are long stretches in any sequence of events where the reflexive interaction is relatively insignificant.

This is the point I failed to make sufficiently clear in *The Alchemy of Finance.* I used the same word—reflexivity—to describe the two-way interaction and the structure of events that permits such interaction. I still do, but I hope I have driven home the point that the reflexive interaction is occasional while the reflexive structure is permanent.

In what you might consider the normal situation, the discrepancy between thinking and reality is not very large and there are forces at play that tend to bring them closer together, partly because people can learn from experience, and partly because people can actually change and shape social conditions according to their desires. These are what I call near-equilibrium conditions.

But there are other circumstances in which people's thinking and the actual state of affairs are very far removed from each other, and have no tendency to come closer together. These are what I call far-from-equilibrium conditions. They fall into two categories. There are cases of dynamic disequilibrium when the prevailing bias and the prevailing trend reinforce each other until the gap between them becomes so wide that it brings a catastrophic collapse. There are also cases of static disequilibrium, although they can rarely be found in financial markets. They are characterized by a very rigid, dogmatic mode of thinking, and very rigid social conditions; neither of them changes, and dogma and reality remain very far apart. Indeed, when reality changes, however slowly, and the dogma doesn't adjust to these changes, thinking and reality drift even further apart. Such conditions can prevail for very long periods of time, as they did—to use a familiar example—in the Soviet Union. By contrast, the collapse of the Soviet system may be taken as an example of dynamic disequilibrium.

We may envisage dynamic and static disequilibrium as the two extremes, with near-equilibrium conditions in between. I like to compare these three states of affairs to the three states in which water can be found in nature: liquid, frozen, or steam. Those three states are very different in character, and the behavior of water is very different in those three states. The same applies to the thinking participants. In what we might consider their normal state, the two-way feedback mechanism that I call reflexivity is not very important; it can be disregarded. When they approach or reach those far-from-equilibrium conditions, reflexivity becomes important and we have boom/bust sequences.

How do you draw the line between near-equilibrium and far-from-equilibrium conditions?

That's the $64,000 question. The borderline is blurred. There are almost always forces at work that would take us into far-from-equilibrium territory. They are resisted by countervailing forces. Usually, the countervailing forces prevail, but occasionally they fail. That is when we have a change of regime or a revolution. I am particularly interested in these occasions, but I would be lying if I told you I have a well-developed theory that can explain them and predict them. I am still at the exploratory state. I can do better in the financial markets than in dealing with history in general, because financial markets provide a more clearly defined space and the data are quantified and publicly available.

Let's stick to financial markets right now. Can you explain your boom/bust theory?

I tried to do it in *The Alchemy of Finance*, but obviously I didn't do a very good job. What most people got out of it is that market prices are influenced by the participants' bias. If that were all, it would be too obvious to discuss. A boom/bust process occurs only when market prices find a way to influence the so-called fundamentals that are supposed to be reflected in market prices.

Look at the various examples I used in the book. In the conglomerate boom, conglomerates used their overvalued shares as currency to buy earnings which, in turn, served to justify the overvaluation. In the international lending boom, banks used so-called debt ratios to measure the borrowing capacity of debtor countries, such as the ratio of the debt outstanding to the Gross National Product or the ratio of debt service to exports. They considered these debt ratios as objective measures, but it turned out they were influenced by their own activities: for instance, when they stopped lending, the Gross National Product deteriorated, and so on. This short-circuit between the so-called fundamentals and the valuation placed on them does not occur very often, but when it does it sets in motion a process that initially may be self-reinforcing but eventually becomes self-defeating.

Usually some error in the act of valuation is involved. The most common error is a failure to recognize that a so-called fundamental value is not really independent of the act of valuation. That was the case in the conglomerate boom, where per-share earnings growth could be manufactured by acquisitions, and also in the international lending boom where the lending activities of the banks helped improve the debt ratios that banks used to guide them in their lending activity.

But it is not always so. The Japanese land boom was not an error: it was a deliberate and far-sighted effort to encourage savings and depress living standards for the greater glory of Japan. The Japanese seem to use reflexivity as a policy tool, probably because they come from a different intellectual tradition. Manipulating the so-called fundamentals seems to come naturally to them, while we put our faith in the invisible hand. Now we are trying to imitate them, just as they are getting caught up in a web of their own weaving.

Does reflexivity follow a predetermined pattern?

Absolutely not. But in order to become noticeable it must be at least initially self-reinforcing. If a self-reinforcing process goes on long enough it must eventually become unsustainable because either the gap between thinking and reality becomes too wide or the participants' bias becomes too pronounced. Hence, reflexive processes that become historically significant tend to follow an initially self-reinforcing, but eventually self-defeating, pattern. That is what I call the boom/bust sequence. Reflexive interactions that correct themselves before they reach boom proportions don't become historically significant; yet they may occur much more frequently than full-fledged booms that result in busts.

Is there a specific boom/bust pattern?

I have established one, based partly on observation and partly on logic, but I want to emphasize that there is nothing determinate or compulsory about it. First, the process may be aborted at any stage. Second, the model describes the process in isolation. In reality, many processes are going on at the same time, interfering with each other, and boom/bust sequences are punctuated by external shocks. Only rarely does the actual course of events resemble the isolated model. Still, the model establishes a certain sequence, with certain stages, and we could not have a boom/bust process in which the key stages are out of sequence. So, if and when it occurs, it does follow a specific pattern.

What are the key stages?

Usually the process starts with a trend that is not yet recognized. When it becomes recognized, the recognition tends to reinforce it. In this *initial phase*, the prevailing trend and the prevailing bias work to reinforce each other. At this stage, we cannot yet speak of far-from-equilibrium conditions. That happens only as the process evolves. The trend becomes increasingly dependent on the bias and the bias becomes increasingly exaggerated. During this period, both the bias and the trend may be repeatedly tested by external shocks. If they survive the *tests*, they emerge strengthened until they become seemingly unshakable. We may call this the *period of acceleration*. A point comes when the divergence between belief and reality becomes so great that the participants' bias comes to be recognized as such. We may call this the *moment of truth*. The trend may be sustained by inertia, but ceases to be reinforced by belief so that it flattens out—let us call this the *twilight period* or the period of stagnation. Eventually, the loss of belief is bound to cause a reversal in the trend that had become dependent on an ever stronger bias; this trend reversal is the *crossover point*. The opposite trend engenders a bias in the opposite direction, causing a catastrophic acceleration that qualifies as a *crash*.

The chart on page 74 shows that the boom/bust pattern has an asymmetrical shape. It starts slowly and accelerates gradually to a wild excess that is followed by a twilight period and then by a catastrophic collapse. When the process is complete, neither the trend nor the bias remains the same. The process does not repeat itself. There is a regime change.

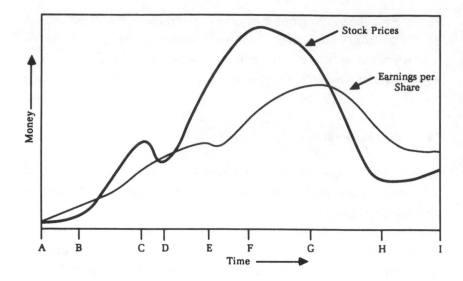

Have you been able to identify boom/bust patterns in history as well as in financial markets?

Yes. It doesn't happen very often because usually there are too many different processes going on and interfering with each other. But occasionally a process is so important that it overwhelms all the others. That was the case with the rise and fall of the Soviet Union; that may be the case with the integration and disintegration of Europe.

How does the boom/bust pattern apply to the Soviet Union?

The Soviet system was all-embracing: a form of government, an economic system, a territorial empire, and an ideology. It was also almost completely isolated from the outside world. That is why the pattern applies. But the Soviet Union was rigid: both the prevailing bias—Marxist dogma—and the prevailing system were rigid. Therefore the acceleration period, where the bias and the trend became almost unshakable, manifested itself in excessive rigidity. This period was reached under Stalin, especially after the system survived the severe test of the Second World War. After Stalin's death came the moment of truth: Kruschchev's speech to the 20th Congress. But eventually the regime reasserted itself, and a twilight period began. Dogma was preserved by administrative methods, but it was no longer reinforced by a belief in its validity. Interestingly, the rigidity of the system increased even further. As long as there had been a live totalitarian at the helm, the communist party line could be changed at his whim. But now, that flexibility was lost. At the same time, the terror also abated, and a subtle process of decay set in. Every institution started to jockey for position. Since none of them enjoyed any real autonomy, they had to engage in a form of barter with the other institutions.

Gradually an elaborate system of institutional bargaining replaced what was supposed to be central planning. At the same time, an informal economy developed that supplemented and filled in the gaps left by the formal system. This twilight period is what is now called the *period of stagnation.* The inadequacy of the system became increasingly evident and the pressure for reform mounted. Gorbachev became the party chief. This was the crossover point. Reform accelerated the process of disintegration, because it introduced or legitimized alternatives while the system depended on the lack of alternatives for its survival. Economic reform demonstrated the need for political reforms. With the advent of *perestroika* and *glasnost,* the process of disintegration entered into its terminal phase, leading to a catastrophic acceleration, which has culminated in the total collapse of the system.

The fascinating feature of this sequence is that it does not lead from near-equilibrium to far-from-equilibrium conditions, but from extreme rigidity to the other extreme—revolutionary change.

So it is different from the boom/bust process in financial markets.

Not really. I can identify at least one case in the financial markets that is similar. Believe it or not, it is the United States banking system. It has also gone from extreme rigidity to extreme changeability. The process was similar but inverted: It started with a bust and ended with a boom.

The United States banking system broke down in the 1930s. It became highly regulated. The structure of the industry was practically frozen by regulation. Expansion across state lines was prohibited, and in some states, even branch banking was outlawed. Managements were traumatized. Safety became the paramount consideration, overshadowing profit or growth. A dull business attracted dull people, and there was little movement or innovation in the industry. Bank stocks were ignored by investors.

These conditions prevailed until the early 1970s. By then, changes were brewing underneath the calm surface. A new breed of bankers was emerging who had been educated in business schools and thought in terms of bottom-line profits. The spiritual center of the new school of thinking was First National City Bank of New York, and people trained there were fanning out and occupying top spots at other banks. New kinds of financial instruments were being introduced, and some banks were beginning to utilize their capital more aggressively and putting together very creditable earnings performances.

There were some acquisitions within state limits, leading to the emergence of larger units. Banks typically leveraged their equity 14 to 16 times, with the Bank of America running as high as 20 times. The better banks showed a return on equity in excess of 13 percent. In any other industry such a return on equity, combined with per-share earnings growth of better than 10 percent, would have been rewarded by the shares selling at a decent premium over asset value, but bank shares were selling at little or no premium. Analysts of bank shares were aware of this relative undervaluation, but they despaired of seeing the situation corrected because the underlying changes were too gradual and the prevailing valuation too stable. Yet, many banks had reached the point where they were pushing against the limits of what was considered prudent leverage. If they wanted to continue growing, they would need to raise additional equity capital.

It was against this background that First National City hosted a dinner for security analysts one evening in 1972—an unheard-of event in the banking industry. I was not invited, but it prompted me to publish a report that recommended purchase of a bouquet of the more aggressively managed banks. It argued that bank stocks were about to come alive because managements had a good story to tell and they had started telling it. "Growth" and "banks" seemed like a contradiction in terms, I wrote, but the contradiction was about to be resolved by bank shares being awarded growth multiples.

Bank stocks did, in fact, have a good move in 1972 and I made about 50 percent on my bouquet. Some of the more alert banks managed to raise some capital. If the process of raising capital at a premium over book value had become established, banks could have expanded on a sound basis and the evolution of the banking system would have followed a near-equilibrium path. As it happened, the process had hardly started when the first oil shock occurred in 1973. Inflation accelerated, interest rates rose, and a 13 percent return on capital was no longer sufficient to enable banks to sell shares at a premium. In the aftermath of the first oil shock, there was a tremendous increase in the flow of funds to the oil-producing countries. It was the beginning of petrodollar recycling and the great international lending boom of the 1970s that ended with the Mexican crisis of 1982. As you can see, the United States banking system also went from one extreme to the other, having missed the chance to settle down to near-equilibrium growth in 1972. The fall and rise of the United States banking system parallels the rise and fall of the Soviet Union.

That is fascinating. I would never have thought of drawing a parallel between the Soviet Union and the American banking system.

It is amusing. But don't be carried away by the analogy. It is very rare to find isolated boom/bust sequences in the real world. Both the Soviet system and the American banking system were significant enough and isolated enough to exhibit the features of a full-blown boom/bust sequence. Therein lies the similarity. They are interesting as theoretical specimens because they show that the boom/bust process does not only go from near-equilibrium to dynamic disequilibrium, but it may also include static disequilibrium; in that case, the period of acceleration manifests itself as a period of increased rigidity. But don't expect to see many full-blown boom/bust sequences in the real world. They are few and far between. Systems do not operate in isolation. Every system has subsystems and is itself part of a larger system called reality. The various systems and subsystems interfere with each other.

There has been a recent development in science, variously called the science of complexity, evolutionary systems theory, or chaos theory. To understand historical processes, this approach is much more useful than the traditional approach, which is analytical. Unfortunately, our view of the world has been shaped by analytical science to a greater extent than is good for us. Economics seeks to be an analytical science. But all historical processes, including the financial markets, are complex and cannot be understood on the basis of analytical science. We need a whole new approach and my theory of reflexivity is just a first step in this direction. The boom/bust pattern should not be taken too seriously. It serves the purposes of illustration, and should not be used as a mold into which reality must fit. There are many different processes going on at the same time, some of which are dynamic, others static, others near equilibrium. The interaction between them gives rise to yet other processes that fall into the same categories.

This is getting terribly abstract. Could we have some specific examples?

Gladly, but first, I should like to make only one general point. In the case of a disequilibrium, economists talk about shocks and exogenous—or outside—influences. By demonstrating the existence of more or less isolated boom/bust sequences, I hope I have shown that disequilibrium is not necessarily introduced from the outside; it is inherent in the imperfect understanding of the participants. In other words, financial markets are inherently unstable and the idea of a theoretical equilibrium that would prevail if only . . . is itself a product of our imperfect understanding.

78

5

THEORY IN ACTION

Can you explain exactly how you apply the boom/bust theory in financial markets? Let's take the case of your most famous exploit. How did you take advantage of the sterling crisis?

Sterling, as you know, was part of the European Exchange Rate Mechanism (ERM), and that mechanism functioned in a near-equilibrium condition for a fairly long period of time. It was actually a very clever, sophisticated system that allowed for frequent adjustments and the adjustments were not severe enough that speculators like me could make a lot of money out of them. So it was a near-equilibrium system, about as good as an exchange rate mechanism can get.

Then came the collapse of the Soviet Union and the reunification of Germany, and the system was thrown into a dynamic disequilibrium. According to my theory, every exchange rate regime is flawed. There was a latent flaw in the ERM as well, but it became blatant only as a consequence of the reunification. The flaw was that the Bundesbank played a dual role in the system: It was both the anchor of the ERM and the constitutional protector of the stability of the German currency. During the near-equilibrium period, the Bundesbank could fill both roles without any problems, but the reunification of Germany, which caused the exchange of the East German currency for deutschemark at a very high, excessive rate, created a conflict between

79

the two roles of the Bundesbank: its constitutional role and its role as anchor of the ERM.

The Ostmark/deutschemark exchange rate had more to do with political objectives than with economic reality?

Right. And the tremendous injection of capital from West Germany into East Germany set up strong inflationary pressures within the German economy. The Bundesbank was duty-bound—by the constitution, not just by law—to counteract it by pushing up interest rates and it did so with considerable vigor. This was at a time when Europe in general, and Britain in particular, were in the depths of a recession. The high German interest rate policy was totally inappropriate to the conditions that prevailed in England. A conflict arose between the two roles of the Bundesbank—and, under the constitution, there was no doubt which role would take precedence. Pursuing a resolutely tight monetary policy at a time when the rest of Europe was in recession disqualified the Bundesbank from serving as the anchor of the ERM. That threw the ERM, which had been operating near-equilibrium, into dynamic disequilibrium.

Other conflicts exacerbated the situation. There was a conflict between Chancellor Kohl and the Bundesbank about the exchange rate between the East German mark and the deutschemark, and about the way the government deficit was financed. But the conflict went much deeper.

When the Soviet Union collapsed, Chancellor Kohl went to President Mitterrand of France and said that he wanted to accomplish the reunification of Germany in a European context. They both agreed that the structure of the European Community needed to be strengthened. Prime Minister Thatcher, of course, disagreed. Strenuous negotiations ensued and finally resulted in the Maastricht Treaty. Among other things, the Treaty established a mechanism for creating a common European currency, which turned out to be a very flawed concept indeed.

The proposed common European currency (EMU) was the death knell of the Bundesbank, because the Bundesbank was going to be superseded by a European Central Bank. One might say that the European Central Bank was the spiritual successor to the Bundesbank, but that is scant consolation for an institution that is extremely powerful and enjoys its power. Institutions seem to have an innate desire to perpetuate themselves. They cling to the preservation of the species even more tenaciously than other organisms do. The Maastricht Treaty endangered the very existence of the Bundesbank.

So there was conflict over these three issues: one, that Germany needed a different monetary policy than the rest of Europe; two, that the Bundesbank advocated a different fiscal policy for Germany than the one that Chancellor Kohl actually adopted; and three, that the Bundesbank was fighting for its institutional survival. In my view, of the three conflicts, the third was the least understood and the most decisive. The conflicts simmered for a while; after all, the reunification occurred in 1990 and the crisis came to a head only in 1992. But anyone aware of this drama could watch it unfold.

Describe the events that led up to September 1992. When did you first get an idea that a breakdown in sterling was imminent?

I got my first hint from Bundesbank President Schlesinger in a speech he gave at a prestigious gathering. He said that investors were making a mistake when they thought of the ECU (European Currency Unit) as a fixed basket of currencies. He was alluding particularly to the Italian lira as a currency that was not too sound. I asked him after the speech whether he liked the ECU as a currency, and he said he liked it as a concept but he didn't like the name. He would have preferred it if it were called the mark.

I got the message. It encouraged us to short the Italian lira, and, in fact, the Italian lira was forced out of the exchange rate mechanism shortly thereafter. That was a clear sign that sterling was also vulnerable. Also, the profit we made on selling the lira short gave us a cushion for taking a risk on sterling. I don't remember the exact sequence of events. I'm blessed with an extremely poor memory, which allows me to deal with the future rather than the past. I remember the "no" vote on the Maastricht Treaty in Denmark and the frantic weekend negotiations prior to the French referendum. As the pressure on sterling built up, it became really exciting. The climax was finally reached when the British government increased the interest rate by 2 percent in order to defend sterling. This was an act of desperation that signaled to us that the British position was untenable. It encouraged us to continue selling sterling even more aggressively than we did before. That was the end: Interest rates were raised at noon. By the evening, sterling had to quit the ERM.

Your critics say that England did the right thing by raising interest rates 2 percent and it would have worked if you hadn't ganged up on the situation and shorted sterling all afternoon.

Well, first of all, it was an untenable move, because if it hadn't been untenable, then our "ganging up on it" wouldn't have pushed Britain out of the ERM. Second, we were not the only ones playing and the process would have unfolded more or less the same way even if I had never been born. We may have played a role at the very end, when the Bank of England raised interest rates, because at that point market participants might have hesitated and our decisive reaction might have got the herd going again. We may have slightly accelerated the process, but I'm sure that it would have occurred in any case.

Now, can you relate this again to your theory?

An institutional structure—the ERM—which had been operating near-equilibrium for a period of time—was thrown into dynamic disequilibrium. Another element, which I haven't yet mentioned, aggravated the situation. It was a flaw in the market participants' perception. If you recall, institutional investors expected the European currencies to be unified in one continuous process, so they concluded that exchange rates would fluctuate even less than they had in the past. Everyone rushed out to buy high-yielding bonds in the weaker currencies. This made the ERM more rigid than it had been before, and set it up for a radical break rather than a gradual adjustment.

You were recognizing that everybody was looking at a situation of modest incremental changes and you saw an enormous discrepancy building up, so your insight here was that this was a disequilibrium of major proportions, and that's why you thought this was one of those few instances where you should increase your leverage to the maximum.

That's right. I was prepared for a regime change, whereas other people were acting within a prevailing regime. And that is where I think my awareness that conditions can undergo revolutionary change was useful. If you recall, the British government assured the public up to the last minute that the ERM was rock-solid. They may have influenced some investors, but they certainly didn't convince us.

And you turned out to be right. Sterling did break, and you made a tremendous profit on it. But you also got a tremendous amount of attention, more attention than you ever did before, and not all of it was favorable. As profitable as that exercise was, you got attacked for it. What is your response to that?

I fight for many causes in my life, but I don't particularly feel like defending currency speculation. I consider it a necessary evil. I think it is better than currency restrictions, but a unified currency would be even better. My defense is that I operate within the rules. If there is a breakdown in the rules, that is not my fault as a lawful participant but the fault of those who set the rules. I think that is a very sound and justified position, and I have absolutely no moral qualms about being branded a speculator. But, as I say, I don't feel like waging a campaign trying to defend speculation either. I have better battles to fight. I think that it behooves the authorities to design a system that does not reward speculators. When speculators profit, the authorities have failed in some way or another. But they don't like to admit failure; they would rather call for speculators to be hung from lampposts than to engage in a little bit of soul-searching to see what they did wrong.

Was this a case of your carrying the theory of reflexivity to a new level? The idea is that a participant can influence the outcome, but here the participant really instigated the outcome. Your theory told you, "Look, here's a situation that's vulnerable; if you participate in this in sufficient size, you can make the outcome predetermined."

It was not so predetermined. In retrospect, it was predetermined, but not in prospect. Believe me, speculation is not without risk, and the outcome is far from assured. In any case, we did not act autonomously. We followed the orders of our master, the Bundesbank. Perhaps we understood better than others who our master was and we had better ears in picking up the signals than others did. But there is no doubt in my mind who was the master of the hunt. We might have been wrong in believing that the Bundesbank was determined to break the ERM in order to preserve itself as the arbiter of monetary policy in Europe, but it proved to be a fertile fallacy.

By the way, the game is not over. The European Monetary Union is still a threat to the institutional existence of the Bundesbank, and the hunt is in full swing even as we speak. The dollar is weakening, partly because of the Mexican crisis and partly because of an apparent softening in the United States economy. The Bundesbank is talking tough. It just published its quarterly report, which ignores the latest international developments and holds out the prospect of further tightening in Germany. The result is a strengthening of the German mark against all European currencies. The French franc is weakening because of the scandals and the decline in Balladur's popularity. In the aftermath of the Mexican crisis, there is a flight of capital from Italy. As these countries try to shore up their currencies, they sell dollars, further depressing the dollar/mark. It's a self-reinforcing circle that is further reinforced by the Bundesbank. We have entered another period of currency volatility. We look to the Bundesbank for our cue, because it is by far the most powerful force in the currency market.

This contradicts the generally accepted opinion that the speculators are more powerful than the authorities.

In the case of the Bundesbank, it does. We do the dancing, but they call the tune.

You are widely credited with being able to influence markets.

After the sterling crisis, I became known as "the man who broke the Bank of England." That is what gave me the reputation that I can move markets. But at the time of the sterling crisis, I was just a member of the crowd—maybe larger and more successful than most—but still just one of many. Even now, my influence is largely illusory. A market move may become associated with my name, as happened once with gold. But if we try to move against the market, we get trampled on. That happened to us more than once, most recently with the yen.

The fact remains that the market pays attention to what we do and what I say. What we do is usually obscured by false rumors. But the fact that my statements may move markets puts me in a very peculiar position. I must be very careful about my statements. It complicates my life considerably.

I don't see why.

Because I believe that financial markets are inherently unstable, I must be careful not to create instability. For instance, when the French franc came under attack, I really believed I could have toppled it if I joined the fray. This led me to behave rather foolishly. I chose to abstain from speculating against the franc in order to be able to express what I thought were constructive suggestions. This had doubly unfortunate results: I lost what was a profit opportunity, *and* I annoyed the French authorities even more with my comments than I would have done by speculating against the franc. It taught me a lesson: Speculators ought to keep quiet and speculate.

In the end, you said that you were no longer going to refrain from buying and selling francs, and you did make some money in the French franc.

Not much. The profit opportunity by that time was rather minimal.

But now when you see another profit opportunity, you don't hesitate to seize it.

That's right. I learned my lesson last time. But I make a point of refraining from public comment. Perhaps I shouldn't be talking with you, either, but by the time this book is published, events will have unfolded and what I am saying now cannot affect the markets.

But you do make public comments.

Only with the public interest in mind. For instance, I advocate a common European currency. According to my theory, all exchange rate mechanisms are flawed. The only way to preserve the common market is to have a common currency. And I rather suspect that it may not be possible to establish a common currency by a process of gradual convergence, because the trend is toward divergence. It will require a political decision, a discontinuity, the setting of a target date.

We talked about the sterling crisis as an example of disequilibrium in Europe. But in the late 1980s, a bubble developed in Japan that was certainly the Far Eastern version of this disequilibrium phenomenon. I wonder if you could interpret that for us and give me some feeling for where we are in terms of how Japan fits into the boom/bust sequence.

Well, that's a rather painful question because I saw a financial bubble developing in Japan in the mid-1980s and I speculated that it had to bust. I went short in the Japanese stock market because I expected the crash of 1987 to start in Japan. But in actual fact it started in the United States and I found myself short in Japan, and long in the United States, and I got badly hurt in the market at that time. But, the nature of the boom/bust process was very clear.

Japan had a very high savings rate, a strong currency, and extremely low inflation and interest rates, and a very highly priced stock market that enabled Japanese companies to raise capital at a very low cost, and that gave them a competitive advantage. At the same time, Japan had a limited supply of land, which was reinforced by rigid regulations such as the Sunshine Laws, which restricted the building of high-rise buildings. So there was a physical shortage and the cost of housing went up much faster than wages. This induced people to save even more in order to buy a house. You had a self-reinforcing process at work to maximize savings and to minimize the rise in living standards. It was a machine designed to make Japan the leading economy in the world, while keeping the Japanese working hard with very little reward. It was a very efficient machine that did, in fact, give Japan a competitive advantage in practically everything. But, like all these self-reinforcing processes, it had a flaw in it. It exacerbated the difference between people who owned a house, and people who didn't own one. This became a divisive social force. The resentment against the system grew until eventually there was a political upheaval, an end to the dominance of the Liberal Democratic

Party and the beginning of a regime change. Preceding this point, there was a tremendous land boom that was even greater than the boom in stocks. It was eventually punctured, and there was a big bust in the real estate market that was even bigger than the decline in the stock market.

I misjudged somewhat the timing of this bust, and I got hurt in 1987. There was an artificial extension of the boom after 1987. The Ministry of Finance prevented a bust in 1987 by propping up the market. Then it embarked on a deliberate policy of providing liquidity to the world. I remember meeting a Japanese official who spelled it out to me. He said that the crash of 1987 won't have consequences similar to the crash of 1929 because Japan was ready to step into the breech and supply liquidity to the world. They wanted their financial clout to match their industrial clout. As you will recall, after 1987, Japanese banks became the major lenders in the world; Mitsubishi Real Estate bought Rockefeller Center. But this time the Japanese overreached themselves. The Japanese financial bubble continued to swell and the overseas lending and investment boom came to a bad end. When the Japanese Central Bank finally deflated the financial bubble, Japanese banks were left with an awful lot of bad debts from which they are still suffering. Most financial investments abroad have gone sour, which has been an important factor in the recent large-scale repatriation of capital. When the bear market finally came, we were still around to take advantage of it. It came in 1990, as I recall. But I must give the Japanese authorities credit: they managed to deflate the bubble without a bust. It was perhaps the largest bubble every deflated in an orderly manner rather than through a catastrophic collapse.

Is the decline in the Japanese stock market over?

We thought so, until quite recently. We were playing the Japanese market from the long side during much of 1994.

What made you bullish on Japan?

We thought that Japan had already gone through a tremendous adjustment. After all, the Japanese economy had been in a recession for three years or so. Land prices had declined, banks had gone through the wringer, and the stock market had dropped by well over half. Japan had adjusted to the changing circumstances by transferring a lot of its production capacity, which requires cheap labor, to other East Asian countries that have plenty of cheap labor.

We formed a hypothesis at the beginning of 1994 that the Japanese market was going to go up, because the Japanese economy was about to start recovering. There was a tremendous amount of liquidity in the system and we felt some of that liquidity would go into the stock market. And in fact, we made some money on the long side in Japanese stock markets.

Did you see it as the beginning of a new boom/bust sequence?

Not at all. There were several countervailing forces at work. On the one hand, there was the prospect of cyclical recovery, which implied higher stock prices. On the other hand, there were important structural changes going on that had negative implications for the valuation of stocks that may or may not have run their course. The recovery was cut short by the strength of the yen that depressed earnings and economic activity. There was no well-defined trend. We had no clear idea what the eventual outcome would be. We were just feeling our way. We saw it as a market for trading, stockpicking—or abstaining.

When you don't have a clear view, you prefer to stay out.

That's right. Remember, fully developed boom/bust sequences are few and far between. Markets tend to move in fits and starts, adopting a thesis and then abandoning it. We try to catch them if we can, but if we can't, we are better off not trying.

How did this apply to your trading in Japan?

As I told you, we made some modest money on our thesis of a cyclical recovery. We sold out because of the strength of the yen. Then we tried again and we lost some money. We took our loss in 1995. On balance, we are about even. It goes to show that when you are confused it is best to do nothing. You are just going for a random walk and that is when you are liable to get mugged because you don't have staying power. You are likely to be faked out by some stray fluctuation because you lack the courage of your convictions. As my friend Victor Niederhoffer says, the market always destroys the weak—that is, investors who don't have well-founded convictions. You need some convictions to avoid getting faked out, but having the courage of your convictions could get you wiped out if your convictions are false. So I prefer to take a stand only when I have well-founded convictions.

You tend to take a stand when the market is confused, but you have conviction.

That is the case in Japan today.

What do you expect?

We think the market is just about ready for another leg down.

Why is that?

Mainly because of the yen. The yen had been in a trading range of Y95 to Y105 to the dollar. The stock market was also in a trading range. But just recently, the yen broke out of the trading range and we expect the stock market to follow. There is a concerted attempt to keep the stock market from falling below 16,000 on the Nikkei index before the end of the Japanese fiscal year—which is at the end of March—but I don't believe the effort can be maintained indefinitely. After all, the attempt to keep the yen within a trading range has also failed. The strong yen is depressing both earnings and asset values. This could bring another leg down in the stock market similar to the one that occurred between 1989 and 1993. It would mean that the effort to preserve the present financial regime in Japan is not succeeding and further far-reaching changes in the financial structure are in the making.

That is quite a shocking prediction.

It is not a prediction. It is a hypothesis, and a tentative one at that—after all, we were playing the Japanese market on the long side until earlier this year—but we are currently willing to back it because the risk/reward ratio is very favorable.

What do you mean by the present financial regime?

One dominated by the MOF (Ministry of Finance) and populated by institutions—banks, brokers, trust banks, insurance companies—that take their signals from the MOF instead of the market. It is part of an overall system based on dominance, and it has been gaining dominance within the system. The MITI (Ministry of Trade and Industry) used to be much more influential in the early stages of the Japanese industrial miracle, but in recent years, the MOF has become the kingpin of the power structure. Its performance has been nothing short of disastrous. The industrial sector has been churning out a tremendous surplus and turning it over to the financial sector. The financial sector has wasted it. The grand adventure to follow in the footsteps of nineteenth-century Britain and become the financier of the world misfired; and the domestic asset bubble has also been deflated. The financial sector had been loaded with hidden assets—the fruits of the industrial miracle—but the assets have been dissipated. The process has taken so long because there were such large assets to dissipate. I don't believe that either the MOF or the financial institutions fully realize what has happened to them. They are uneasy, but they are not fully aware of their predicament. Yet it is not surprising that the financial sector should have performed so badly. They are guided by book values, not by market values; consequently, they are following the wrong signals. They are accustomed to work according to regulations and the MOF is accustomed to issue regulations. They are bureaucrats and bureaucrats are not cut out to operate in a market environment. Incidentally, there is a similarity with France—think of the Credit Lyonnais.

I could never understand what Japanese financial institutions were up to. They were always responding to some regulation, not to the real world. There are many examples, but they are all too technical, and I don't fully understand the regulations involved. For instance, the MOF introduced a rule that allowed financial institutions to carry Japanese government bonds at cost, but foreign bonds had to be marked to market and exchange losses, if they exceeded 15 percent, had to be recognized. This was an important factor in the repatriation of capital by Japanese financial institutions and the strength of the yen. Apparently, private placements and over-the-counter bonds do not have to be marked to market and therefore they fetch a premium—the opposite of what you would expect.

You can't dance to your own tune and do well in the market. On top of that came the invention of derivative instruments. One of the main uses of derivatives is to circumvent regulations. When foreign brokers brought derivatives to Japanese financial institutions, it was like the white man bringing firewater to the Indians. I don't know the extent to which Japanese financial institutions have derivatives on their books, but it further complicates the already complex system of juggling the books.

Why should the system come apart? The Ministry of Finance has every reason to hold it together and so far they have always succeeded.

Because of the yen. The authorities have done everything to keep it down and they failed. The strong yen is having a detrimental effect on earnings and on economic activity. The effect is the opposite of a financial bubble; the proper name is deflation. Domestic prices are falling; profit margins and sales volumes are shrinking; workers' bonuses are cut and consumers are retrenching. Real interest rates are very high, but the authorities are powerless to do anything about it. Very reluctantly, they are thinking about cutting the discount rate but that creates new problems. A large part of the population is living on its savings and a reduction in the Postal Savings rate would cut into their income. In addition, insurance companies, having sold large amounts of annuities guaranteeing, say, 4¾ percent, are all operating at a loss and eating into their capital. They need to raise cash. The stock market is still selling at, say, 50 times earnings and yielding less than 1 percent. Who can absorb the selling of securities? Foreigners, strangely enough, have been buyers recently and the rise in the value of the yen has partially offset their losses on stocks. Will they continue buying with the yen where it is?

That is Japan. What about the United States market?

The outlook is good and getting better.

Let me ask you about the role of mutual funds in the United States. More money has been invested in equity mutual funds than ever before. The mutual fund industry has grown since the 1950s from $50 billion to $2 trillion. There has been a tremendous amount of enthusiasm shown by individual investors since 1990.

But a lot of them are unseasoned.

Most of them are naive and inexperienced, but they have not had bad experiences so far. There are excesses in every market cycle, and this is the excess that is building up now. How would you interpret this excess in terms of your theory?

This is a very clear-cut case of a potential boom/bust sequence. You may add to your case that investors can switch between different kinds of funds at short notice, so you could change from equity funds to money market funds with one phone call. The tremendous influx of money has been triggered by the decline in interest rates, which reduced the income that you could get from money market funds and from bank certificates of deposits. Many buyers of mutual funds are new to the stock market and do not fully realize the risks involved. Now that interest rates have risen again, there is a potential for people to start switching back to money market funds. On the one hand, stocks have stopped appreciating because of rising interest rates, and on the other hand, the yield on money market funds has been rising. There's no question that this has been a boom, and therefore it has the potential for a bust. But you must remember that there is nothing determinate about the sequence of events, so a boom is not necessarily followed by a bust. There has to be something specific to trigger it. It is quite possible that you will not have the kind of downward acceleration that is typical of a bust; this excess could perhaps be worked off by a gradual switching of funds against a background of sustained economic growth.

But you are quite right to identify this as a danger point at the present time. You can also identify Fidelity Fund, or, more specifically, the Magellan Fund as the epicenter, just as Morgan Guaranty and Citibank were at the heart of the "nifty-fifty" boom/bust sequence in the 1972 to 1974 period.

But the risks represented by the Magellan Fund are already in the headlines; they are unlikely to catch the market unaware. That doesn't mean that an unraveling process may not occur. Some really significant developments can be clearly foreseen, yet they happen—like the outbreak of the Second World War or the international debt crisis of 1982. There is such a crisis unfolding in the emerging markets. A significant portion, perhaps as much as a quarter, of the inflow into equity mutual funds went into emerging market funds toward the end of the boom in 1994. Emerging markets are, by definition, narrower and less seasoned, and the relative weight of United States mutual funds is correspondingly greater. The unwinding process has already begun and, in my opinion, it has a long way to go. It was precipitated by the crisis in Mexico. As far as the domestic stock market is concerned, I am less certain of a bust because I am not sure what would trigger it. Indeed, the Mexican crisis has extended the duration of the bull market.

The Mexican situation seems like a classic boom/bust sequence. One of the aspects of it is that so many of the people who were most heavily invested in Mexico did not even realize that the currency was egregiously overvalued. Explain the Mexican situation and more importantly its significance to the emerging markets in general and even to the more mature markets.

Foreign investing usually involves boom/bust sequences. I have been in the foreign investment business from the beginning of my career. I have seen many cycles. And I concluded early on that foreign investors acting as a herd always prove to be wrong. This applied to the United States investors buying European securities in the late 1950s and early 1960s that came to a bad end with the Interest Equalization Tax in 1962. It was true of United States institutions buying Japanese securities that turned out to be a false move in 1972. It was true of Japanese institutions investing abroad in the late 1980s and early 1990s. The repatriation of these funds has accounted for the strength of the yen in 1994. And it is certainly true of this global investing mania that reached its climax in December 1994. It's the biggest foreign investment boom that I have ever seen and the corresponding bust is likely to be equally significant. It is the closest thing to 1929 I have experienced in my lifetime.

Are you saying that Mexico is the first domino to fall and that there will be many others?

It is certainly having repercussions, especially in Latin America. The extent of the damage is difficult to estimate, but it is going to be quite significant, in the real world as well as the financial markets. In my view, it could easily lead to a breakdown not just of the international financial system, but of the international trading system as well.

How were investors caught so unaware by what happened in Mexico? The problem must have been developing for several years?

Well, it was certainly visible since the beginning of 1994. Rudy Dornbush, a professor at MIT who had actually been the teacher of the technocrats who were running Mexico, was quite explicit as early as February 1994 that Mexico needed to devalue.

But he was ignored. And the market kept on doing better and the investors had the same arrogantly confident attitude toward Mexico that they had toward emerging growth stocks in the late 1960s.

In retrospect, it's really quite easy to explain. Mexico wanted NAFTA to be enacted and running a big trade deficit was a good way to get domestic support in the United States for NAFTA. Then came the elections in Mexico. Mexico had become more democratic than it had been in the past and therefore the elections were no longer a foregone conclusion. The previous president, Miguel De La Madrid, could afford to take all the unpleasant measures before he handed over power to Salinas because, as you know, the election of Salinas was widely regarded as rigged. But during Salinas' term, democracy reared its ugly head and Salinas was afraid that he might damage the prospects of his successor by devaluing before the elections. You will recall that you had the Chiapas uprising in January 1994 and the original candidate for president, Colosio, was murdered. The political situation was quite unstable in Mexico, and it was felt that a devaluation might have an adverse effect on the elections. After the elections and before he handed over power, Salinas could and should have devalued, but he was running for the position of head of the World Trade Organization, so he didn't want to blot his copy book. And worst of all, these technocrats who had done an outstandingly brilliant job of levitation, bringing Mexico from the third into the first world with the help of foreign investments, began to believe in their own magic. That is the worst thing that can happen to magicians. They thought that they could continue to support the boom even as the gap between image and reality was becoming unsustainably wide. Investors became leery of holding peso-denominated debt; so the Mexican government started borrowing in dollars rather than in pesos. This made them much more vulnerable to devaluation. The devaluation actually came too late, after Mexico had lost practically all its foreign currency reserves. Mexico was left with a dollar debt that was unchanged in dollar terms, but greatly increased in peso terms. This made both the fiscal position of the government and the credit-worthiness of much of the private sector suspect. The 15 percent devaluation, instead of providing an adjustment, precipitated a panic flight of capital. And then, within a day, the entire exchange rate regime was swept away. The peso lost its moorings and fell by another 25 percent or so. And that precipitated a crisis.

As I listen to you I am struck by how the countries that are supposed to have the best financial management end up with the greatest financial difficulties. Mexico was supposed to have an outstanding team; and you impressed me by what you said about the MOF in Japan.

And do you remember Delfin Netto in Brazil? He was the architect of the great Brazilian boom of the 1970s until it all came apart in 1982. He who lives by the sword dies by the sword. I used to be impressed with how well both the Japanese and the Mexicans understood the theory of reflexivity. Now I can see they forgot the most important point: a recognition of their own fallibility.

This kind of thing could take several years to resolve, couldn't it?

The question is whether it can be resolved at all. The United States and the international monetary authorities felt, I think rightly so, that if

Mexico defaulted or rescheduled again—it last happened in 1982—it would unsettle the entire international market. So they embarked on a rescue operation. But the operation was botched.

What went wrong?

They moved too slowly, they did not coordinate their efforts properly and they did not mobilize sufficient resources. Had they acted sooner and more resolutely, they would have needed less resources. But they missed the chance to reassure the market and stabilize the peso by a show of force. Getting a rescue package together took too long. The United States Treasury felt obliged to seek Congressional approval but Congress balked and they had to resort to the Exchange Stabilization Fund, which could have been used in the first place. They also failed to mobilize support from Europe and Japan. In the meantime, the situation continued to deteriorate. The peso depreciated in a self-reinforcing fashion because the more it fell, the more precarious the position of the banking system became, encouraging further flight of capital. In the end, even the international monetary authorities got cold feet and attached a rubber band to the rescue package. What was supposed to be $52 billion may add up to much less.

Do you think Mexico will take the necessary steps internally to resolve the situation?

Under pressure from abroad, they have already taken the bitter pill. The Mexicans fought it as much as they could. Interest rates have been raised to 50 or 70 percent. That is a self-defeating remedy. There is going to be a tremendous depression in Mexico with incalculable political and social consequences.

It should be recognized that the problem presented by this Mexican crisis was much more intractable than the crisis in 1982, because in 1982 the debt was held by the banks. The monetary authorities could exert pressure on the banks and the banks could be persuaded to forego interest payments, or more exactly, to re-lend enough of their interest receipts to ensure that the interest was paid. Voluntary lending was replaced by what I called the "collective system of lending," and it worked. But you can't exert the same kind of pressure on market investors, because once they get paid off they have absolutely no inducement to reinvest their money in the country concerned. So market debt is much more intractable than bank debt.

What should have been done? Should we not have intervened at all?

Ideally, we should have allowed Mexico to convert its dollar-denominated treasury bills, the so-called Tesobonos, into longer term obligations and then we should have provided a rescue package to allow the Mexican banking system to survive. Why should the United States Treasury bail out sophisticated investors who were receiving a hefty risk premium on their Tesobonos? The holders of Tesobonos should have been obliged to take the consequences. The amount required to bail out Mexico would have been much smaller and the international institutions would have had more ammunition to come to the rescue of other countries. But such a scheme would have been very difficult to orchestrate. Would the United States Treasury have been able to provide support to Mexico if the interests of United States investors had been damaged? Would Mexican banks have been able to continue borrowing after the Mexican government had rescheduled its debt? Could a panic in other financial markets have been avoided? In retrospect, it would have been better to face those uncertainties than to engage in a rescue operation that failed. These were daunting questions and the authorities would have been criticized just as much as they are now.

What is going to happen now?

That is a question I shouldn't answer because, whatever I say, it will be superseded by events. The financial crisis is at its height right now. The

99

rescue package is too tenuous to reassure the market and the Mexican government is shell-shocked. Only the high interest rates stand in the way of capital flight, but they are doing great damage to the banking system and the real economy—and that serves to encourage further capital flight. If the financial crisis passes, there are bound to be political and social repercussions that can be expected to climax just about the time this book is published, in August or September, when the full effects of the depression are felt—workers get three-months' severance pay in Mexico. If that crisis also passes, there are going to be repercussions in the United States, because the economic survival of Mexico depends on its ability to develop a big trade surplus with the United States. That has some positive implications for the United States stock and bond markets—it will help cool off the economy and keep some prices under pressure—but politicians are likely to focus on the negative effects—the loss of jobs and unfair labor competition. It is likely to become a big issue in the 1996 elections. If the country swings toward protectionism, we could have a replay of the 1930s. We shall see.

If the Mexican situation is as serious as you say, what will be the repercussions in other places?

Latin America is already devastated. Debt instruments offer astronomical yields. The stocks in Brazil have fallen by up to 70 percent. The country that is next in line after Mexico is Argentina. Argentina operates a currency board system. It is a very rigid regime, reminiscent of the nineteenth-century gold standard. Local currency is issued only if an equivalent amount of dollars is deposited with the currency board, and banks must maintain a minimum reserve requirement with the currency board against their deposits. This provides an automatic defense for the exchange rate because if pesos are changed into dollars or if deposits are withdrawn from the banks, interest rates are driven up. Theoretically, all local currency could be exchanged for dollars without any effect on the exchange rate, only interest rates would rise to astronomical levels. That is already happening. The economy is, for all intents and purposes, dollarised but, even in dollar terms, interest rates are unsustainably high because deposits are being withdrawn from the banking system. The danger is not devaluation but a banking crisis, because the banks will not be able to collect the interest, let alone the principal, from their customers. As interest rates rise, bond and stock prices fall, precipitating margin calls. Forced liquidation reinforces the panic. That is where we are today. The crisis has revealed a flaw in the currency board system: There is no lender of last resort. That is what was missing in the gold standard in the nineteenth century, that is what led to the development of central banking and the eventual abandonment of the gold standard. It is happening again. The Argentine authorities are providing a lifeline to the weaker banks by prevailing on the stronger banks to transfer some of their minimum reserves at the currency board. But that is a dangerous recipe: A few rotten apples can contaminate the whole box. When the Mexican crisis comes to a head, Argentina will also reach a climax.

But, in contrast to Mexico, where I am on the fence, I am convinced that Argentina can be saved. It is a classical liquidity crisis and there is a classic remedy: a lender of last resort. Since it is missing locally, it needs to be provided internationally. That is what the international financial institutions are there for. The Inter-American Development Bank is already working on a $1 billion loan for the restructuring of provincial banks; the IMF ought to modify its usual practice and use its $2 billion standby facility to underwrite a deposit insurance scheme; the World Bank ought to chip in and the Bank of International Settlements ought to provide a bridge loan. To top it off, the currency board is allowed to hold a portion of its assets in dollar-denominationed bonds; by going into the market at the critical moment, it could reverse the trend in the bond market, absorb the forced sales, relieve the banks, and bring down interest rates. This is a rescue package that could work!

And what about Brazil?

Brazil is not in serious trouble. It has a slightly overheated economy and a slightly overvalued currency. There has been a 1929-type stock market crash and the external debt is depressed by panic selling. But the trade balance can be corrected. The exchange rate has been ratcheted down and the trade surplus is likely to reappear. Brazil is a large and largely self-contained economy: It could survive on its own. If Argentina survives, so will Brazil.

So the storm will pass.

If Mexico is saved, it will. But it will leave a lot of debris. And there will be a fallout in other parts of the world. The boom in emerging markets is over: There is no return to the conditions that prevailed prior to the crash.

Do you foresee other financial crises?

There are other countries with high debt ratios that already are under pressure: Italy, Sweden, Canada, Hungary, Greece, just to mention the most obvious. These pressures are likely to intensify, especially if Mexico goes down the drain.

You didn't mention any countries in Asia.

I should have mentioned the Philippines. And I am concerned about China.

How about China? Of all the emerging markets, China is the most dynamic. What do you think?

I formed a hypothesis soon after the Tiananmen Square massacre that communism in China will be destroyed by a good old-fashioned capitalist crash. Five years have passed and my hypothesis is about to be tested.

Can you explain your hypothesis?

The communist regime lost its legitimacy, its "mandate from heaven" in the Tiananmen Square massacre. Since then, it has been tolerated only because it promises material prosperity. If it fails to deliver on its promise, it may not be tolerated. That is why it is unable to dismantle inefficient state enterprises; that is why it can't control inflation. So far, it has been able to assure economic progress by attracting foreign capital. If the flow is reversed, all hell may break loose. Political turmoil could reinforce the flight of capital and vice versa. The saving grace is that almost all the foreign capital is in the form of direct investments and direct investments may not be influenced by the turmoil in emerging markets. Only Hong Kong is susceptible to the direction of portfolio investment. Hong Kong is vulnerable, but it is far from certain that there will be a decline in direct investment in China. New commitments are falling and the disbursement of existing commitments is just about peaking. It needs a pickup in new commitments for China to pass the test.

What about the rising tigers?

Most other Asian countries are much better situated than Latin America because they enjoy high domestic saving rates. Several of them have recently raised interest rates. It is likely to cool off their economies and contribute to a worldwide slowdown.

Do you expect a worldwide slowdown?

Yes. How can you avoid it, with so many dislocations?

There is a lot of turbulence in currency markets.

Yes, there is so much going on, so many different factors are at play that it is difficult to keep them apart. There are many reasons why the dollar is weak and why the yen and the deutschemark are strong. Some of the factors overlap, others are quite separate. Let me try and disentangle them for you.

The yen came under upward pressure because of the repatriation of capital. At times of panic, international investment tends to return to home base. Much of the international portfolio investment came from the United States; but most of the countries where it was invested belong to the dollar zone: Their flight was largely neutral as far as currency rates are concerned. By contrast, the repatriation of Japanese capital has had a direct effect on the yen/dollar rate; and the effect was greatly magnified by the impact of currency options.

As I mentioned before, the yen had been trading in the range of Y105 to Y95 to the dollar. Japanese exporters were so confident that the range would be maintained for the rest of the fiscal year ending in March 1995 that they bought so-called knock-out put options in very large quantities. When I say large quantities, I mean tens of billions of dollars' worth. Knock-out put options are very strange animals; they give you the right to sell a currency at a certain striking price, but you lose that right the moment the market price falls below a certain point. In this case, the striking price on the typical contract was Y105 to the dollar or the top of the trading range and the upset price was Y95, or the bottom of the trading range—a very attractive proposition to the exporters provided the dollar stays within the range. It was also attractive to the sellers of the options because it enabled them to sell additional "out of the money" put and call options at Y105 and Y95 to the dollar. When the dollar fell below Y95, the option writers had to cover their yen commitments in a hurry and the Japanese exporters found themselves without a hedge for their dollars. Their combined selling drove the dollar down to Y88 in a couple of days. It was a crash in the currency market comparable to the crash of 1987 in the stock market and for much the same reason: When there is a large imbalance in option positions, it can cause a crash.

The strength of the deutschemark comes from quite different sources. The German economy is oriented to the production of capital goods and demand has been strong from all parts of the world. Interest rates in Germany have probably bottomed and could turn up. This has created strains in the exchange rates with other European currencies. Italy is in the throes of a continuous political crisis; France faces presidential elections; the conservative government of the U.K. is on its last legs, and the economy is also beginning to turn down; Spain has its own troubles. The flight to quality was exacerbated by the crash in emerging markets and the Bundesbank was not at all unhappy to see the prospects of a unified European currency fade away. To the extent any country wanted to support its currency vis-à-vis the deutschemark, it had to dip into its dollar reserves, putting pressure on the dollar.

The weakness of the dollar was to some extent the inverse of the strength of the yen and the deutschemark, but it also had other causes. The most significant was the Mexican crisis; indeed it was the Mexican crisis that touched off the turbulence in currency markets. Mexico was seen as a United States liability; and when the United States Treasury was forced to dip into the Exchange Stabilization Fund, it was practically advertising that the dollar was defenseless. The swing in the balance of trade with Mexico would moderate economic growth, and competition from Mexican exports would moderate inflation in the United States. At the same time, the threat of a banking crisis in Mexico would prevent the Federal Reserve from raising interest rates. Underlying these considerations was the prospect that the rate of growth may be slowing down in any case. The defeat of the balanced budget amendment also affected sentiment and precipitated a selling climax of the dollar. What is most disturbing is that central banks, particularly in Asia, have begun to diversify their dollar holdings. This has shaken the international monetary system to its foundation. It is as if the continental plates started moving against each other.

It seems that we are faced not with one boom/bust process, but a whole slew of them.

How right you are! Boom/bust sequences rarely occur in isolation. I managed to isolate a few in *The Alchemy of Finance* but usually there are a number of processes going on concurrently and they interact. Usually they are perceived as external shocks, but in truth they may form integral parts of each other. For instance, the emerging market mania formed an integral part of the Mexican boom and the Mexican crisis was a necessary element in the ending of the mania. If it hadn't been Mexico, it would have been something else, but then, events would have taken a different course. By the same token, the Mexican crisis may have preempted some other event that would have affected the Magellan Fund. Similarly, the overindebtedness of Canada and Italy was unsustainable in any case, but if Mexico defaults or reschedules, it is likely to accelerate the crisis in those countries. Still, the present situation is unusual because there are so many dynamic disequilibria at play at the same time.

Let's see. There is the emerging market boom and bust, the Mexican boom and bust, a separate story for each of the Latin American countries, the story about the yen and the Japanese market, the possibilities of a capitalist bust for Chinese communism, the tensions in Europe...

And underlying it all, there is a process of disintegration in the world that extends both to political and security issues and to economic and financial issues. Co-operation among the monetary authorities is much weaker than it was at the time of the Plaza Accord. You don't hear much about an emergency meeting of the G7 although there would be a lot to discuss. Each country pursues its own interests, sometimes individual institutions pursue their institutional interest, with little regard for the common interest. Yet, financial markets are

inherently unstable and liable to break down unless stability is introduced as an explicit objective of government policy.

Few people would agree with you.

I realize that, but it follows directly from my theory of dynamic disequilibrium. Paul Volcker put it very well, "Everybody would agree that excessive volatility is harmful, but there is no constituency for dealing with it." Governments are preoccupied with their self-interest and the private sector; the commercial banks and investment banks actually benefit from volatility, not only because they have greater trading volume, but also because they can sell hedges and options. They profit coming and going. I would add that hedges and options tend to amplify market volatility by engendering automatic trend-following behavior. Recent experience indicates that so-called knock-out options are particularly pernicious in this regard. They relate to ordinary options the way crack relates to ordinary cocaine.

Do you think they should be banned?

Yes. I would not have said that a few months ago, when I testified before Congress, but we have had a veritable crash in currency markets since then. As I have said before, knock-out options played the same role in the 1995 yen explosion as portfolio insurance did in the stock market crash of 1987, and for the very same reason. Portfolio insurance was subsequently rendered inoperable by the introduction of so-called circuit breakers. Something similar needs to be done now with knock-out options.

How would you go about it?

All derivatives traded by banks ought to be registered with the Bank for International Settlements (B.I.S.) in Basle through the various national regulatory agencies. The B.I.S. could study them, gather data, establish capital requirements and, when necessary, discourage them by raising capital requirements or ban them altogether. I think knock-out options would fall into the last category.

I am surprised that you, as a market participant who is supposed to benefit from volatility, should advocate such drastic action.

I should like financial markets to survive.

Part Two

Geopolitics, Philanthropy, and Global Change

with
Krisztina Koenen

6

THE PHILANTHROPIST

Why do you give away many millions of dollars in Eastern Europe? Do you have a guilty conscience? Are you hoping to make up for something?

Not at all. I do it because I care about the principles of open society and I can afford it. It is a unique combination.

But you are widely accused of earning unconscionable profits as a financial speculator. You took money from every British taxpayer when you speculated against sterling.

Profits, yes; unconscionable, no. When you speculate in the financial markets, you are free of most of the moral concerns that confront an ordinary businessman. When the markets are functioning normally, no single anonymous investor can cause any perceptible change. There would have been a sterling crisis without me. My position changed when I became something of a guru after the sterling crisis, but that is a recent development. Before that, I did not have to concern myself with moral issues in the financial markets.

Rockefeller established his foundation when he was accused of making monopoly profits. He hoped to improve his public image with his foundation. Many large firms have set up foundations for similar reasons. It was different in my case; when I set up my first foundation

111

in 1979, I had no public image. At that time I was a small fry in the market, managing a fund with $100 million dollars of capital; today we have more than $10 billion.

Perhaps you didn't have a public image when you started, but you certainly have one now. Has being a well-known philanthropist helped you in your business?

Perhaps. It gives me better access. But, frankly, I don't need access for business purposes. Indeed, I am fearful that it may warp my judgment. I made my career without hobnobbing with the rich and powerful and now that I can hobnob, I don't have time for it. The main advantage I have is that people like to be associated with me. That goes for people who propose business deals, as well as members of my management team. My being a philanthropist is not the only reason, but it undoubtedly contributes to the good spirit in the firm.

Then what are the real reasons for your philanthropy?

Some 15 years ago, when the fund had reached a size of $100 million dollars, and my personal wealth had grown to roughly $25 million, I determined after some reflection that I had enough money. After a great deal of thinking, I came to the conclusion that what really mattered to me was the concept of an open society.

How would you define an open society?

I wouldn't define it. Popper taught me that concepts shouldn't be defined; they should be explained. In my philosophy, open society is based on the recognition that we all act on the basis of imperfect understanding. Nobody is in possession of the ultimate truth. Therefore, we need a critical mode of thinking; we need institutions and interests to live together in peace; we need a democratic form of government that ensures the orderly transfer of power; we need a market economy that provides feedback and allows mistakes to be corrected; we need to protect minorities and respect minority opinions. Above all, we need the rule of law. Ideologies like fascism or communism give rise to a closed society in which the individual is subjugated to the collective, society is dominated by the state, and the state is in the service of a dogma that claims to embody the ultimate truth. In such a society, there is no freedom.

I can also give you a more personal view: An open society is one in which a person like me can live and prosper. As a Jew in Hungary I was hunted by the Nazis, then later I had a foretaste of communist rule in that country, so I know whereof I speak. I emigrated to England when I was 17 and it was as a student at the London School of Economics that I came to understand the difference between open and closed society.

What was the purpose of the foundation?

To open up closed societies, help make open societies more viable, and foster a critical mode of thinking. But I learned how to run a foundation only gradually. I was very leery of foundations. I had some strong prejudices against them. I still do. I think that charity tends to turn the recipients into objects of charity, and that is not what it is intended to accomplish. I call this the paradox of charity. I also think that philanthropy is basically a corrupting influence; it corrupts not only the recipient, but also the giver, because people flatter him and never tell him the truth. It's the role of the applicant to find a way to get money out of the foundation, and it's the role of the foundation to prevent people from taking advantage of it. To protect itself from people who want to take, a foundation needs to be either very bureaucratic and have very strict rules, like the Ford Foundation or the state, or it should keep a low profile, working quietly in the background. I chose the latter alternative, you know: "Don't call us; we'll call you." I intended, in theory, to make all the activities and all the donations anonymous. I made a deliberate effort to keep my ego out of it, because I felt that the foundation must justify its existence by what it accomplishes; if it only served for ego gratification, my ego would not be gratified. It is ironic that today I run one of the largest foundations in the world and I am personally, deeply involved.

What were you giving money to?

My first major commitment was in South Africa. Here was a truly closed society based on the separation of races. I thought the best way to undermine the apartheid system was to enable the blacks to stand up to the whites on an equal footing through education. I had a Zulu friend, a lecturer at a university in New York, who went back to South Africa. I went to visit him in 1980. Through him I met a number of South African blacks and I got to know them as friends. I also visited Cape Town University whose Rector, Stuart Saunders, impressed me with his commitment to educating black students. In a somewhat misguided fashion, I thought that Cape Town University was an institution based on the principles of open society, seeking to treat people equally. The tuition was paid by the state. I thought that by helping to put black students into Cape Town University, I would get the state to pay for their education, so that I would be taking advantage of the apartheid state.

It didn't quite work out that way. The University as a whole was by no means as open-minded as the Rector. I gave 80 scholarships to blacks as my opening effort, but the number of black students increased by less than 80. The University was obviously redirecting some of its own funds to other goals. I went back to South Africa the next year and met with the students, and they were exceedingly alienated, hostile, and resentful. I decided to see the first 80 students through, but not to continue the program. It was a great pity because, if it had continued, there would now be a greater number of qualified blacks to lead and develop the country. I tried other projects in South Africa, but I came to the conclusion that instead of me taking advantage of the apartheid state, the apartheid state was taking advantage of me. The system was so insidious that whatever I did made me an accomplice of the system. I continued a few projects, like supporting the training of black journalists and some human rights programs but, basically, I did not do a lot more in South Africa, which I now regret. And, belatedly, I have set up an Open Society Foundation there.

What else did you do in the early days?

In that same year, 1980, I started giving scholarships to Eastern European dissidents. I also began my support of human rights organizations, Poland's Solidarity, the Czechoslovak Charta 77 dissidents (through a foundation in Sweden), and the Sakharov movement.

That was a period in which no one dared to hope that any essential change could be effected in Eastern Europe. It was in December of 1981 that General Jaruzelski staged his putsch in Poland. The Chartists in Czechoslovakia were only a small, isolated group. What did you hope your foundations might accomplish?

My aim was to support the people who had staked their lives on fighting for freedom, for open society.

Then you did not envision imminent change in the political situation in Eastern Europe?

No. I was putting my money into something that other people had staked their lives on. I supported these people to carry on whatever they were doing, for it was they who were taking the risk and the responsibility. I had no projects of my own, no grandiose schemes. I did not believe for a second that I could change the regime. But I did have a certain perspective. I knew that communist dogma was false because it was a dogma. If one could foster alternatives, open the door for other ideas, the falsehood of that dogma would become obvious. By undermining the dogma one would, in fact, weaken the regime. I did not

115

expect that the communist system would collapse, but I did want to weaken it from within by making alternatives available and supporting critical thought.

You were running all these programs yourself?

Yes, everything was done purely on a personal basis. I got involved in Human Rights Watch, which was called Helsinki Watch at that time, and I attended their weekly meetings. I view it as a kind of learning period. Aryeh Neier, who was the head of Human Rights Watch, is now the president of my foundation. But, at that time, Open Society Fund was really a very small and experimental activity. After the South African attempt, my main focus was on giving an opportunity to dissident Eastern European intellectuals to come to the United States. A dozen or so dissidents were invited at any one time, and I got to know some of them. Their acquaintance helped me a great deal, for at that time I was unfamiliar with the problems of the region. After all, I had left it many years before.

Does your commitment have nothing to do with your Hungarian background, then?

It does have something to do with it. I speak the language, after all, and my roots are in Hungary. But it was not because I was born in Hungary that I decided to support the dissident movement there. Among the people who received scholarships from my foundation, there were at least as many Poles as Hungarians. Yet it was from the Hungarians that I learned the most and with whom I established the best personal relationship.

Was that why you set up the first of your Eastern European foundations in Hungary?

Yes. The dissidents told me that the way I selected the candidates was beginning to have a harmful effect. It was secretive, and people were being rewarded for being dissidents. In a sense, the scholarships served to discredit them; they could be accused of making a living out of their opposition to the regime. The dissidents were morally upright people with an integrity you don't find very often, so their opinion carried a lot of weight with me. In 1984, I approached the Hungarian Ambassador here and I asked him whether it would be possible to set up a foundation in Hungary, which could then give out scholarships on a competitive basis and engage in other cultural and educational activities. To my considerable astonishment, my proposal met with a positive response. Obviously, the Hungarian officials regarded me as a businessman who could be a useful contact for them in America and who would give them money without too many strings attached, the proverbial American uncle who was naive enough to let himself be used.

Did you have any full-time people by that time?

The foundation here still had no full-time employees and, in effect, it was run out of my home. Susan, my wife, was then the chief administrator, and she did a very good job running it. There was no overhead whatsoever. Or rather, it was extremely expensive, depending on how I value the services of my wife.

When did you get your first full-time employee?

Later in 1984, with the establishment of the Soros Foundation in Hungary, which was separate from the Open Society Fund because the Hungarian government could not accept the name Open Society. That foundation had an office here in New York and a full-time person in charge. But the Open Society Fund did not. It continued to be run by Susan for several more years.

In 1984, when this was happening, the government in power in Hungary was still strictly communist. In Hungary of all places, you are

**now frequently accused of having collaborated with that regime in
the interest of your foundation. Is that true?**

Of course we collaborated: The communists wanted to use me, and I
wanted to use them. That was the basis of our collaboration. The big
question was who would get the better of the other. The arrangement
we worked out was as follows: a joint commission was set up between
the Hungarian Academy of Sciences, an institution still completely
under the control of the communist party and government at the
time, and the Soros Foundation in New York. We had an agreement
ensuring that both sides had veto power over expenditures. Monies
could be spent only on programs approved by both chairmen. I was
one of the chairmen, the vice-secretary of the Academy of Sciences
was the other.

Who ended up getting the better of whom?

In Hungary, there is no question that we won. I had wonderful advisors. One of them was, and is, Miklos Vasarhelyi, the one-time press
spokesman for the Imre Nagy government of 1956. He is a man who
was nearly sentenced to death for his part in the revolution and spent
several years in prison. The Hungarian foundation's success can be attributed to a great extent to his political wisdom and skill and the universal respect he enjoyed. Back then I did not take a step without first
consulting him. He understood the situation much better than I, and I
suspect much better than the responsible Hungarian authorities as
well. We knew what we were doing and they did not.

But right at the start you wanted to quit?

After we had already signed the agreement establishing the foundation, we had a disagreement on how it should be run. Our idea was
that the employees should be independent and selected by us. However, the government expected that the decisions of the commission

would be carried out by a rather dubious organization called the Union for International Cultural Relations. They were an arm of the Ministry of Security established to serve as the counterpart of IREX, the American cultural exchange organization. At that point, Miklos Vasarhelyi insisted that I should not make compromises, that we needed our own staff. That led to a meeting—my first—with Gyorgy Aczel, the all-powerful Party boss for cultural affairs. We couldn't come to an agreement so I told him I was quitting. He said that I should not leave with bad feelings, whereupon I responded that I couldn't help having bad feelings, after all the effort I had wasted. I was then already at the door. He asked me, "What is it you really want?" "An independent secretariat," I replied. Ultimately we reached the same compromise with respect to the secretariat that we had regarding the chairmen. Each side appointed its own responsible person and they had to co-sign all documents.

How much money were you giving away at that time?

The endowment was $3 million a year, but we did not spend all the money in the first years. One of our first projects was to offer photocopying machines to cultural and scientific institutions in exchange for Hungarian forints. We needed forints in order to give out local grants, but the photocopying machines also did a lot of good, so the same money was put to work twice. The project was a great success because it was a perfect way to undermine the Party control of information. Up until then, the few existing copying machines were out of reach, literally held under lock and key. Each user had to be approved. As more and more photocopying machines became available, the Party apparatus lost control of the machines and the dissemination of information.

Why didn't the Party forbid the project?

The institutes desperately needed the machines for their work. The Hungarian state did tighten the regulations, but, with so many machines, it could not enforce them. We then used the local currency we got from the institutes to support all kinds of unofficial initiatives.

The Hungarian foundation at that time was exempt from all the ills that befall normal foundations. All the paradoxes connected with philanthropy were resolved because the foundation became an institution of civil society. It did not have to protect itself because it was under the protection of the people whom it supported. The foundation didn't need to be bureaucratic; it didn't need to have any procedures for controlling, reporting, and evaluating, because the grant recipients would have been ashamed to take advantage of the foundation. If there was abuse, somebody would tell us about it.

There were a number of reasons why the foundation worked so well. First of all, there was a tremendous shortage of hard currency and the dollar was worth a lot more than the official rate. It was worth even more to cultural institutions that were flush with local currency, but had little access to hard currency. We joked about an exchange rate for "culture dollars."

On the local currency side, people practically volunteered their efforts for tiny grants because the foundation was empowering them to do what they wanted to do anyhow. So almost nobody had to be paid for their work. All they needed was some material support, like a photocopying machine, or an opportunity to do some research abroad. We were also using the facilities of the state for nonparty activities because most of the people were actually employed by the state. Courses, meetings, performances could be held without paying rent. That was another way in which the impact of the foundation was magnified. Ultimately, we were accused of being an alternate Ministry of Culture and Education and we considered this the greatest accolade we could possibly get. Don't forget, we were spending $3 million a year and, with that, we affected the workings of the entire educational and cultural establishment, which had a budget hundreds of times greater.

Didn't they try to stop you?

Yes. The question was seriously debated in the Party. But even there we had our sympathizers.

Who were they, and what made them sympathetic?

They were mainly on the economic side. The ones responsible for ideology were opposed to the foundation. My main government supporter was Ferenc Bartha, who was, at that time, in charge of economic relations with foreign countries. The government held him responsible for the foundation, and he definitely wanted it to be a success. He hoped to help change the political system without exposing himself. He was a technocrat who, along with a number of other economists, Marton Tardos, for example, wished for reforms.

The foundation was very circumspect. We carefully balanced projects that would annoy the ideologues in the Party, with other projects that they couldn't help but approve, and we made sure that there was always a positive balance. We engaged in patriotic cultural programs and widely beneficial social programs to offset the distribution of copying machines. The Party was particularly alarmed at our grant program for writers because it increased their independence. We were even accused of having fomented the Writers Union's rebellion against the Party.

Looking back, do you consider your activity in Hungary as a success?

That was the most fantastic, marvelous time we ever had. The foundation enabled people who were not dissidents to act, in effect, like dissidents. Teachers, university professors, and researchers were able to indulge in their nongovernmental activities while keeping their jobs. So it was really a very successful operation, and a wonderful spirit prevailed. Nothing that we have done since quite compares with it. The foundation was clean and well run. I visited from time to time and discussed the strategy; the next time I visited, it was implemented. I don't know how they did it. Perhaps it was because the foundation was the only game in town and all the intellectual energies of civil society were available to it. After the liberation in 1989, people had many other opportunities; but from 1984 to 1989, the foundation was really the center of intellectual life in Hungary.

You speak of that time with a great deal of nostalgia.

I'm sure that everyone involved looks back on it with nostalgia, for we achieved a tremendous amount with very little money. And we felt good, fighting evil. Never again have circumstances been so favorable. Later, after the changeover, the Hungarian foundation had a lot of trouble adapting to the new reality.

At that time, was the work of the foundation more important to you than making money?

Not at all. I was actively running Quantum Fund. That was the time when I was engaged in the real-time experiment that forms part of *The Alchemy of Finance,* and it was certainly a lot more important to me. The foundation work was still very much a sideline, even though I was actively involved in it. I did not identify with it; I looked for no recognition. I felt the foundation belonged to the Hungarians; that was the secret of its success. There was no publicity, which also contributed to the success. The "agitprop" of the Communist Party in Hungary put out the word that the media should ignore the foundation. Therefore, there were no press reports, although we were allowed to advertise our programs. Most people found out what was going on by word of mouth. Here was the only institution in Hungary that actually did something worthwhile without talking about it, whereas all the official organizations always talked about things that they didn't actually accomplish. So, in a way, the image of the foundation was established by the lack of publicity. And I was firmly determined not to take any personal credit, because I genuinely felt that the people running the foundation were putting themselves on the line, and I was merely providing them with the means. I admired them for doing what they achieved, so it was really their creation, not mine.

But it was your money that was making it possible.

Yes, I found all this very, very gratifying, but, as I said, the foundation was something apart from me that I admired almost as an outsider. It's very different from my involvement today.

After your success in Hungary, you expanded the scope of the foundation, didn't you?

Yes. I tried my hand in China, starting in 1986. I also set up a foundation in Poland soon after, based on "Okno" (Window), an underground cultural organization associated with Solidarity. Then came the foundation in the Soviet Union in 1987, when Sakharov was allowed to return to Moscow. After the Revolution of 1989, there was an explosive growth in the number of new foundations. That is when the foundations became a network.

By now you have foundations in 25 countries, most in Eastern Europe. What exactly do your foundations do?

It is impossible to say. The transformation of a closed society into an open one is a systemic transformation. Practically everything has to change and there is no blueprint. What the foundations have done is to change the way the transformation is brought about. It has mobilized the energies of the people in the countries concerned.

In each country, I identified a group of people—some leading personalities, others less well known—who shared my belief in an open society and I entrusted them with the task of establishing the priorities. I had an overall vision and, with the passage of time, I learned from the experience of individual foundations. I reinforced the initiatives that were successful and abandoned the ones that were not. I tried to transfer the successful programs from one country to the others and I also introduced regional programs. But I did not impose anything from the outside. I gave the foundations autonomy and I exercised control only through the amount of additional money I made available.

Open society is meant to be a self-organizing system and I wanted the foundations not only to help build an open society, but also to serve as a prototype of open society. We started in a chaotic fashion and order emerged out of chaos gradually. The scope for the foundations was practically unlimited. We tried to choose projects that made a real difference. What they were, depended on the need we identified and on the skills we could bring to bear. The priorities are rapidly shifting. For instance, travel grants were usually effective in the early days, but they are less so today. Our main priorities are education, civil society, law, the media, culture, libraries and the Internet. But these categories do not describe adequately the scope of activities. The activities came first and the categories afterwards. Nobody knew everything we were doing, and I liked it that way. I derived the greatest satisfaction from activities I knew nothing about, that I ran across accidentally. I had managed to mobilize other people's energies—things were happening that I did not think of, indeed, could not think of, because often they were beyond my comprehension. It gave me a sense of liberation. Finally, I broke out of my isolation and connected with the real world. When I found out about the various activities of the foundations, I didn't like everything I saw, but I derived great satisfaction from the fact that, unbeknownst to me, all these activities were going on.

Can you give me some examples?

I met Wiktor Osiatynski, a brilliant political scientist, who had been treated for alcoholism by Alcoholics Anonymous. He introduced AA first to Poland and then to other countries. He had a tremendous impact, for instance, in the treatment of alcoholics in Polish prisons. We introduced a new approach to health education and I visited a workshop of teachers from various countries who were spending a week together. Their enthusiasm was overwhelming. But, perhaps, the most relevant is the network of contemporary art centers we have established. I really don't like most of the art in the centers, but I realize that I am not competent to judge. You may consider it weird, but in my view, it is an essential feature of an open society that not everything should be to my liking. If I tried to control the content of every program, I would not be creating an open society. I could certainly not have expanded the foundation network as fast as I did. Our growth was exponential.

How could you finance it?

It so happened that the dissolution of the Soviet Union coincided with some wonderful years for Quantum Fund. The amount of money I had available exceeded the capacity of the foundations to spend it well. The combination of a revolutionary opportunity with ample financial resources was explosive. The foundation network grew dramatically in five years. It dwarfed the growth rate of Quantum Fund.

How did you manage it?

We operated with what Janos Kornai calls "soft budgetary constraints," which are disastrous for an economy, but can work wonders for a foundation. A foundation is, in a sense, the inverse of a business. In business, it is the profit that counts; in a foundation, it is the way the money is spent. With soft budgetary constraints, the foundations can concentrate on what really counts.

It sounds as if your foundations were running out of control.

In a sense, yes. But I demanded high standards of performance and also high ethical standards. I wanted the foundations to be lean and clean. But if they enjoyed my confidence, I was willing to authorize any number of new projects at short notice. That is what I mean by "soft budgetary constraints."

Money is only one of the components necessary to success, and, under certain circumstances, money can do more harm than good. If a foundation has nothing but money, it has no justification for its existence other than a self-serving one. I am constantly subjecting the foundations to severe critical examination.

How can you test them?

One of the ways is to keep the overhead low, to ensure that people working for the foundation are not in it for the money. Even then, an unlimited supply of money for programs can spoil them. For instance, I made a terrible mistake in Russia. After several false starts, we finally had an incredibly successful program for the transformation of the humanities. Originally, I provided $5 million for the program, and it made a real impact on the entire educational system of the country. But I got carried away. I increased the budget to $15 million and I was planning to raise it again to $250 million. The temptation was too big for the program administrators, and what had been a lean operation became corrupt. It nearly destroyed the foundation.

You already mentioned that the foundations have not been every-where as successful as in Hungary. What kinds of problems have they had?

All the foundations are different. No two of them have the same problems. In China, for example, the foundation became embroiled in the country's internal political struggle. That was in 1988. The hard-liners tried to destroy Prime Minister Zhao Ziyang and Party Secretary Bao Tong by attacking the foundation. Zhao defended himself by transferring the foundation from the supervision of the internal political police to the external political police. The external political police took no chances: it put its own people into the foundation. In effect, the foundation was run by the secret police. When I got wind of it, I tried to close the foundation and the Tiananmen Square massacre gave me an excuse for doing so. Poor Bao Tong is still in jail and reportedly very sick.

In the beginning, I had a lot of trouble with the Polish foundation as well. Probably I was to blame, for I was trying to reproduce the success of the Hungarian foundation. I felt that I had a solid base of support in Poland because I had supported the Solidarity movement and its cultural arm, "Okno," which was also illegal. In trying to replicate the Hungarian formula, I relied on the Okno people, assuming that they knew how to run a foundation. I thought all I had to do was to make a deal with the government and give them some money and they could take it from there. But it didn't turn out that way. The Okno people had no idea what to do; they couldn't even manage to get a telephone line installed. After the revolution of 1989, I placed the foundation in the hands of Zbigniew Bujak, the Solidarity hero. But that didn't work too well, either. We later found the right man to act as executive director, but by then a major conflict developed between me and the foundation. I was still expecting it to function like the Hungarian one, as a grant-giving organization, open to all, empowering people to pursue their goals, serving as a support mechanism for civil society. But the people involved in the foundation had a different vision. They wanted an operating foundation with priorities and programs of its own. It turned out that they were right and I was wrong. Their format was better suited to the new era. Over the years, the Polish foundation—Stefan Batory—has become one of the best foundations in the network.

The Bulgarian foundation is very similar to the one in Poland, but I didn't have the same trouble setting it up. It arose fully armed like Pallas Athene. I had the assistance of the American Cultural Attaché, John Menzies, who had worked in Hungary and understood what the foundation stood for. He prepared everything and all I had to do was to bless it. That is not to say we didn't have some problems. For instance, one of the board members, who had been the head of a human rights group, turned out to be a rabid nationalist, violently anti-Turkish and anti-gypsy.

The Russian foundation is quite another story. I could write a whole book about it. Let me just say that I wanted it to lead the revolution, but it got caught up in the revolution instead. It went through the same revolutionary turmoil as Russian society at large.

It suffered as many setbacks?

I began organizing the Russian foundation, or more correctly the Soviet foundation, in 1987. I first went to Moscow as a tourist, hoping to convince Andrei Sakharov to head it. He strongly advised me against going ahead, because he was convinced that the money would end up in the coffers of the KGB. But I persisted, and I managed to assemble a governing board. It was truly an odd collection, for it included people who normally wouldn't even speak to each other: on the one hand, the historian Yuri Afanasiev and the sociologist Tatyana Zaslavskaya, and on the other hand, the writer Valentin Rasputin, who has since become an extreme nationalist. Such a combination would be unthinkable today.

The management of the Cultural Initiative Foundation, as it was called, fell into the hands of a reformist clique of Communist Youth League officials and they proceeded to form a closed society for the promotion of open society. I tried to prevail on them to be more open-minded, but they couldn't shake off their Soviet mentality. When I became aware of it, I had to organize a putsch to remove them. This came just before the August 1991 putsch. But the man who organized it, my lawyer in Moscow, then turned the foundation into his personal fiefdom so I had to organize a second putsch to get rid of him. The foundation then languished until we started the Transformation Project—an ambitious program to replace Marxist-Leninist teaching in schools and universities. With the full cooperation of the ministries, we made tremendous strides within a very short period—

commissioning nearly a thousand textbooks, training school princi-
pals, giving grants to innovative schools, introducing a new curricu-
lum in economics, sponsoring Junior Achievement. The project was
so successful that I decided to throw a large amount of money at it
and that was the cause of the next crisis. This happened at the height
of the robber-capitalist episode in the first half of 1994, when shares
of Russian enterprises were given away in a mass-privatization
voucher scheme and could be bought for a song. Money was in incredibly short supply and less reputable banks paid as much as 10 percent a month for dollar deposits. Everybody with money was making
money hand-over-fist. The temptation must have grown too strong
for the administrators of the program. We discovered an enormous
bank deposit—some $12 million—in a less-than-first class bank and,
although we recovered it and suffered no loss, we undertook a thorough audit. We got rid of our key operating personnel and the foundation has still not recovered from it. With three reorganizations, we
lost five valuable years. I learned from bitter experience how difficult
it is to run a foundation in a revolutionary environment.

**But you said you were a specialist in just such revolutionary situa-
tions.**

I was able to recognize when things were going wrong. I could correct
mistakes, but I couldn't find the right people to get things done. Perhaps if I had learned Russian and devoted full-time, I could have done
a better job.

**This sounds like a tale of woe. Yet your foundations in the former
Soviet Union are reputed to be very successful.**

Rightly so. I was speaking only of the Cultural Initiative Foundation in
Moscow, which we are phasing out and replacing with a new organiza-
tion. I am also responsible for the International Science Foundation
(ISF), which has as its mission saving the best of natural science in the

former Soviet Union, and a companion program, The International Science Education Program (ISEP). These are mega-projects, much larger than the projects we normally undertake. I gave ISF $100 million and we spent it in less than two years. We gave emergency grants of $500 each to some 30,000 scientists, which was enough to support them for a full year. We organized a grant program, on the model of the National Science Foundation, that allocated the bulk of the money. We also provided travel grants and scientific journals, and we are currently working to make the Internet available not only to the scientific community, but to all users: schools, universities, libraries, hospitals, the media. The Science Education Program, with a separate annual budget of more than $20 million, is reaching an even larger number of people than the ISF. Everything is done according to clearly defined rules. It's very efficient and it has had a tremendous impact on the scientific community.

Why did you decide to spend such large amounts on science in the former Soviet Union when you practically excluded natural science from the regular activities of your foundations?

I wanted to prove that Western aid can be effective, and natural science was the best field in which to prove it, for a number of reasons. Soviet science represented an outstanding achievement of the human intellect, a somewhat different strain from Western science, that deserved to be preserved. Scientists had been, and remain, in the forefront of the struggle for open society. Also, the effort had a reasonable chance of success, because there are reliable criteria by which merit can be judged, and the international scientific community could be mobilized to assist in the selection process.

We proved our point. The programs were a resounding success. We recently came under attack by the Russian counterintelligence service, and the Duma instituted an investigation. The entire scientific community rose up in our defense and what started out as an attack ended up as a triumph for the foundation.

Most of the other foundations in the former Soviet Union are doing well. The one in Ukraine is particularly strong. It has succeeded in the role I would have liked the Russian foundation to play. A whole network of other institutions has grown up around it, each working in a different area. They are all related to the foundation in one way or another but independent: an institute that trains public servants, a private university, a foundation for the development of legal culture, a media center, a center for modern art, an economics institute, a privatization institute. The foundation is helping to supply Ukraine with the infrastructure necessary for a modern state—and an open society. If Ukraine survives as an independent state, the foundation will have made a real contribution to its success.

What made you focus on Ukraine to such a considerable extent?

It was a combination of factors. I recognized the importance of an independent and democratic Ukraine. As long as Ukraine prospers, there can be no imperialist Russia. I was able to help Ukraine, because I had very capable and reliable collaborators: Bohdan Hawrylyshyn, who retired as dean of a business school in Geneva in order to set up a business school in Kyiv, and Bohdan Krawchenko, a professor from Canada who went to Ukraine to do research. I put them in charge and they built the foundation. We started early, establishing the Ukrainian Renaissance Foundation in 1989, well before Ukraine became independent in 1991. When independence came, we decided to push ahead with all possible speed. Our explicit objective was to blaze the trail for the Western aid we hoped would follow. Again I can say that we accomplished our goal.

I must admit I started with very ambivalent feelings about Ukraine. I knew the fate of Hungarian Jews deported to Ukraine during World War II because one of them returned and gave me boxing lessons when I was about 13. His stories made a deep impression on me. When Ivan Dzuba, a Ukrainian writer who later became Minister of Culture, asked me to set up an Open Society Foundation in Ukraine, I confronted him with those stories. He said the objective of the foundation would be to build a different Ukraine where those kinds of atrocities couldn't happen. I accepted that as a worthwhile goal.

In Prague, in the Czech Republic, everything seems to have miscarried for you.

As I said earlier, I had supported the dissidents of Charta 77 through a foundation in Sweden since 1980. Altogether I gave it some $3 million. I was its main source of support. When the Velvet Revolution took place, I suggested to Frantisek Janouch, who ran the foundation in Sweden, and to Prince Karl von Schwarzenberg, who headed the International Helsinki Federation for Human Rights in Vienna, that we should now set up a foundation inside Czechoslovakia. We met in Prague in December 1989. I remember that Schwarzenberg, a member of what had been the Czech royal family, still had difficulty getting a visa, because the Czech Embassy in Vienna had not yet fully adjusted to the new situation. There was a wonderful, peaceful, Christmastime atmosphere in Prague, one that I shall never forget. However, the foundation we set up was not properly grounded in civil society. From the very beginning, outside help was regarded with suspicion. There was a lot of grumbling on the part of people who had received support from Janouch, and much more on the part of those who hadn't. People did not know that I had supported Charta 77 long before the revolution, and no one understood what this strange person from America wanted to accomplish. The problem was that my support had gone through emigrants, and there was a lot of mistrust of emigrants. Old quarrels kept breaking out and, instead of living in the present, people were mainly concerned with settling the disputes of the past.

There was also conflict between the foundation and the Charta 77 organization, for Charta 77 was of the opinion that the foundation ought to belong to them. These conflicts ultimately consumed all of the foundation's energy. I warned Janouch a number of times to put the past to rest and to devote himself to the present. When that didn't do any good, I stopped my support for the foundation in Prague. It was the most disappointing experience in all my philanthropy.

You not only support the foundations, you also finance the Central European University. Why do you feel this university is necessary?

I used to be opposed to setting up permanent institutions and I never wanted to invest in bricks and mortar. But, after the revolution of 1989, I recognized the need for an institution that would preserve and develop the spirit of that revolution. As a revolution, 1989 was incomplete. It destroyed communism, but it did not give rise to a new form of social organization. The Velvet Revolution was fought in the spirit of open society, but the concept of open society was not elaborated, either in theory or in practice. There was a gaping intellectual need and I set up the CEU in the hope that it might meet that need. It is not meant to propagate the concept of open society, but to practice it. The aim is not only to educate a new elite, but also to reach a new understanding.

The university came into existence in a revolutionary fashion—without any planning and without the proper legal structure. Classes started in September 1991, a few months after the decision to set up the university was made. By now, order has emerged out of the chaos and the university has been transformed into a solid institution. We have an outstanding faculty, combining eminent names with names that will become eminent in the future, a first-class president and a distinguished board of trustees. I was very active during the founding period, personally making decisions, but I have relinquished authority to the board. Our degrees have been accredited by New York State and the quality of instruction was deemed high enough that even students in the first academic year were awarded Masters degrees. Retroactively, I believe that is a unique accomplishment in the history of education: six months to start an accredited M.A. program. The university will receive at least $10 million a year from me for running expenses for at least 20 years. In the fall of 1995, classes will begin in downtown Budapest, in an attractive building that we built.

Originally it was planned that the university would have branches in both Budapest and Prague. Did your plans for the Central European University in Prague also miscarry?

That's a long story. I was anxious not to start the university in Hungary. Since I am myself Hungarian, the university would have immediately become a Hungarian one. The Czech government offered us a building and I gratefully accepted it. After the 1991 election, the new government reneged on the obligations undertaken by the previous government. I was partly to blame because I didn't pay enough attention to the legal documents. There were strong voices opposed to the idea of the university, including Vaclav Klaus, the new prime minister, and not enough support for it, so I decided to close our branch in Prague. It was not primarily a question of money. The university in Budapest cost me a lot more. I felt that the university in Prague did not have enough local support. On principle, I don't want to inflict my philanthropy. I want the people involved to develop a sense of commitment and to show an ability to fend for themselves.

Why was Klaus opposed to the university?

That is a complicated question. The university was the initiative of the previous government of dissident—and ineffectual—intellectuals whom he detested. That government gave us a building and the Klaus government reneged on that obligation. He did not like an intellectual center for Eastern Europeans in Prague, because he wanted to move toward the West. He would have been happy to see Eastern Europe fall into the ocean, because then the West would take him on board more readily. But there was more to it than that. He felt a personal animosity toward me. It troubled me, because I did not need him as an enemy. It all became clear recently, when he accused me of advocating a new form a socialism. He believes in the pursuit of self-interest and, accordingly, he finds my concept of open society—which requires people to make sacrifices for the common good—objectionable. Now I know why we are opposed to each other, and I am happy to acknowledge it. In my view, Klaus embodies the worst of the Western democracies, just as the pre-revolutionary Czech regime represented the worst of communism. I am opposed to both extremes.

Did you give up everything in Prague?

No, we haven't abandoned Prague. President Vaclav Havel offered space for the university in the president's castle. I was delighted to accept his offer, because it showed that the university had some support after all. We are planning a major new initiative in Prague, a department that combines international relations with ethnic relations. We have moved the former research institute of Radio Free Europe to Prague and it will also be connected with the university. The headquarters of the Central European University, however, will be in Budapest, with branches in Prague and Warsaw.

Who is allowed to study at the university?

We accept graduate students from East and West, but most of them come from Eastern Europe to whom we give full scholarships. The various disciplines of the humanities are represented, and the language of instruction is English. Currently, many of the teachers come from Western universities, but I hope this will gradually change. The program is somewhat different from traditional universities. There is more room for original research. Teaching, research, and involvement in practical projects mutually reinforce each other.

How is the foundation doing in Hungary? You mentioned that it had difficulties in adapting itself to changed conditions.

That is true. After the regime change, we were no longer the only game in town. Before 1989, we had a decisive influence on cultural life; after, there were many other sources of support for cultural activities, and we lost our preeminent position. Our financial situation also deteriorated. Cultural institutions were no longer flush with local currency and the "culture dollar" lost its value. We could no longer work with volunteers. We had to pay people, we had to become a professional organization.

There was a short period prior to the first democratic elections in April 1990 when we enjoyed a privileged position. We were the very embodiment of liberation, compared to the reform communist government that had lost the support of the people. The government wanted to work with us, hoping that our legitimacy would somehow rub off on them. They gave us matching funds. That was the high point in the history of the foundation. Once free elections were held, the new government had legitimacy, and we lost status. After that, there was a certain tendency in the foundation to live in the past and resist change.

Why did the free elections cause the foundation to lose status?

For a very simple reason: The new government didn't like us. Although the foundation had taken great care not to have any preferences in party politics, not to develop into a clique, most of the people associated with the foundation were members or sympathizers of a party that ended up in the opposition after the first free elections, namely the Free Democrats. Which is no surprise, for the political program of the Free Democrats comes closest to the concept of open society.

I can explain the situation in more general terms. Communism sought to establish a universal closed society. Many people rejected it because it was universal, because it denied them their national identity, and for that reason they adopted a nationalist program in opposition to it. Others rejected it primarily because they wanted an open society. In Hungary, they divided fairly precisely into the Democratic Forum, which won the elections, and the Free Democrats, which lost them.

To make matters worse, the Democratic Forum had a rabidly nationalistic anti-Semitic wing. I came into direct conflict with them, which did the foundation a world of good. It regained its sense of mission.

Have conditions improved under the new socialist-liberal government?

For the foundation, yes. Now it can work with the government, which it couldn't do before. Programs that have been successful in other countries can now be instituted in Hungary as well. That is especially true in the areas of education and public health.

Is it not a problem for you to stand so close to the government? You have even received a decoration.

It doesn't bother me in the least. I don't lose my critical faculties. The problem is in the opposite direction: in most countries, I come under increasing criticism. Some of the attacks are so vile and vicious that they are hard to take.

Why is that?

Because they don't like what I stand for. The idea of open society, in general, is coming under attack.

You once referred to yourself as a "stateless statesman." How far can a foundation established in a foreign country—by a citizen of another state—really go? What do you see as the limits of your involvement?

A legitimate and very important question. I always rely on the people who actually live in the country. It is they who decide what is best for their country. If I did not do so, I would be an intruder from the outside. I support the concept of open society. That doesn't stop the people who are opposed to this concept from regarding me as an intruder. President Tudjman of Croatia accused me of supporting traitors and called the concept of open society a dangerous new ideology. So my activities are controversial, to say the least. The greater the opposition, the greater the need for the foundation.

You are accused of meddling in internal affairs.

Of course, what I do could be called meddling, because I want to promote an open society. An open society transcends national sovereignty. At the same time, an open society cannot be imposed from the outside. The people within the country who are on the board of the foundation have to take responsibility for its actions and I rely on their advice to the greatest possible extent.

In practice, I often find it difficult to decide what position to take, because the political situation differs from country to country and, as relations between countries deteriorate, a position that is appropriate in one country may be unacceptable in another. For instance, when I took a strong stand on Bosnia, my statements endangered the foundation in Yugoslavia. I try to be circumspect, but I don't always succeed. I don't know how it will work out. In the good old bad days, my situation was easier because I was anonymous; now I have a high profile.

Are there some things that you would never do with your foundations? Are there limits you would never overstep?

Yes! I support the concept of open society, but I am categorically opposed to supporting political parties. I have no difficulty supporting a democratic movement if it is fighting an undemocratic regime. But my foundations would never support a political party and never have. It would be against the law governing United States foundations.

To be precise, however, I have to say that in any given situation, it may be very difficult to draw the line between a democratic movement and a political party. Take a country like Romania. There we supported all the independent newspapers by supplying them with newsprint at low prices. President Iliescu subsequently accused me of supporting the opposition. My response was that I was supporting a pluralistic, free press. We agreed to disagree. I use this example only to illustrate how difficult it is to determine just how far one should go.

There are plenty of people who don't want an open society in Central and Eastern European countries; they want a closed one. That was once true of the communists and today it is equally true of the nationalists. If someone wants a closed society, it is only natural that he would like to force people like me out of the country.

In many countries, the foundations have unquestionably become a force in the cultural realm, and now you have declared that you also want to do business in Eastern Europe. Haven't you and your foundations become too powerful for these countries, which are, as a rule, small and weak?

No fear. I am unlikely to invest significant amounts of money. The foundations are another matter. In some countries, they have become very influential, perhaps too influential for their own good. But I am aware of the problem and I have taken steps to prevent the foundations from becoming a monolithic block. We have many checks and balances within the foundation network. We are so decentralized and diffuse that the real problem is that the left hand doesn't know what the right hand is doing.

The country where the foundation is the most powerful is Ukraine. The foundation supports roughly two dozen independent organizations, each with its own board of directors. It is much more like a network than a power structure with a uniform direction.

But they are linked by a very powerful bond, they all receive money from you.

Correct.

The Eastern European countries are very weak. In such circumstances, the weight of a strong organization is even greater. And that is especially true if one adds your business ventures. Couldn't the foundations one day find themselves in a situation where they are stronger than the state? That would run counter to the idea of open society.

A foundation will never be able to compete with the state, no matter how weak a state might be, because a state has powers of coercion. Without such powers, a foundation may run afoul of a government, but it cannot replace the government.

You couldn't topple a government?

No. You confuse the power of ideas with political power.

How about the power of money?

I am fully aware of it. We have very strict rules to ensure that awards are made on the basis of merit and not on the basis of connections. We consider transparency in the process of making awards even more important than the awards themselves. In Romania, for instance, that is how the foundation established its reputation. Nobody had ever seen scholarships awarded on merit. Even in the media program, which was confined to independent newspapers, we took great care to treat them equally. We are often accused of buying people or buying influence, but usually by people who cannot imagine acting any other way. We would never do that; it would defeat our purpose.

I recognize that people may profess certain ideas or propose certain programs just to get money out of the foundation. That applies to all foundations and it is the job of the foundation to protect itself. I also recognize that a foundation may become too powerful when civil society has no other sources of support. I guard against it by respecting the autonomy of the people who receive support. The best protection is to spend my money while I am alive.

That means that we have to trust that you continue to be one of the "good guys."

In the sense that power shouldn't go to my head, you are right. For that purpose, I must rely on my critical faculties and my willingness to surround myself with people who are not hesitant to tell me when they disagree with me. But think of this: If we had not always respected the autonomy of those receiving assistance, we could not have established our reputation. If we had ever tried to tell people what to do, people would not have come to the foundation in the first place. Think of this, also: What conceivable use would I have for a myriad of Eastern European vassals? I ran up against that problem in China. According to Chinese morality, if you help someone he becomes obliged to you for life. In a sense you own him, but also he owns you. He expects you to continue helping him forever because, if you don't, you lose power. That is why I would never dream of restarting the foundation in China.

You said earlier that you did not plan to invest in Eastern Europe, not only because you have enough money already, but also because it could lead to conflicts between your business goals and your philanthropic ones. Why have you changed your mind?

Because the situation has changed.

Do you no longer have enough money?

No, that's not it. My rule not to invest in countries where I had foundations was a simple rule to deal with a complex situation. It was convenient, because it avoided any possibility of conflict of interest. Today the rule is no longer tenable. The Eastern European financial markets are developing, and it is my business to operate in financial markets. On what grounds can I deny my investment fund the possibility of being involved in this market? Moreover, Eastern European countries are in desperate need of foreign capital. I shouldn't abstain from investing merely for personal convenience.

Are your foundations and the possibility of conflicts of interest not reason enough to stay out of the Eastern European markets?

No, not any longer. Originally I was worried that my investments might be held hostage in order to influence the behavior of my foundations. Now the foundations are strong enough to be able to resist such blackmail. There is still a risk, to be sure, but much less so than before.

Besides, my experience shows that people take me much more seriously as an investor than as a philanthropist. So if I really want to have an influence in these countries, I can do better as a potential investor. In Romania, for example, the government was at first extremely hostile to my foundation. However, after my role in the sterling crisis, President Iliescu urgently wanted to see me, and the foundation has also had a somewhat easier time since then. But I have no intention of investing in Romania at present.

One problem remains. I might be accused of exploiting my political influence for financial gain. To guard against it, I invest only on behalf of my foundations and not for profit whenever this possibility arises. For instance, I am currently working on an investment fund for Ukraine in order to reinforce the privatization effort there. So I rest easy on that score. It troubles me more that if I invest in a country in

142

which I have a foundation, I immediately fall into the same category as a Robert Maxwell or an Armand Hammer, whose foundations were part of their business activity. I find the comparison somewhat repugnant. But I have always put substance ahead of image. The fact is that my foundations predated my business activity in the region by more than 10 years. You have to be very gullible to believe that I set up the foundations just to prepare the ground for entering the market as an investor.

But by refraining from making investments, you could have reduced the grounds on which you can be attacked.

Yes, I could have. But I deliberately chose to expose myself. To be a selfless benefactor was just a little too good to be true. It fed my self-image as a godlike creature, above the fray, doing good and fighting evil. I have talked about my messianic fantasies; I am not ashamed of them; the world would be a grim place without such fantasies. But they are fantasies. And to be godlike is to be removed from humanity. The great benefit of the foundation to me personally was that it brought me in touch with humanity. But the explosive growth of the foundation and the sheer size of the operation brought with it the danger that I would become estranged from humanity once again. I became an awesome figure, and I could see, particularly in Russia, that people simply could not understand what I was all about. Previously I never needed to explain my motivation to people who shared my objectives, but in today's Russia, people are so caught up in the fight for survival that the pursuit of an abstract good like open society seems hardly credible. I made the decision to start investing last year at the height of the robber capitalist episode. It seemed to me that to appear as a robber capitalist who is concerned with cultural and political values was more credible than to be a disembodied intellect arguing for the merits of open society. I could serve as a role model for the budding robber capitalists of Russia. And by entering the fray as an investor, I descended from Mount Olympus and became a flesh and blood human being.

143

My descent was more rapid than I intended. I entered the Russian market—the ultimate emerging market bubble—just before it burst. I realized this almost as soon as I entered and I tried to get out, but it was more difficult than getting in so we got stuck with part of our investment and I have egg on my face. From godlike, I have become all too human.

Did you lose money in your investments in Eastern Europe?

On balance, we are about even. We did well in the Czech voucher privatization.

Do you feel that Eastern Europe needs this kind of investment? Isn't Quantum much too large for these countries that are so extremely short of capital?

The countries of Eastern Europe need financial markets. As investors in financial markets, we contribute to their development. Of course we don't do that as a public service, we do it to make money. It may not be in the interest of these countries that we take away the profits we make there, but that's the nature of financial markets. It is much worse, both for us and for them, if we don't make any profits. In any case, the rumors that are circulating about the extent of our investments are exaggerated. In all of Eastern Europe we have invested at the most 1 or 2 percent of our capital. Admittedly that is not insignificant for Eastern Europe, but it is almost too little for us to justify the effort. With our $10 billion, we are like a supertanker that can put in to only a few deep ports. The fact that the Eastern European markets are so small is indeed a limitation.

Do you make the investment decisions yourself?

Only the strategic decisions whether to get engaged or not.

You have been accused of playing by your own rules and changing the rules when it suits you.

I plead guilty. I do not accept the rules imposed by others. If I did, I would not be alive today. I am a law-abiding citizen, but I recognize that there are regimes that need to be opposed rather than accepted. And in periods of regime change, the normal rules don't apply. One needs to adjust one's behavior to the changing circumstances.

Look at the tremendous changes I have gone through on a personal level. Consider my career as a philanthropist. In the beginning, I avoided any personal involvement. I sought to remain anonymous and shunned publicity. Later, when the revolution gathered momentum, I accepted the fact I was deeply involved. After 1989, I actively sought to gain a hearing for my views. That alone was a major change. At the same time, I continued to abstain from doing business in Eastern Europe. Now, I have given that up too. The reversal from my starting point, when I dissociated myself from my philanthropy, is complete. I accept everything that I do, whether as an investor or as a benefactor, as an integral part of my existence. And I am very happy about it because in a sense my whole life has been one long effort to integrate the various facets of my existence.

There is a remarkable parallel in the evolution of my attitude toward philanthropy and my attitude toward making money. At first, I didn't want to identify myself with my business career. I felt there was more to me than making money. I kept my private life strictly separate from my business. Then I went through a rough patch in 1962, when I was practically wiped out, and it affected me deeply. I had some psychosomatic symptoms, like vertigo. It made me realize that making money is an essential part of existence. Now I am completing the process by doing away with the artificial separation between my activities as investor and as philanthropist.

The internal barriers have crumbled and I am all of one piece. It gives me a great sense of fulfillment. I realize that I cut a larger-than-life figure and I feel ambivalent about it. On one hand, I find it gratifying, but on the other, the sheer magnitude of my activities, both in business and in philanthropy, makes me uneasy. I must admit that I wanted it that way and I probably could not feel all of a piece if I weren't larger than life. It makes me feel somewhat abnormal, and that is the source of my malaise. Still, it is much better to have abnormal accomplishments than to harbor abnormal ambitions. For the first 50 years of my life, I felt as if I had a guilty secret; now it is out in the open and I am proud of what I have accomplished.

I have another interpretation of the changes that have taken place in you: You are a person primarily interested in beginnings, in stormy, revolutionary times. Those times are now over in Eastern Europe. It is my feeling that the prosaic routine that now faces the foundations can no longer hold your interest. You are simply bored. Over the long haul it is surely more interesting being a fund manager than a philanthropist. In this respect, the fund manager has won out over the philanthropist.

What you say about the adventure of beginnings and about prosaic routine is correct. But I don't believe you are right about the victory of the fund manager. It would be more correct to say that I would like to transcend both roles. I would like to change my relationship with the foundations in the same way as I have changed it with my funds. I would like to distance myself from the management of the foundations as I have from the management of the funds: set the strategy and be available in case of need, but delegate authority and responsibility to others. I would like to free myself from these daily burdens, so as to be able to explore new boundaries. I am pushing against the boundaries of understanding. There has been a tremendous increase in my capacity, both in making money and in giving it away. I am concerned that my capacity to think, to comprehend a fast-changing world, has not kept pace.

All in all, would you say that your foundations in Eastern Europe are a success? Has it paid off giving away so much money?

Absolutely. The way I run the foundations, I come in contact mainly with the problems, but as I travel around, I get a strong sense of all the wonderful things the foundations are doing.

You mentioned that now, in the post-revolutionary period, the foundations have to work differently from before, in a communist regime. What had to change?

The foundations had to become more professional. It is a change I have had difficulty accepting. In the beginning, I wanted to have an anti-foundation foundation, and for a time I succeeded: the Hungarian foundation was exempt from all the ills that beset normal foundations. Then came the revolution and I rose to the challenge. There was an opportunity to change the world and I threw everything into the effort. The revolution is now cooling off, but the mission is not accomplished. The need for the foundations remains as strong as ever. Yet to continue without becoming an institution would be very detrimental. To operate without bureaucracy would render us wasteful and capricious. I have come to realize that we require a solid organization, a bureaucracy if you will. I have become reconciled to the fact that we must switch from a sprint to long distance running.

How long do you expect the foundations to continue?

As long as the money lasts, but I want them to spend the money as quickly as possible.

147

And how long will that be?

I envisage a minimum of eight years, but it may be much longer. It depends on how the Quantum Fund performs. The Central European University is endowed for a longer term, but even the foundations may outlive me. I now recognize that the mission of these foundations, building open society, cannot be accomplished in one revolutionary leap. I have started thinking in biblical terms: forty years in the wilderness.

But why shouldn't the foundations exist forever?

Because they are bound to stray from their original goals. They are institutions with a mission, and institutions tend to put their institutional interests ahead of their original mission.

How can you presume that the foundations could ever become superfluous? Even Western societies, which function more or less properly, could benefit from having an open society foundation.

Eastern European societies will surely need the foundations for a long time. But I have to assume that the foundations are going to degenerate. They should not be endowed by the money of a dead man who cannot exercise critical judgment.

I am certain that in 10 or 40 years, people will look around for new sponsors so as not to let your foundations go under.

It is happening already and I am very pleased about it. It means that the foundations are proving their right to exist.

What has changed in the foundation network?

The greatest change is that we now have a budget. Up to now everyone who had a good project that fit our criteria received money, and if it

148

didn't work out, he or she didn't get any more. It was chaotic, appropriate to the confusion of the revolutionary process in Eastern Europe. That method is no longer appropriate. We now have to plan ahead for the whole year. That changes the character of the foundations.

We have also gone from explosive growth to consolidation. 1995 will be the first year that I cannot finance the foundation out of current income and must dip into principal.

How do you feel about that?

I don't mind, indeed I quite enjoy it. I am following in my father's footsteps, who lived up his capital. But the foundations are not as happy. It is a hard landing. You have accused me of following my own rules and changing the rules to suit my needs and I pleaded guilty to the charge. I like changing my modus operandi to the circumstances; it makes me feel on top of the situation. But organizations don't take to change so kindly. They like stability. I have learned that the hard way. For instance, the Hungarian foundation that performed so brilliantly under the communist regime simply could not adjust to the new situation. And it remains to be seen how the network reacts to the changes currently underway.

And how are you going to adjust?

I am showing exemplary behavior. I recognize that I am not an organization man. I am ready to delegate everything that has to do with organization to those who are more qualified, but I retain the right to formulate strategy. I am determined to preserve as much of the spirit of the foundations as possible.

7

THE STATELESS
STATESMAN

What do you see as the economic future of the Eastern
European countries? They have become free and independent at a time when even the strongest Western
economies are experiencing major crises, and facing problems that
will only be overcome, if at all, over a long time.

At the time of the Revolution, in 1989, the Western democracies were
doing very well. Their failure to follow a far-sighted, generous policy
toward Eastern Europe cannot be blamed on economic difficulties. It
is the other way round. The present-day difficulties of the Western
world may be partially attributed to its failure to adjust to the collapse
of the Soviet Union.

As to the economic future of the region, one has to draw a sharp
line between Central Europe, that is to say Poland, the Czech Republic, and Hungary on the one hand and the former Soviet Union on the
other. There are a number of countries that lie between them: Slovakia, Romania, Bulgaria. Central Europe has made good progress toward a market economy. I am basically optimistic that this direction
will continue, unless political or military developments intervene.
The same can be said about the Baltic States, Estonia, Latvia, and
Lithuania, though with less confidence. They have stable currencies

and although conditions are very difficult, these countries have survived the worst and are moving in the right direction. Slovenia has also made the grade.

In the former Soviet Union, the situation is very different. The Soviet system has collapsed, but no new system has taken its place. The prevailing trend is still downward, toward disintegration and decay. It is impossible to say how far it may go. There have been precedents: the "time of troubles" at the end of the sixteenth century and the Russian Revolution. Between 1913 and 1917 industrial production fell by 75 percent; between 1917 and 1921 it fell by another 75 percent—that is the kind of decline that is in the cards. I used to speak of a "black hole" that would destroy civilization.

But industrial production has more or less stabilized.

That is true. Many industrial enterprises—those that are still functioning—have learned to fend for themselves. The economy is like an octopus whose head has been cut off. The tentacles have adapted themselves to a more or less independent existence—I say more or less because many tentacles are still attached to the state budget and feed off it.

Something very interesting and unexpected happened in Russia in 1994. The shares of state-owned enterprises were distributed to the public practically free in a mass privatization scheme. This divided the enterprises into two classes: those whose shares had value and those that did not. Roughly speaking, the energy and raw materials producers fell into the first class, the energy users into the second class. The division had been there before, but the voucher privatization scheme made it more obvious. It also engendered a feeding frenzy. Shares representing claims on natural resources could be bought at a tiny fraction of their potential value. Oil in the ground sells for $2 to $3 a barrel in the rest of the world; in Russia, it could be bought for 2 to 3 cents. This attracted some enterprising investors from home and abroad and touched off one of the weirdest stock market booms in history. The amounts involved were relatively insignificant—a few hundred million dollars—but the rate of appreciation was phenomenal. Some shares rose tenfold in a matter of a few months—between March and August of 1994. The market was rudimentary: There were no clearing and custodian arrangements and share registries were not properly administered. Banks and brokers suffered from an acute shortage of capital—they gladly paid 10 percent a month or more for dollar deposits.

Is that when you changed your mind and started investing?

Yes, that is when I lifted the ban on investing. I couldn't resist the temptation. Here was an embryonic financial market with tremendous upside potential. Why should we stay away from it? But when I went to Moscow, in the early fall, and took a look at what was going on, I was appalled: it had all the earmarks of a bubble about to burst. I gave the order to sell, but I got the classic answer: to whom?

At any rate, there was a moment in 1994 when one could see the faint outlines of a new order rising out of the ashes of the old. It resembled the robber capitalism that prevailed in the United States in the nineteenth century, but it was much worse because the legal infrastructure was much more feeble. There is much talk about the Mafia, but the Mafia is nothing else but the privatization of public safety— the most successful privatization effort in Russia.

Has law and order completely broken down?

No, but the public authorities are also working for private profit. What we call Mafia is really an interwoven network of alliances between entrepreneurs and officials. It is the seamy side of free enterprise.

153

Surely you don't find it attractive?

I find it repulsive, but it may be better than the alternative. People act as robber capitalists because that is the only way they can become capitalists in a lawless society. Many of them are educated, decent people who don't like it any better than I do. Given half a chance, they would become upright citizens. In the United States, the corruption in Chicago and Boston and the New York of Tammany Hall engendered a public outcry for clean government. The same would happen in Russia—because Russians really care about honesty—if only robber capitalism succeeded.

But that is not at all certain because it is being destroyed even before it got started. The enterprises whose shares rose tenfold in the summer of 1994 did not get a red cent out of it—all the profit went to the people who bought the shares and resold them. It is only in the second stage of privatization that the proceeds would accrue to the enterprises, but the bubble has burst and it is doubtful whether there will be a second stage that really amounts to something. Undoubtedly, some energy companies are going to try, because their managements discovered that they can actually raise money by selling shares and are preparing feverishly, but I don't think they will get very far.

Why are you so pessimistic?

Partly because the emerging markets boom—in which Russia was the last and most outlandish entrant—has burst and partly because of political developments inside Russia.

Consider the political implications of a robber-capitalist regime in Russia. The natural resource producers would prosper but the military-industrial complex would decay. The prosperity of the natural resource sector would lead to an import boom because consumers prefer imported products to locally produced goods. The service sector—banking, financial services, distribution, trade—would also develop, but there would be practically no market for producer goods. But that is the sector that constitutes the bulk of the economy. The old Soviet economy was incredibly distorted: The producer goods industry, including military goods, was called Sector A and it accounted for 75 percent of industrial production; light industry, called Sector B, was only 25 percent. In a market economy, the proportions are reversed. The energy-using industry would be penalized because oil and other raw materials are worth more when they are sold in world markets than when they are transformed into products at home. But the military-industrial complex carries tremendous political clout. Already, the political struggle can be boiled down to a conflict between these two interest groups. The energy-producing sector is represented by the Prime Minister, Viktor Chernomyrdin, the military-industrial complex by Oleg Soskovets, First Deputy Prime Minister. The actual state of play is, of course, much more complicated—the mayors of Moscow and St. Petersburg and the other local potentates are not so easy to fit into the picture—but the main political battle is going to be fought along these lines. It is a battle that the energy users are favored to win. Not only do they carry much greater political weight, they also have a strong political argument: They can appeal to nationalist sentiment. Robber capitalism would lead to the hollowing out of the Russian economy. The bulk of industrial workers would lose their jobs and would have to be redeployed. In any country, there would be a political outcry. Russia is no exception.

No sooner has robber capitalism reared its ugly head than political forces have coalesced against it. Soskovets has been gaining ground against Chernomyrdin since the middle of 1994. Even the attack on Chechnya, however badly it was bungled, plays into the hands of the military-industrial complex. The robber-capitalist goose is going to be devoured before it can lay any golden eggs.

Can you explain the invasion of Chechnya?

I have no special insight. Clearly, it was designed to exploit the strong popular prejudice against Chechens, who are associated with the Mafia in the public mind, and to regain some measure of popularity for President Yeltsin. But it was incredibly mismanaged. It started out as a covert intelligence operation, a so-called internal uprising, which misfired and turned into a full-scale military invasion. It will have incalculable consequences.

What do you expect?

Almost anything. The struggle for power has intensified to a point where almost anything can happen. In a country where people are prepared to steal anything, the state itself is up for grabs. Until now, it was not worth grabbing because the economy was unable to support the state mechanism. Those who tried, failed—remember the abortive coup in which incompetent bureaucrats tried to oust Gorbachev. But time has passed, people have recovered their wits, and even the economy has stabilized. It is worth making the effort and the effort is currently underway. A rather sinister group has gathered around President Yeltsin, bent on seizing power. The most visible person among them, and probably their leader, is General Korzhakov, head of the presidential guard and Yeltsin's long-standing drinking partner. The presidential guard is being expanded into a private army and already there have been some ugly incidents. It is rather scary when members of the presidential guard, wearing ski masks, attack the security guards of a banker who controls a television network that is critical of the President; when a key figure in the state-owned television network that has shown a large degree of independence during the siege of Grozny is murdered; when the son of a prominent dissident is killed in a suspicious car accident the same day that the dissident is speaking out about the abuse of state power. There seems

156

to be a concerted campaign to silence or intimidate the independent media before the elections.

I don't see why a dictatorship—if that is what is in the making—should be incompatible with robber capitalism. Indeed, that is the essence of fascism.

That is a very penetrating observation. But I don't think you can take the victory of fascism in Russia for granted. The battle has just begun. People are not going to give up their new-found freedom without a fight. The media have shown the invasion of Chechnya in its full horror and people have been shocked, much like Western public opinion was shocked by the gory pictures from Bosnia. Indeed, the effect was much greater because people in Russia were exposed to it for the first time. I don't expect the great masses to be aroused to action—they remain long-suffering and passive—but I do expect the media to fight for its hard-won independence with messianic zeal. No wonder that the recent atrocities were directed at people connected with the media!

Do you really believe they can resist the pressure?

If there is no countervailing pressure, probably not.

Where would the countervailing pressure come from?

From abroad, to start with. People in Russia really care what the world thinks of them. Yeltsin himself cares a great deal. He may be under the control of a small, sinister group around him, but he can't be happy about it. The German Chancellor, Helmut Kohl, called him a number of times about Chechnya and he tried to respond. Unfortunately, his orders were not obeyed. That is how we were treated to the spectacle of Yeltsin announcing the suspension of bombing without any effect. Kohl is demonstrating real understanding and concern with the internal situation in Russia. I wish I could say the same thing for our own administration.

There is a factor at play whose importance is not properly appreciated: the military. The military has stayed out of politics so far, but Chechnya has been a traumatic experience. Commanders have refused to obey orders. Large numbers of body bags have been sent home. The army is deeply divided and deeply hurt. When the military becomes politicized, it happens very fast and it profoundly changes the political landscape. That is what happened just before the outbreak of the Spanish Civil War and that is what is happening in Russia today.

So you expect civil war?

I expect the military to play a more active political role than before. And whoever makes a grab for the control of the state is liable to run into resistance. Whether events will deteriorate into full-scale civil war, it is impossible to say. Almost anything may happen, civil war not excluded. One thing is certain: Political instability is not conducive to investment. That is why I give both robber capitalism and fascist dictatorship a relatively low probability, at least in the near term, and increasing instability a much higher probability. We are approaching the conditions I had in mind when I spoke of a black hole.

I am still at a loss as to why you should want to invest in conditions like these.

Conditions in 1994 were very different. It is characteristic of revolutions that conditions turn around completely; that is why they are called revolutions. I anticipated the conditions that prevail today, but the emergence of robber capitalism last year caught me by surprise. It ran counter to the normal evolution of financial markets. Normally the establishment of a legal infrastructure comes first; direct foreign investment next; and the development of foreign portfolio investment last. In this case, the order was reversed: foreign portfolio investment came first and it acted as a catalyst for the emergence of robber capitalism. I could recognize it when I saw it. I was particularly impressed by the way Boris Jordan, working for Credit Suisse First Boston, helped to develop the market. He did not try to hog the market, like some other players, but left room for others and tried to develop the institutional infrastructure. It reminded me of my youth, when I pioneered the opening up of the Swedish market and other markets and I didn't want to be left out. But, for a number of reasons, including my ban on investing where I have foundations and the role change involved, I was a little slow on the uptake. Instead of first in, first out, we were last in, first out, and instead of a profit, we have a loss.

How do you feel about your foundations in Russia?

Concerned. I committed large amounts of money—the International Science Foundation alone cost me more than $100 million—and it may have been largely wasted if Russia goes down the drain.

But you tell me you anticipated the current turn of events.

That's right. I did everything I could to prevent the present turn of events and I have no regrets on that score. It was well worth trying, even if it didn't succeed, because so much was at stake. But now that my worst expectations are coming true, I am at a loss as to what to do. I cannot pull up stakes because I would be abandoning those whom I wanted to support in their hour of need. At the same time, it goes against the grain to throw good money after bad. I am caught in a trap of my own making. I console myself with the thought that in the case of societies, there is life after death. Some of the seeds we sow may survive no matter what happens to Russia in the near term.

Are you trying to extricate yourself?

No; the fight is not yet over.

But you cut your losses on your investments.

That's different. I invest for profit; philanthropy is for a cause, even if it turns out to be a lost cause. I can't quit now. I have a strategy and I shall adjust it as events unfold.

What is your strategy?

The International Science Foundation was meant to be a one-time emergency operation: $100 million to keep alive, during a period of economic dislocation, a scientific establishment that is outstanding by international standards and has been the mainstay of independent thought and action in the former Soviet Union.

The Science Foundation has accomplished its mission. The money that was meant to be spent in two years was committed in 18 months and the program was so highly appreciated that the various governments concerned—Russia, Ukraine, and the Baltic States—offered matching funds in order to get me to continue it. I accepted their offer and committed additional funds for 1995, but I will not extend the program into 1996 unless I also get matching funds from Western sources. I think it is inappropriate that I should be the sole Western source of support for Russian science, especially as European and American governmental programs failed to use the money allocated. The scientists are urging me to lobby for governmental support but I refuse to do so. Let them lobby! We are slowly winding down the operation. The international travel program is already shutting down. The same strategy applies to the science education program that started a year later and, barring outside support, will wind down a year later. But I intend to continue the supply of international scientific journals because the publishers have offered such favorable terms that I consider it matching funds. I shall persevere with the Internet program, which is just beginning to pick up momentum, even if I don't get outside support because I consider it so important for establishing the pre-conditions of open society. I am trying to make the most of the transformation of the humanities program—we are printing millions of textbooks this year—and I shall continue our effort to keep alive the so-called "thick journals," the cultural journals that have played such an important role in Russian history. I am also ready to embark on new programs for the support of culture, civil society, and the media, but not on the scale people in Russia have come to expect of me. I intend to continue along these lines as long as civil society supports the foundations and the authorities tolerate them. But I can't help feeling despondent about the prospects.

Do you think events could have taken a different course?

I am convinced of it. It was well within the powers of the Western democracies to slow down the disintegration of the Soviet Union and lay the foundations of an open society before the closed society collapsed. All it would have taken was some positive reinforcement for Gorbachev's policies of glasnost and perestroika. He was dying for it. He had a naive belief that, once he provided an opening, the free world would rush in to help. But the Western governments lacked the vision and the political will. In the spring of 1989, at an East-West security conference at Potsdam, I proposed a new version of the Marshall Plan, this time to be financed mainly by the Europeans. My proposal was "greeted with amusement," as the *Frankfurter Allgemeine Zeitung* reported. If it had been taken more seriously, history would have taken a different course.

Aren't you overestimating the potential for Western intervention in what were, after all, the internal affairs of the Soviet Union?

Not at all. I speak from personal experience. As early as 1988 I proposed to the Soviet authorities a study group to establish what I called an "open sector" in the Soviet economy. I was not as well known as I am today; I was practically a nobody; nevertheless, I received a positive response. Admittedly, the cooperation of the Soviet authorities was haphazard at best but, when I insisted, Prime Minister Ryzhkov issued an order obliging the relevant officials to attend.

What was the outcome?

Negative. I was thinking of creating a market-oriented sector within the centrally planned economy, a sector not too far removed from the consumer and not too far down the chain of production. Food processing, for instance. I had in mind a kind of embryonic market economy that would grow within the body of a centrally planned economy. But it didn't take too many meetings to discover that the mother's body was too diseased to support a healthy embryo.

Aren't you contradicting yourself? If the centrally planned economy was doomed in 1988, what could Western assistance accomplish?

It could have slowed down the process of disintegration. It could have given people a sense of material improvement and built support for economic reform. It wouldn't have taken much. For instance, the introduction of tampons would have generated a great deal of enthusiasm among women who had to rely on the most primitive sanitary devices; or electronic gadgets would have motivated the younger generation. At the time I am speaking about, the Soviet Union still enjoyed a first class credit rating because it had always paid its obligations punctiliously. In those years, the Soviet Union borrowed tens of billions of dollars.

Why didn't it have the desired results?

Because no conditions were attached or, more exactly, the conditions were designed to benefit the lenders, not the recipient. Germany lent tens of billions to gain Gorbachev's consent to the reunification of Germany. I remember a $5 billion credit from Italy for the promotion of Italian exports. Exporters had to pay 5 percent to the brother of Italy's then-Foreign Minister, Gianni De Michelis, who is now in jail. But no thought was given to the effect on the Soviet economy. If the lenders had insisted, they could have dictated whatever conditions they wanted. The Soviet authorities were eager to be told what to do. I saw that in connection with the Open Sector Task Force but, of course, I was not in a position to impose conditions because I wasn't lending billions of dollars. But I would have imposed conditions and I would have enforced them. That was a time to be intrusive. It would have been appreciated.

Would it have worked?

Probably not. Nothing worked at the time. There would have been slippage. But there would have been also some positive results and that could have changed the course of history. What Gorbachev lacked was a modicum of success.

Was it possible to keep the Soviet Union together? And would it have been desirable to do so?

I am sure it would have eventually disintegrated, but I am convinced that it would have been better if the process had been slower and more orderly. Look at the dissolution of the British Empire; it took half a century to accomplish and it wasn't without conflict, but the effect was almost wholly beneficial.

But Great Britain was the motherland of democracy.

That is all the more reason why the Soviet Union needed more time for its dissolution. I do not make myself popular today when I say that it would have been better if the Soviet Union had not collapsed, just as it would have been better if Yugoslavia had not broken up. It would have made possible the transition from a totalitarian system to a free and democratic one. There would have been demands for autonomy, and eventually there would have been an independent Ukraine, for instance, but it would have occurred over a longer period of time. Ukraine would then have been a more stable and viable country when it became independent. To come into the world as a viable organism, a fetus needs nine months. The new countries arising out of the Soviet Union did not have enough time to develop. They are all premature births, and one has to wonder whether they will survive.

I was a great supporter of the so-called Shatalin Plan, or the 500-Day Program as it is also known. I was involved in it from its inception. I met with Nikolai Petrakov, Gorbachev's economic adviser, on the day the task force was formed. I provided a group of eminent international economists to critique the plan, sponsored a group of lawyers to help design the necessary legislation, and brought the authors, under the leadership of Grigory Yavlinsky, to the 1990 Annual Meetings of the IMF and the World Bank in Washington.

The idea behind the Shatalin Plan was to transfer sovereignty from the Soviet Union to the constituent republics but, at the same time, to transfer back certain critical elements of sovereignty from the republics to a newly created entity, the Inter-Republican Council. In theory, it would have replaced the Soviet Union with a new kind of union that would have been more like the European Union. In practice, it would have pitted the new authority, the Inter-Republican Council, against the old, Soviet authorities. Since the old political center was almost universally despised, the new political center would have gained popular support by doing battle with the old one.

It was a brilliant political conception that was not properly understood. Had it received international support, I am sure Gorbachev would have endorsed it. Even without Western endorsement, it was touch and go. I remember Leonid Abalkin bragging to me how he managed to sway Gorbachev against the plan. He would be the 13th member of a council uniting 12 republics; each member would have a firm territorial base except him; therefore, he would become the least powerful member of the Council. That argument won the day. But a year later, Yeltsin used the Russian state as the power base for toppling Gorbachev and dissolving the Soviet Union. If Gorbachev had accepted the Shatalin Plan, he could have remained in power and the Soviet Union could have been reformed, instead of disintegrating.

You say you were initially involved in the Shatalin Plan. Did you remain involved in the reform process after the dissolution of the Soviet Union?

Not in Russia. I was friendly toward Yegor Gaidar and I would have been ready to help him, but I came to the conclusion that the reform was moving on a false track relatively early on. It happened in April 1992 when I discovered that the enterprises were accumulating receivables at a rate that was roughly half the rate of industrial production. This meant that roughly half the production was exempt from the monetary control that was the cornerstone of Gaidar's policy. Half of industry ignored monetary signals and continued producing according to the old system of "state orders" irrespective of getting paid. This was a shocking discovery. I confronted Gaidar when he came to see me one night in New York, and he admitted it. Then he delivered a rousingly optimistic speech in Washington later that week. I started advocating publicly that Western aid should be tied to the creation of a social safety net. This would have enabled the Russian government to put enterprises that failed to obey monetary signals into bankruptcy. My proposal did not make much headway.

None of the policies you supported seem to have been implemented. Wasn't that frustrating?

Yes, it was. But the policies I could implement on my own succeeded. I tried to demonstrate my social safety net proposal in a pilot scheme. That was the origin of the International Science Foundation. We distributed $500 a year to some 30,000 scientists and I had the satisfaction that it worked. Privately I suggested a similar scheme for military officers, but I was not willing to fund it. It might have cost $500 million, but it would have made a difference.

165

You are very critical of Western policy. What would you recommend to the IMF today?

I would not like to be in their shoes. But then, I don't like being in my own shoes very much, either.

Can you be more explicit?

I think it is too late to have a real impact on the course of events in Russia. Russians may have had exaggerated expectations of the West, but now they are disappointed and disillusioned. Our influence has been greatly reduced. Even the progressive elements have turned anti-Western. Aleksandr Yakovlev, who had been the architect of glasnost and the former Chairman of Ostankino, the state television, complained to me bitterly about the policies of the United States.

But you are actively engaged in Ukraine.

Yes. That is where it is possible to make a difference and I am doing my utmost to bring it about. And, for the first time, I don't feel frustrated. I have a sense of accomplishment. For the first time since 1989, the Western powers did the right thing: in the communiqué of the 1994 Naples Summit, they promised $4 billion in aid if Ukraine embarks on a reform program. This happened to coincide with the election of a new president, Leonid Kuchma.

The previous president, Leonid Kravchuk, was an opportunist who realized that the problems of Ukraine exceeded his capacity to deal with them and he did not even try. All he wanted was to stay on top, bobbing along like a cork in a turbulent sea. He had been the chief ideologist of the Ukrainian communist party and he felt it opportune to change horses from communism to nationalism. For a while, it worked; he was elected with a greater majority than practically any other president: more than 60 percent. He sought to maintain his popularity by playing up the conflict over the Black Sea Fleet

166

and other nationalist themes, but he was undercut by the collapse of the economy.

Kuchma is made of a different fiber. The manager of an important enterprise in the military-industrial complex, he is oriented toward problem solving. He realizes that Ukraine cannot survive as an independent country the way things are going and he is determined to do something about it. The Naples Summit offered him a lifeline and he resolved to seize it. He had no deep understanding of the market mechanism, but he understood very clearly what $4 billion could do for Ukraine because that was the cost of Ukraine's energy imports. On this occasion, the promise of economic aid did what it was supposed to do: It changed the direction of economic policy. The main credit goes to senior United States Treasury officials, who inserted an actual amount into the communiqué.

Ukraine was, and remains, in a highly precarious state. The economic collapse has been much greater than in Russia, partly because Ukraine is deficient in energy and partly because there has been no serious attempt at macro-economic stabilization or structural reform. In accordance with my boom/bust theory, this actually makes it easier to engineer a change of direction. I was well placed to assist and I rushed to offer my assistance. We put in place a small team of experts, under the direction of Anders Aslund, to help the Ukrainians develop their economic reform program and deal with the international donor community. The cooperation was successful because it was based on mutual trust and an initial agreement with the IMF was put in place in record time. Success is far from assured; the process could be derailed at any point and already we have had to exert ourselves several times to put the train back on the rails, but I have a strong sense that it is moving in the right direction.

Are you confident that the reform program is going to succeed?

Not at all. I can see some glaring deficiencies in it. As it stands at present it suffers from the same flaw as the Gaidar program in 1992: the emission of currency is reasonably well controlled but the budget and the behavior of the state-owned enterprises remains out of control. The spending ministries continue to spend and the enterprises continue to operate at a deficit; the liabilities continue to accumulate, and wages, receivables simply remain unpaid. This is unsustainable but it can be fixed. It requires structural reforms and I hope they will not be long in coming. In contrast to the Gaidar times, I can do more than just predict failure.

This must be a novel experience for you.

Yes, and it is very satisfying.

Why do you think it comes so late in the day? You have been trying since 1988.

Because it takes time to catch up with revolutionary change. This applies to the international authorities; it applies to the Ukrainians—for instance, Roman Shpek, one of the first graduates of Hawrylyshyn's business school is a key player on the Ukrainian team—and it applies to me.

But you pride yourself on understanding revolutionary change better than others.

It took time to establish my credentials. I have also learned to be calmer and bide my time. In the early days, I was too eager and jumped on every opportunity. Now, I am ready to abstain or withdraw. I don't need to score.

Are you personally so engaged in any other country?

Macedonia. It is the last surviving multi-ethnic democracy in the Balkans. It can survive as an independent country only if it has a government devoted to the principles of open society—otherwise, the ethnic tensions between its Macedonian and Albanian communities would tear it apart. It is the victim of an illegal and unjustified blockade by Greece, which is a member of the European Union. The Western democracies should have gone to the aid of Macedonia, but they did not. The United States stationed some peacekeeping troops there, but nothing was done to provide economic relief. I stepped into the breach. I provided a $25 million loan that allowed Macedonia to buy oil and I provided a subsidy for an airlift of its export of early vegetables. I continued to agitate for a more constructive policy toward Macedonia but to little effect. As the economy deteriorated, so did ethnic relations. Tensions reached the breaking point recently. Albanian radicals established a so-called university without government permission. It was a political provocation aimed at creating an illegal parallel structure for ethnic Albanians similar to the structure that Albanians have established in Kosovo. I pleaded with President Gligorov personally not to be provoked, but I failed. He deployed the police and there has been a fatality. Both the Albanian and the ethnic Macedonian populations are becoming radicalized. The ethnic Macedonian inhabitants of the Albanian region are increasingly attracted to the way Milosevic has handled the Albanian problem in Kosovo. The government is failing to provide firm leadership. The situation is liable to deteriorate and I am distressed. Nobody could have done more than I did in the way of early warning and prevention, but it didn't help. I can see the third Balkan War in the making. I am at a loss as to what to do. I intend to go to Macedonia and appeal to their better judgment. But I have some doubt whether they have a better judgment.

You have said that you consider the rise of nationalism the greatest threat to the region.

Yes. Communism represented the idea of a universal closed society. That idea has failed. There was a small window of opportunity for the idea of a universal open society to take hold. But that would have required the open societies of the free world to sponsor that idea. Because open society is a more advanced form of social organization than a closed society; it is impossible to make the transition in one revolutionary leap without a firm helping hand from the outside. The Western democracies lacked the vision and the opportunity was lost. Universal closed society has broken down and no new unifying principle has taken its place. Universal ideas generally are in disrepute. People are preoccupied with their personal survival. They can be aroused to a common cause only by a real or imagined threat to their collective survival. Unfortunately, such threats are not difficult to generate. Ethnic conflicts can be used to mobilize people behind the leadership and create particular closed societies. Milosevic has shown the way and he has many imitators.

Do you consider the threat of nationalism universal?

There is something self-contradictory in your question because nationalism ought to be, by definition, particular. Yet it has a universal aspect. It is catching. It flourishes in the absence of a universal idea, such as human rights or civilized conduct. The rise of nationalism and ethnic conflicts indicate the lack of international law and order. In that sense, it is universal. Nationalists are kindred souls. Milosevic and Tudjman understand each other; they can make music together.

As far as Russia is concerned, you are quite pessimistic. I am therefore surprised by the optimism you have expressed regarding the countries of Central Europe. Their prospects are surely better than those of the former Soviet Union, but it seems to me by no means certain that they are irreversibly on their way to a market economy and free society.

I am surprised that you are surprised. The communist system is gone and these countries—with the exception of Slovakia—have definitely committed themselves to democracy and market economy. My main concern is whether the European Union will be open enough to accept them.

Aren't you worried that former communists are once again in power both in Poland and in Hungary?

Not particularly. Communism as an ideology is well and truly dead. At the height of the revolution, former communists were repudiated by the electorate. Their return to public life is a welcome broadening of the democratic spectrum. That is not to say that I agree with their policies. On the contrary, I think they are harmful. But, in the case of Poland, the agrarian party is worse than the former communists. In the case of Hungary, I had high hopes when the socialist-liberal coalition was formed, but I have been somewhat disappointed with the prime minister, Gyula Horn.

Why?

Because he hasn't changed. When I got to know him, around 1987, I considered him the most dynamic member of the government; by 1989 he struck me as almost reactionary because conditions had changed but he had not. The overarching problem of Hungary is its accumulated debt. The debt was accumulated during the Kadar era, when Horn's political attitudes were formed. He brings those attitudes to his job now. He would like to maintain economic growth by accumulating more debt. But the music has stopped. After Mexico, Hungary is facing a financial crisis. This is so obvious that I don't see any harm in saying so publicly.

You once proposed a solution to the debt problem.

That was during the elections of 1990. I saw an opportunity to draw a line under the debt incurred by the communist government and turn over a new page. At a time of discontinuity, when a legitimate government is replacing an illegitimate one, such a move is possible. But the opportunity was lost and it will not recur.

Would it not be possible to obtain some relief even now?

No. The old debts and the new debts have been intermingled and bank debt has been replaced by market debt. Even to talk about it would make matters worse. At the same time, I don't know how Hungary is going to refinance its debt in view of market conditions.

Doesn't that contradict the optimistic view you expressed earlier?

Not really. I think Hungary has made the grade, both politically and economically. It has a severe debt problem, like many other countries, which has suddenly turned more acute because of the bust in international investing. It will probably force Hungary to take some painful measures that it would have otherwise deferred and, if it does, I hope it will be rescued by Germany because Germany owes Hungary a particular debt. But a financial crisis could destroy the country, so there is reason to be wary.

Poland does not have a serious debt problem because it has defaulted and its debt has been restructured. I consider Poland one of the healthiest countries in Europe today. Its economy is growing but, even more importantly, it has the right spirit. I have the impression that public life is less corrupt and people remain more concerned with the common good than in many of the former communist countries. I am particularly impressed with the intellectual atmosphere surrounding the Stefan Batory Foundation.

That is a strange view. Most people would consider the Czech Republic and Hungary ahead of Poland.

They may be ahead, but Poland is coming up fast. I am interested in the rate and direction of change. My only concern is that Poland may be losing momentum because of political developments. It is unfortunate that the electorate rejected the previous Solidarity-based government just when it got its act together.

Many people would say that the improvement is greatest in the Czech Republic, especially since it got rid of Slovakia.

The Czechs have undoubtedly benefited from the separation from Slovakia, but the Czechs' gain has been Europe's loss. Meciar is trying to align Slovakia with Russia. His ambition is to become the first outpost of a new Russian empire. If he succeeds, it bodes ill for Europe: Slovakia will become a dagger pointed at the heart of Europe. So much for the unabashed pursuit of self-interest.

Is Romania also going to become a trouble spot?

Not necessarily. Romania is a devastated country without the prerequisites for an open society. It has a crypto-communist regime that has unfortunately felt obliged to align itself with some extreme nationalist parties. This carries with it the seeds of trouble, but the trouble may be contained because the regime does not want to be cut off from Europe. The democratic forces are weak, but fortunately they never got a chance to run the country.

You say fortunately?

Yes. They weren't ready and they would have failed, as the democrats did in Bulgaria. Or the dissident intellectuals in Czechoslovakia, for that matter. They need time to mature, and I see some signs of maturity. They are more willing to cooperate. Not everyone has to be the head of a party. But they don't have much time left. As a new economic and financial structure emerges, elections will no longer be decided by ideas but by funding and the control of the media. The next elections will be crucial. If the democrats fail to make headway, they may be permanently frozen out of power.

What do you think the West should do to help the countries of Central and Eastern Europe?

It varies from country to country and from time to time. Central Europe needs access to markets and membership of the European Union more than anything. Romania needs assistance with the establishment of democracy and independent media, especially television. Generally speaking, the further you go East and South, the greater the need for technical assistance and other forms of aid.

You have been very critical of Western policies. How could the delivery of aid be improved?

The trouble is that technical aid is provided by bureaucracies with all their negative features. Bureaucrats are sometimes very decent, well-intentioned people, but they are confined by rules. We joke inside the foundation that Western aid is the last remnant of the command economy, because it is designed to satisfy the needs of the donors, not the needs of the recipients. The foundations try to reverse the order by seeking to respond to the needs of the country concerned. In Ukraine, our technical experts work for the Ukrainians: they are selected by them and can be fired by them. But as the foundations become increasingly bureaucratized, the joke is increasingly on us.

I would sum it up like this: Western assistance has gone through three phases. In the first phase, we should have offered assistance, but we didn't. In the second phase, we promised it, but we didn't deliver. In the third phase, we delivered, but it didn't work. We are now in the third phase.

My foundations have developed a very useful concept for delivering assistance. You have to find a local partner you trust; you have to empower him to carry out his mission, but you had better retain the pursestrings.

174

Do you think you have changed the course of history in Eastern Europe? Would it have taken a different course if you hadn't been there?

Only marginally. Take Hungary, for example. Although the foundation helped to undermine the communist regime—we sponsored writers who then overthrew the communist writers' union; we sponsored youth leaders who then formed the first noncommunist youth league, and so on—the regime would have collapsed without the foundation. After all, it collapsed in other countries where we had no foundation. We can claim a lot more credit for the smoothness of the transition. We did lay the groundwork for an open society. The same applies to other countries. The full impact of our work may be felt only in the future.

Can you envisage developments that would cause you to withdraw from certain countries?

Easily. I am surprised it hasn't happened already. As local conflicts proliferate, our stance in one country is liable to displease another country. Communications and travel may also become more restricted. There is a vicious campaign being waged against my foundation in Yugoslavia even as we speak. But I shall not leave willingly. The more my people come under pressure, the more determined I am to stand by them. I am more likely to be expelled by indifference. That was the case in Prague, where the foundation was neither attacked nor supported—although recently it has shown some signs of revival.

We may also reach closure because we run out of money, although that is at least eight years away. With the exception of the Central European University, I don't want my foundations to last forever.

THE FUTURE OF THE UNITED STATES AND OPEN SOCIETY

You have recently said that you are turning your attention from Eastern Europe to the West. Why is that?

The regime change in Eastern Europe is now five years old. At the height of the revolution, almost anything was possible. I attempted to seize the revolutionary moment, but on the whole, the outcome has not corresponded to my expectations. The pattern that is emerging is not a pattern of open societies. If anything, the trend is in the opposite direction. I haven't given up hope, but I recognize that the trend is set and it will take a long time and a great deal of effort to change the direction.

In the meantime, there is another regime change unfolding. It is less clearly recognized than the revolution that occurred in the former Soviet Union, but it is no less far-reaching in its implications. The stable world order that prevailed during the Cold War has broken down, and no new order has taken its place. While everybody is now aware of the revolution that has occurred in the former Soviet Union, the revolutionary transformation in international relations has still largely escaped our attention. People who have been directly affected by the collapse of the Soviet system could not help but realize that they are living through revolutionary times. The rest of the world was less directly affected; therefore, it will take them longer to become aware of the profound change that has occurred in the world order.

The Cold War was not an attractive order, but it had a large element of stability built into it. There were two superpowers, representing two diametrically opposed forms of social organization, locked in deadly combat. But they were obliged to respect each other's vital interests because they were operating in conditions of mutually assured destruction.

The system came to an end because one of the superpowers disintegrated from within. No new system has taken its place. The process of disintegration is continuing unabated and it is now spreading from the Soviet Union to the Atlantic Alliance. The reason for the disintegration is that the open societies of the free world do not really believe in the concept of open society. They are not willing to make the effort and the sacrifice that would be necessary for the concept of open society to prevail. My goal in Eastern Europe was to promote the concept of open society. I now feel that I must switch my attention to the world at large.

That is a very ambitious goal. How do you propose to go about it?

Honestly, I don't know. I merely recognize that confining my attention to Eastern Europe is not enough. The transition from closed to open societies in Eastern Europe failed because the free world failed to provide sufficient support. I thought that I would blaze the trail, I would lead and others would follow. But now that I look back, I find that there was practically nobody behind me. I ask myself what went wrong.

Perhaps you were too idealistic.

I admit it. But I don't believe I overestimate the importance of ideals. Only when people believe in something can they move the world. The trouble is that people simply don't believe in open society as a goal worth fighting for.

But you yourself have said that open society is too complicated a concept, too full of contradictions to serve as a unifying principle.

How right you are. People may be willing to fight for king and country. They may be prepared to defend themselves against a real or imagined national or ethnic injury, but they are unlikely to rise to the defense of open society. If there was any doubt about it, Bosnia has proved the point.

What went wrong in Bosnia in your opinion?

That is too broad a question. I shall confine myself to the behavior of the Western world. It is clear that people in the West failed to understand what the Bosnian conflict was all about. It was not a civil war between Serbs, Croats, and Bosnian Muslims. It was a case of Serbian aggression and the use of ethnic cleansing as a means to an end. On a more profound level, it was a conflict between an ethnic and a civic concept of citizenship. Appropriately, the conflict has pitted the Serbian country folk against the city dwellers of Sarajevo and the other towns of Bosnia.

It is less clear whether the failure to understand what is at stake was deliberate or unintentional. Undoubtedly, there was a great deal of obfuscation by Western governments that were determined not to get involved. There was a lot of loose talk about how the Balkans were a hellhole of ethnic conflicts that was contradicted by the fact that three nationalities and four religions coexisted in Sarajevo for the last 400 years. But there was also a genuine lack of understanding and a genuine incapacity to deal with the problem on the part of the Western governments because they haven't learned to think in terms of open and closed societies.

Professional diplomats and statesmen are trained to deal with relations between states. They are intellectually unprepared to deal with a situation where a state like Yugoslavia disintegrates. First, they tried everything to keep it together. Secretary Baker paid a visit to Belgrade just a week or so before Slovenia and Croatia seceded from Yugoslavia. I met with Ambassador Warren Zimmerman shortly thereafter and he told me that the United States could have no objections if the Yugoslav army would keep Yugoslavia together by force, provided that federal elections were held within, say, six months.

When it proved impossible to keep Yugoslavia together, the international community tried to treat the constituent republics as if they were full-fledged states. Here the Germans must bear the brunt of the responsibility because they insisted on recognizing Croatia and Slovenia, which practically forced Bosnia and Macedonia to opt for independence, because otherwise they would have remained part of a mainly Serbian state that espoused ethnic principles.

Recognizing Bosnia and Macedonia and admitting them to the United Nations imposed certain obligations on the international community that, when the crunch came, they were unwilling to live up to. Here the blame shifts to the British. The United Kingdom held the presidency of the European Union when the full horror of ethnic cleansing was revealed on television—the Western governments had been aware of it for some time, but suppressed the information. The British government could not stand idly by; yet they were determined not to get militarily involved. The solution they devised was a particularly nefarious one: they proposed to send United Nations peacekeeping troops where there was no peace to keep. The British knew what they were doing and they remained consistent throughout; the United States and the French wavered between expediency and lofty principles.

The outcome was the most humiliating, debilitating experience in the history of Western democracies. The United Nations troops were given an impossible mandate. Their mission was to deliver humanitarian aid to the civilian population, and in order to do so they had to have the agreement and cooperation of all the warring parties. This required the United Nations troops to be neutral between the aggressors and the victims. Since the Serbian aggressors sought to achieve their goals by hurting civilians, the United Nations troops effectively became their tools. They acted like KAPOs in the concentration camps. Just as a small example, they prevented mail from the outside from reaching the civilian population of Sarajevo. This was an outrageous position to be in. Different commanders reacted differently. The French general Morillon went beyond the call of duty in defending the population of Gorazde. The British commander Sir Michael Rose tried to find fault with the Bosnians in order to justify taking a neutral stance. It was worse than Munich, because Munich was appeasement before the fact, Bosnia was appeasement after the fact.

After the humiliation of Munich, we were ready to fight for freedom and democracy and open society in World War II, and our concept of freedom was a universal one. Our goal was not merely to defend our country, but to spread those ideas throughout the world. We did a pretty good job with our erstwhile enemies, Germany and Japan. And we stood up to the communist threat pretty resolutely, but after the dissolution of the Evil Empire we seem to have lost our bearings.

What has changed?

I believe our concept of freedom changed. It was replaced by a narrower concept—the pursuit of self-interest. It found expression in the rise of geopolitical realism in foreign policy and a belief in laissez-faire in economics. The doctrine of geopolitical realism holds that nations are best advised to pursue their self-interest as determined by their geopolitical position. Any commitment to universal moral principles is an encumbrance that may lead to defeat in the Darwinian fight for survival. According to this point of view, advocating the values of an open society might have been a wonderful propaganda tool for embarrassing the Soviet Union; but beware of believing your own propaganda. In economics, the doctrine of laissez faire holds that the freedom of market participants to pursue their self-interest leads to the most efficient allocation of resources. Again, in the Darwinian fight for survival, the most efficient economy will prevail.

I believe these doctrines are inadequate and misleading. They emphasize the importance of competing within the system, but pay no attention to the preservation of the system itself. They take an open society, in which people are free to compete, for granted. Yet, if there is any lesson to be learned from the dissolution of the Soviet Union, it is that open society cannot be taken for granted: The collapse of a closed society does not automatically lead to the creation of an open society. Freedom is not merely the absence of repression. Open society is not merely the absence of government interference; it is a sophisticated structure that rests on laws and institutions and requires certain modes of thinking and standards of behavior. The structure is so sophisticated that it is hardly visible and it is easily taken for granted. In a closed society, the role of the authorities is pervasive; as a society becomes more open, the authorities become less intrusive: that is why it is so easy to ignore the structure that supports an open society. But the experience of the last five years has shown how difficult it is to bring about an open society.

So you hold the Western powers responsible for the failure of the former Communist countries to evolve into open societies?

Yes, to a large extent. Admittedly, even if the West had done all the right things, it would have been a long and arduous process with many missteps. But at least the formerly communist world would be moving in the right direction. And even more importantly, the Western democracies would also have a sense of direction. Europe, in particular, needed Eastern Europe to give it spiritual, moral, and emotional content. Without it, Europe is floundering. The European Union is a jumble of complicated rules and bureaucratic maneuvering. The idea of a European union used to fire people's imagination. Young people, especially in Germany and France, but also in the other countries, felt

182

good about overcoming their historical differences and belonging to the same political entity. They are becoming increasingly disaffected, as all the voting patterns show.

You spoke about the coming disintegration of Europe.

Yes, I gave a speech on the subject in Berlin in September of 1993. And everything that I said then seems to be coming true. Look at the changes that have occurred. On the one hand, a number of new countries have been admitted to the Union. On the other hand, the British government has become almost entirely obstructionist.

Germany is facing east and France is facing south, and it is only their dogged determination not to fall out with each other that keeps Europe together. Tensions within the monetary systems are rising again. It is only a matter of time before people will start advocating protection from undervalued currencies, bringing into question the very existence of the common market.

How about the United States?

We are suffering from an acute crisis of identity. We used to be a superpower and the leaders of the free world. The two terms were synonymous; we could use them interchangeably. But the collapse of the Soviet Union has changed all that. We can be one or the other, but we cannot be both. We lack the economic clout and the economic interest to maintain such a dominant position. We are no longer the main beneficiaries of the international trading and financial system; we cannot afford to be the policemen of the world. In much of the nineteenth century, England held a pre-eminent position; it was the banking, trading, shipping and insurance center for the world. It had a colonial empire that spanned the globe. It could afford to maintain a fleet of gun boats to be dispatched to any trouble spot. The United States today has the military might, but it has neither the economic interest, nor the political will to become embroiled in far-away conflicts. It can remain a military superpower in order to protect its national interests, but it is questionable whether those interests justify such vast military expenditures. Other countries, like Japan, sheltering under the military umbrella of the United States, may derive greater benefit from our superpower status than we do. Even so, we cannot lay claim to being leaders of the free world, because our national interests do not justify military action in the many trouble spots of the world where intervention is sorely needed. We have withdrawn from Somalia; we had great difficulty in deciding to intervene in Haiti; and we refuse even to contemplate sending ground troops to Bosnia. The only way we could remain leaders of the free world would be in the context of the United Nations where we would act not on our own, but in cooperation with others. But the United Nations has become a dirty word in American politics. Animosity toward the United Nations is so strong, that we are more likely to kill it than to turn it into an effective force for maintaining peace and order in the world.

Don't you feel the animosity is justified?

Frankly, I share the popular sentiment. I see the United Nations as ineffective and wasteful. In my philanthropic work whenever I come up against any United Nations agencies, I give them a wide berth with one exception: the UNHCR (High Commissioner for Refugees). Since the intervention in Bosnia, my feelings have become even more negative. I regard the role of the United Nations as positively evil.

Isn't that going too far?

No, but I must make it clear that I don't blame the United Nations organization as such. The primary responsibility falls on the members of the Security Council, particularly on the permanent members that have veto rights, because the Security Council is merely an instrument in their hand. It is they who decide what the United Nations can or cannot do. To narrow down the responsibility in the case of Bosnia even further, it fell on three Western permanent members: the United States, the United Kingdom, and France. If the three of them had agreed among themselves, they could have carried out whatever policy they wanted.

What could they have done?

They had NATO at their disposal. If they had wanted it, the Security Council could have entrusted NATO with peacemaking in Bosnia. The rest of the members would have gone along. Later on, Russia might have objected, but not in 1992. The Secretary General, Boutros Boutros-Ghali, wrote a letter to the Security Council imploring it not to impose on the United Nations troops an impossible mission. NATO had credibility. On the first occasion when it intervened, the Bosnian Serbs caved in. But the Western powers, each for their own reason, did not want NATO to take charge.

I thought it was Boutros Boutros-Ghali who objected.

That came later on. It was a matter of bureaucratic infighting: Who is in charge? If the Security Council had put NATO in charge, there would have been no problem. As it is, Bosnia has done more to destroy the United Nations than any other crisis. Secretary General Boutros Boutros-Ghali was fond of saying that Bosnia was just one of 17 equally important humanitarian crises. The point he missed is that Bosnia served as a catalyst for the disunity of the Western Alliance. And without Western unity, the United Nations cannot survive.

Why do you say that?

Because the Security Council, where the power to maintain law and order in the world resides, was designed to be effective when the Great Powers agree among themselves. As soon as it was born, the Great Powers fell out with each other and the United Nations could never function as it was designed. It became a public forum where implacable enemies could meet and revile each other and vie for support among the non-aligned nations. On the rare occasions when they reached an agreement, the United Nations could be entrusted with supervising it. This was the origin of the United Nations peacekeeping missions. Perhaps the only exception to this arrangement was the Korean War when the Soviet Union made the mistake of boycotting the meeting at a crucial moment.

Then came Gorbachev. He was a great believer in the United Nations. If you recall, he came to the United Nations and paid up the arrears of the Soviet Union. He gave a speech to the General Assembly in which he outlined his vision for the United Nations, which was a return to the original vision. It was the only part of his program that was properly elaborated, because the ministry of foreign affairs was the only part of the Soviet bureaucracy that genuinely supported reform. He envisioned a grand alliance between the NATO powers and the Soviet Union. The Soviet Union would have supported the Western powers politically, and the Western powers would have supported the Soviet Union economically, enabling it to make the transition to a market economy. This would have allowed the Security Council to function as it was originally designed, because the great powers would have cooperated. But we didn't take him seriously. The Soviet Union disintegrated, and Russia started pretty much where the Soviet Union left off: it was only too eager to cooperate. The United Nations could have become an effective organization for the first time in its history. That is why it was so tragic that Bosnia occurred when it did and the Western allies misused the United Nations the way they did. They had at least five or six years to make the United Nations work, but they completely missed the boat. It is no exaggeration to say that Bosnia is playing the same role for the United Nations as Abyssinia did for the League of Nations in 1935.

So you are giving up hope for the United Nations?

On the contrary, it makes me more convinced that we ought to do everything we can to prevent the United Nations from following in the footsteps of the League of Nations.

But as you have said yourself, the United Nations is discredited. It is part of the Contract with America to reduce and circumscribe United States support for United Nations peacekeeping operations.

We are compounding the mistake we made when we ignored the opportunity presented by Gorbachev. The failure of the United Nations is *our* failure. It is easy to be critical of the United Nations as if it were an organization apart from, and independent of, us. But that is simply not true. The Security Council has been designed to function with the United States acting in concert with the other permanent members. As sole remaining superpower, we have been cast in the leadership role. If the United Nations fails, it is because we have decided that it should fail. We ought to do everything we can to save it.

Doesn't that contradict everything you have said before?

Not at all. We find ourselves in a contradictory situation. On the one hand, we need an international organization to preserve peace and order because we cannot and should not act as the world's policeman. On the other hand, the international organization we have got, the United Nations, is inadequate. Therefore, we must exert ourselves to make it work.

You yourself called the United Nations ineffective and wasteful. Why is that?

Very simple. It is an association of sovereign states. The members are guided by their national interests, not by the collective interest. And the organization is responsible not to one master, but to many. This compounds the defects of bureaucracies because the main objective of a bureaucracy is to survive. Having many masters engenders a can't-do, protect-your-behind attitude. By a process of natural selection, only those whose primary concern is to preserve their jobs will survive in their jobs. But the selection is not natural to start with.

187

Member nations use their patronage power quite shamelessly. Employees enjoy almost complete job security. And that makes it almost impossible to get anything done.

What is the remedy?

That is not so simple. The root cause, namely national sovereignty, cannot be eliminated. If the executive is not responsible to the member nations, to whom is it responsible? We cannot allow a self-governing bureaucracy. In the case of the European Union, which suffers from very much the same defects as the United Nations, one could give a larger role to the European parliament. But in the case of the United Nations, it would be Utopian to contemplate a world parliament. Therefore, the only possibility is to try and get the member nations to put the collective interests above their national interest. But that sounds pretty Utopian, too.

There is no doubt major changes are needed. We cannot have an international organization run for the benefit of its employees. Many functions have become obsolete, but there is no mechanism to discontinue them. The best example is the Trusteeship Council that continues long after the last trusteeship territory has gained its independence. But you cannot expect governments to abdicate their self-interest. You must therefore mobilize public opinion to exert pressure on their governments. You need a thorough overhaul of the way the United Nations operates. But how can public opinion exert pressure, when many of the governments concerned are not at all democratic? And how can you mobilize public opinion? In the first place, there have been countless studies about reforming the United Nations, but they have all fallen flat. You need some simple slogan like "Pro-Choice" or "Right to Life" or the "10 Points" or the "Contract with America." I am looking for such a formula and I would suggest "Reinventing the United Nations"

The United Nations has reached its 50th Anniversary, and as a rule, organizations decay with the passage of time. It would be appropriate to go back to the drawing board and redesign the organization for the next 50 years. It is very difficult to implement changes piecemeal, because they require the consent of all the members. Therefore, the reforms ought to be introduced wholesale. The leading nations of the world ought to get together and propose a new structure and then invite the rest of the members to subscribe to the new Charter, just as they did with the original one. Actually, the Charter itself does not need many changes. What you need is a new start in the way the organization is structured, a sunset clause whereby the existing arguments expire, and a new start is made.

Do you consider this a realistic proposal?

It may not be realistic, but it is doable. It would have been even more doable five years ago.

Why didn't you propose your sunset clause five years ago?

Because I wouldn't have been taken seriously. In fact, I wouldn't have been heard. I was a nobody.

Are you advocating it now?

I haven't quite decided. I am afraid that the United States itself might not subscribe to the new Charter. I doubt whether the United States would enact its own constitution if it came up for a vote.

How do you see the role of NATO? Do you support its eastward expansion?

If there had been a grand alliance between the NATO powers and the Soviet Union, there would have been no problem in admitting the countries of Central Europe into NATO under the umbrella of that alliance. Even after the breakup of the Soviet Union, the same policy could have been pursued with Russia. But we lacked the vision. The "Partnership for Peace" was a watered-down version of that grand alliance, but it didn't work because we were unwilling to back it up with any significant economic assistance to Russia. Now it is too late. Relations between Russia and the West have deteriorated. What is much worse, Russia itself has deteriorated. It is no longer possible to pursue the eastward enlargement of NATO and remain friends with Russia. Russia objects to the enlargement of NATO. When Yeltsin visited Poland in the summer of 1993, he still agreed to Polish membership of NATO and it was only after his generals objected that he withdrew his approval. Since then, the Russian position has crystallized.

I think it would be wrong to appease an intransigent Russia. Poland, for one, ought to be admitted to NATO. But we ought to make every effort to reassure Russia. This might take the form of some kind of treaty between NATO and Russia as the European members of NATO are proposing.

There is a much larger issue concerning NATO. What does it stand for? If a sunset clause is needed for the United Nations, that need is much greater for NATO.

What should NATO stand for?

The original idea of a defensive pact to protect the territorial integrity of the member countries remains valid in theory, but it would hardly justify maintaining NATO. Even if Russia became a nationalist dictatorship, it would take many years before it could rebuild a serious offensive capability. Indeed, one could argue that if it became a nationalist dictatorship, it would take much longer to rebuild that capability than as a market economy. Therefore, it is hard to imagine any real threat to the territory of the NATO countries in practice. By contrast, the situation outside the borders of the NATO countries is very unstable and the instability is likely to increase even further. What is at issue therefore, is the ability of NATO to project its power beyond its borders. That is where not only the political will, but even the political understanding is lacking.

I would propose that NATO should be turned into an instrument for protecting the values and principles of open society, not only within its borders, but also beyond them. This does not mean that NATO would get engaged whenever those principles are violated. It means only that NATO would be available whenever the member countries, acting in concert, call upon it. The values and principles of open society are universal. No member country acting individually can treat the protection of those values as a matter of national interest, but they should treat it as a matter of collective interest. That ought to be the new mission for NATO. If it had been properly formulated, NATO would have been available when the Bosnian crisis erupted, and if it had been available, it would have provided, in all likelihood, a strong enough deterrent to Serbian aggression. And the whole debacle could have been avoided.

Do you think the British would have acted differently?

Conceivably. One of the reasons the British were determined to avoid military involvement was that they were afraid they would be left holding the bag. The Americans said this was a European matter, and the Germans were precluded both by their constitution and their past history in Yugoslavia from intervening militarily. That left only the British and the French. Britain was tied up in Northern Ireland, and simply did not have the troops available even if it had wanted to use them. If NATO had been willing to take on the task, the United Kingdom could have participated up to the limits of its capacity.

But that would have required the United States to contribute ground troops.

Yes. And there is the rub. The United States espoused lofty principles, but was unwilling to commit ground troops. The United States must re-think its role in the world. If NATO's role had been properly defined and explained to the people, I believe American ground troops could and should have been available. I think NATO is much more suitable an organization for projecting American military power into the world on a collective basis than the United Nations for a number of reasons. First, it is created and led by the United States, although American leadership may have to be modified somewhat in the future. Second, it consists of like-minded democratic states, whereas the United Nations is a much more mixed bunch. Third, NATO is effective as a multinational force, while the United Nations simply lacks the command structure needed for a successful military operation. United Nations troops can be used for peacekeeping (Chapter VI in the United Nations Charter); but peacemaking (Chapter VII) is a job for NATO.

Listening to you, it seems to make sense. What are you going to do about it?

Talk about it. Mark Twain said that everybody talks about the weather but nobody does anything about it. If the theory of reflexivity is correct, talking about social or political objectives may be a way of doing something about them.

Ironically, while I have been thinking and talking about these matters, another issue has arisen that is much closer to my field of expertise: The international financial system is in danger of breaking down. The crisis arose while I wasn't watching, but now that it has occurred I am giving it a lot of thought.

Do you see a real crisis looming?

Yes. It is similar to the crisis in the international political system in the sense that it doesn't affect us directly and therefore we are not conscious of it. It is affecting people in Latin America and in the other so-called emerging markets. As I have said before, the crash in emerging markets is the worst since 1929. As long as it is confined to them, the international financial system is not really in danger. But if and when it has a negative fallout in the industrial countries, you could have a breakdown not only in the financial system but also in the international trading system.

That sounds alarmist.

Deliberately so. As I have already mentioned, the Mexican crisis is bound to lead to a radical shift in the balance of trade between Mexico and the United States. If that coincides with a slowdown in the United States economy, there will be a political outcry that may lead to the election of a protectionist president in 1996. The similarity with the aftermath of the 1929 crash would be too close for comfort.

You are predicting a breakdown in free trade.

I am not predicting it, but I can enivisage it. The danger is that people are not aware of the danger. Everybody talks about the global financial markets as if they were irreversible. But that is a misconception. It involves a false analogy with a technological innovation like the internal combustion engine. Once the automobile was invented, it spread like wildfire. It may be improved, it may even be superseded by a superior invention, but it cannot be abolished. Not so with a financial innovation. It differs from a technological invention in the same way that social science differs from natural science.

We came close to having a global financial market based on the gold standard toward the end of the nineteenth century, but the system broke down and by the end of World War II when the Bretton Woods system was established, there were practically no private international capital movements. People don't remember it, but the Bretton Woods system was specifically designed to create institutions that would allow international trade to be financed in the absence of private capital movements. As capital movements picked up, the Bretton Woods system of fixed exchange rates broke down. The international financial institutions created by Bretton Woods—the IMF and the World Bank—have successfully adapted themselves to the changing circumstances and they continue to play an important role. But they are inadequate to the task of maintaining stability in the system. Their resources are dwarfed by the magnitude of private capital movements and they have no regulatory powers. There is some cooperation among governments—the Bank for International Settlement in Basel has been the main instrument for international cooperation—but it is quite limited in scope. The trouble is that the need for greater international cooperation is not generally recognized. The prevailing wisdom about the way financial markets operate is false, and a global market based on false premises is unlikely to survive indefinitely. The collapse of the global marketplace would be a traumatic event with unimaginable consequences. Yet I find it easier to imagine than the continuation of the present regime.

That is quite a dramatic statement. Can you be more specific? Why and how would the international financial markets collapse?

They are quite close to collapsing right now. Take Mexico. The bulk of the Mexican voters did not derive much benefit from Mexico's transition from a third world to a first world country, but they must now bear the brunt of the adjustment. It is touch and go whether the present regime will survive. Whether it does or not, the risks of international investing have been brought home. Even if the crisis abates, the risk premium for other heavily indebted countries will not disappear. It is questionable whether they will be able to live with those high risk premiums. If they cannot refinance their debt they will be facing defaults. It is a self-reinforcing process.

Is there no escape?

There could be individual rescue packages. I have an even better idea. We ought to establish a new international institution to facilitate the

194

financial reorganization of heavily indebted countries. Countries beyond redemption would be allowed to enter into a debt reduction scheme; others would be merely assisted to refinance their debt. The assistance would take the form of a guarantee for newly issued bonds. The international agency, providing the guarantee, would, of course, insist on suitable adjustment policies. It could be financed by a new issue of Special Drawing Rights that would not even be drawn upon if the operation is successful. Having such an institution would prevent market excesses in the future because investors would refrain from lending to heavily indebted countries without a guarantee. It would be an appropriate addition to the existing institutions in response to the growth in international lending that has become unsustainable.

At the risk of becoming too abstract, I should like to make a more general point. We have gone a long way toward opening up the globe to free movement of goods and services and, even more importantly, ideas. The international flow of capital has become largely unrestrained. Even people can move more freely. But the establishment of this global system has not been matched by an acceptance of the principles of open society. On the contrary, international relations continue to be based on the principle of national sovereignty and the internal political regimes of many nations fall well short of the standards of an open society. In the economic sphere, there is practically no recognition that financial markets, particularly the international financial markets, are inherently unstable.

Markets are, by definition, competitive. But unrestrained competition without regard to the common good can endanger the market mechanism. This idea runs counter to the prevailing idea that competition is the common good. Even if the need to preserve the system is recognized, it takes second place to getting ahead within the system. Look at the rhetoric of the last few years: it is all about competitiveness, very little about free trade. With this attitude, I cannot see the global system surviving. Political instability and financial instability are going to feed off each other in a self-reinforcing fashion. In my opinion, we have entered a period of global disintegration only we are not yet aware of it.

It is strange to hear you inveigh against competitive behavior when you are recognized as one of the most competitive people in financial markets.

I am in favor of competing, but I am also in favor of preserving the system that permits competition. Where I am at odds with the latter-day apostles of laissez faire is that I don't believe markets are perfect. In my opinion, they are just as likely to lead to unsustainable excesses as to equilibrium. But my disagreement goes even deeper: I don't believe competition leads to the best allocation of resources. I don't consider the survival of the fittest the most desirable outcome. I believe we must strive for certain fundamental values, such as social justice, which cannot be attained by unrestrained competition. It is exactly because I have been successful in the marketplace that I can afford to advocate these values. I am the classic limousine liberal. I believe that it behooves those who have benefited from the system that they should exert themselves to make the system better. I should like to draw your attention to the fact that it wasn't until I made $20 or $30 million that I set up my first foundation.

So your motivation is to give back something to the system that made you rich.

Not really. Being rich enabled me to do something I really cared about. I never allowed the availability of money to guide me in my philanthropy. I started with $3 million a year, but it took me more than five years until the expenditures reached $3 million a year. There was only a short moment, around 1992, when I had more money to give away than I knew what to do with. Now the shoe is on the other foot. I have an enormous network and I must hustle to keep it going.

You have started some activities in the United States.

Yes. It has always been part of my program to help make open societies more viable, but I got so wrapped up in the revolution in Eastern Europe that I didn't have any time to do anything about it. Around 1992, when the revolution began to cool off, and I still had some unspent money, I started to look around.

What are the problems you see in open societies?

The deficiency of values. It has always been part of my framework of open and closed societies that open societies suffer from a deficiency of values. All that I have seen in the last five years confirms me in that view.

I am aware of grants you have made for the legalization of drugs and the study of the American way of death.

No, it is not legalization of drugs I am supporting, but the development of different approaches to the drug problem. And the same applies to the problem of dying. These are problems where misconceptions and the lack of understanding play a tremendously important role, where well-intended actions have unintended consequences. The remedy is often worse than the disease. That is the insight that has made me focus on these issues.

By remedy you mean that trying to handle the drug problem through law enforcement is worse than the drug problem itself?

That is right. I think that to treat the drug problem as primarily a criminal problem is a misconception.

You think it's a medical problem?

I think that there's a problem of addiction. And of course if you create laws that make drugs illegal, you also have a criminal problem.

It's also a social problem. And to eradicate the social problem would require more money than even you have.

I think that the whole idea of eradicating the drug problem is a false idea. Just as you can't eradicate poverty or death or illness, you can't eradicate addiction. You have addictive personalities and you have situations in which people seek an escape from reality. A drugfree America is simply not possible. You can discourage the use of drugs, you can forbid the use of drugs, you can treat people who are addicted to drugs, but you cannot eradicate drugs. Once you accept this point, you may be able to develop a more rational approach to the problem. The trouble is, it is very difficult to have a rational debate. The issue has become too emotional.

What is your solution?

Let's stick to the problem before we speak of a solution. There is no doubt that drugs are harmful, although there are differences among different drugs. Some are only harmful to the users; others like crack or certain hallucinogens can be dangerous to others; although driving or doing other responsible jobs is dangerous under the influence of most drugs. Some drugs are addictive; others like marijuana are not. Marijuana is relatively harmless, but all you need to do is look at some potheads to realize that they have been impaired. But then, the same is true of alcoholics. All drugs and addictive substances should be discouraged. Preventing children from using drugs, alcohol, and even cigarettes is highly desirable. But does it justify turning drug use into a criminal act? The evidence indicates that it has the opposite effect. It creates drug pushers. And it creates a myth around drugs that tends to attract young people rather than repel them, especially when the myth is so far removed from reality. But the unintended consequences go much further. The criminalization of drugs creates criminals. It creates drug dealers and drug users who commit crimes in order to get their fix. The crimes frighten the citizens and politicians exploit the fears of the voters to get elected. This leads to the war on drugs. It is very difficult to oppose the war on drugs if you are a politician who wants to get elected. The war on drugs creates a law enforcement apparatus that has a vested interest in perpetuating the law enforcement approach. That is how we end up with a remedy that is worse than the disease.

Are you advocating the legalization of drugs?

I am agnostic on this issue. I haven't made up my mind, and in a way I don't really want to make up my mind. I am willing to discuss the issues in private, but I am not prepared to take a public stance because, while I can see what's wrong, I don't see clearly what's right. I can see that the present approach is clearly wrong and is doing more harm than good, but I haven't got any firm views on what would be the right approach. I can see a number of approaches that would certainly be preferable to the present one, like focusing on treatment rather than law enforcement. I could envisage legalization as an effective way to reduce the harm that drugs cause because I'm sure that if you legalize drugs, maybe not all of them, but some of the less harmful or less addictive ones, you could reduce criminality, say, by 80 percent. And the savings this would produce could be used for treatment. But I think that public opinion is so aroused on this issue that a campaign for legalization that goes directly against the prevailing consensus would be counterproductive. That is why I support several initiatives, some of which are adamantly opposed to legalization and others that are more sympathetic and I don't want to have a prescription of my own.

Still, if you were asked, what would you say?

You remind me of an old Hungarian joke from before the 1956 revolution when the communist party was trying to encourage party members to express their opinions more freely. After every meeting, the party secretary asked the members for their own opinions. One member always answered, "I entirely agree with the comrade secretary's opinion." Eventually the secretary said, "Surely you have a private opinion!" He answered, "Yes, but I don't agree with that at all."

On that basis, I'll tell you what I would do if it were up to me. I would establish a strictly controlled distribution network through which I would make most drugs, excluding the most dangerous ones like crack, legally available. Initially, I would keep prices low enough to destroy the drug trade. Once that objective was attained I would keep raising the prices, very much like the excise duty on cigarettes, but I would make an exception for registered addicts in order to discourage crime. I would use a portion of the income for prevention and treatment. And I would foster social opprobrium of drug use.

Let's talk about the Project on Death for a moment. What are your objectives in supporting that project?

Well, here I am applying much the same line of thinking. There's a widespread denial of death in America. It's effectively, not outlawed, but outcast. I know from my own experience that when my father died, I denied it. I refused to face the fact that he was dying. I think that it was a tragic mistake on my part. I think that our whole society is somehow operating in a state of denial and distortion. We have been told all about sex, but very little about dying. Yet dying is even more widespread than sex. It cannot be avoided, but we ought to come to terms with it.

What specific activities are you supporting?

Well, I have found a group of experts, people who have devoted their lives to confronting the issue of dying. I leave it to them to decide what the project ought to do. I have no program, no specific agenda as far as dying is concerned. They do.

Are you trying to enable Americans to be more comfortable with dealing with death in their own family?

Yes. I think if there is any unifying thread, it is to encourage family involvement and to reduce the dehumanizing effect of medical treatment. I believe we should encourage people to die at home with the involvement of the family. I would like people to come to terms with the idea of dying, so it is not such a horrifying experience for the person or the family. In practice, most people die in hospitals. Therefore much of the effort in the project goes to the education of medical personnel.

Would one of the possible results of the Project on Death be that less effort is made to sustain life after it becomes medically futile?

Yes. I think that is very much part of it. The use of technology to extend life when life has no meaning doesn't make sense. It may be more negative than positive because it causes unnecessary pain and suffering, not to mention the expense. Acceptance of death would certainly reduce the effort to extend life at all cost.

How about euthanasia?

The experts are deeply divided and the Project on Death takes no position. I personally think that is a pity, but they may be right: there is a lot of work to be done on the culture of dying without getting embroiled in its most controversial and sensational aspect.

Let's come back to your concept of social justice. How do you feel about the Contract with America?

Well, I understand the feeling of resentment that motivates it and I have some sympathy with it. The welfare system is full of abuses and it has been "business as usual" for too long. It is time for a change. But I am afraid that in this case, too, the remedy is going to be worse than the disease. We are engaged in a swing of the pendulum away from the welfare state. It has considerable force and it is likely to carry quite far. But don't forget, every human construct is flawed. That is true of the welfare state, just as it is true of whatever exchange rate system is in force. The longer a system prevails, the more glaring its deficiencies become. Everyone is aware of the shortcomings of the welfare system. But let me point out a contradiction in the Gingrich program. The aim is to reduce the role of government, but imposing conditions on welfare increases the discretionary power of the bureaucracy, opens the way to abuses and inequities, and increases administrative costs. Replacing federal welfare benefits with block grants to states creates an inducement for states to mistreat their welfare recipients and make them move to other states that treat them better. The poor and infirm are going to get kicked around, literally. We are declaring war on poverty, and it is going to be just as successful as the war on drugs. I hope that when people discover this, the pendulum is going to swing the other way. As I have said before, all human constructs are flawed, but it is rare that when a new vision is offered the flaws are so clearly visible in advance.

You are in a very peculiar position. You're not like someone working for the government or a politician responsible to his electorate. You're accountable to no one. As you use your own money, you can implement any ideas or any programs you want. There are no

controls or checks and balances on any of your activities. Do you have too much power?

What a question! We all want to make an impact on the world in which we live. Beyond a certain point, the acquisition of wealth does not make sense, unless you know what you want to use it for. I want to use it for the social good. In deciding what the social good is, I have to rely on my own judgment. I think the world would be a better place if we all relied on our own judgments, even if we differ among ourselves in our judgments.

There is a new type of public figure emerging on the political scene—Ross Perot in the United States, Berlusconi in Italy—the self-made billionaire with a political agenda. Do you belong to this breed?

There was also a breed of businessmen who did their business by engaging in philanthropic activities in communist countries: Armand Hammer, Robert Maxwell. All I can say is, I hope I am different.

Can you sum up your views on the international political situation?

I can try. I don't have the answers, but my theoretical framework allows me at least to ask the right questions and it provides me with some snippets of insight.

1. We are entering into a period of world disorder and the sooner we realize it the better our chances of preventing the disorder from getting out of hand.
2. The theoretical concepts of open and closed society are particularly useful in understanding the present situation.

3. Communist dogma has lost its sway over people's minds and it is almost inconceivable that it should regain it. On the contrary, the pendulum is swinging the other way, toward laissez-faire.

4. There is a real danger of nationalist dictatorships arising in formerly communist countries.

5. To mobilize society behind the state, you need an enemy. The rise of nationalism is likely to be associated with armed conflicts.

6. Nationalist dogma may intermingle with religious dogma and the trend is likely to spread beyond the confines of the former communist world. You may find Russia or Serbia defending Christianity against Islamic fundamentalism and vice versa.

7. Democracies suffer from a deficiency of values. They are notoriously unwilling to take any pain when their vital self-interests are not directly threatened. Therefore, they are unlikely to prevent the spread of nationalist dictatorships and conflicts.

The present situation has more in common with the interwar period than with the Cold War. There are some notable differences. One is the absence of a Hitler—you only have Mussolini-like figures, such as Tudjman in Croatia and Milosevic in Yugoslavia, but the most important country, Russia, is still up for grabs. Another difference is the European Union, but it has no common foreign policy and it is in disarray. For the rest, the United Nations is increasingly reminiscent of the League of Nations and Bosnia plays a similar role to Abyssinia. But the United States reducing its contribution to peacekeeping operations is not the same as withdrawing altogether.

History does not quite repeat itself, but the patterns that emerge or the regimes that prevail do exhibit certain similarities. I find the pattern that is currently emerging very disturbing. The interwar period led to the Holocaust and the most destructive war in the history of mankind. I do not expect a replay: there is no Hitler on the horizon. Even if a Hitler-like figure came to power in Russia, it would be a long time before Russia could pose a military threat similar to the Soviet Union or Nazi Germany. But the technological capacity to wreak havoc has greatly increased. Russia does have atomic weapons; so will Iran and a number of other countries. Something should be done to change the emerging pattern.

Part Three

Philosophy

with
Byron Wien

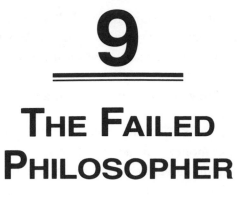

9

THE FAILED PHILOSOPHER

You say thay your ideas are of primary concern to you now. Though your activities may seem diverse—ranging from investing to philanthropy—in fact, they are intimately interconnected by the philosophical underpinnings of your ideas. Can you bring together now your theory of reflexivity, your ideas about investing, and your commitment to an open society?

Let me try. After all, that has been the goal of my life: To turn the disparate elements of my existence into a coherent whole.

Is there a unifying idea behind your varied activities?

I would sum it up in one sentence: I believe in my own fallibility. This sentence plays the same role for me as *cogito ergo sum* (I think; therefore I am) did for Descartes. Indeed, its significance is even greater: Descartes' dictum referred only to the person who thinks, whereas mine relates also to the world in which we live. The misconceptions and misunderstandings that go into our decisions help shape the events in which we participate. Fallibility plays the same role in human affairs as mutation does in biology.

This idea is terribly important to me. It has guided me in my life even before I could reduce it to a single sentence. Whether it can have the same significance for others, it is not for me to say.

How has the belief in your own fallibility guided you in your life?

In practical terms, both in making money and in giving it away. But my life is not about money. For me, money is a means to an end. I focused on money in my career because I recognized that there is a tendency in our society to exaggerate the importance of money, to define values in terms of money. We appraise artists by how much their creations fetch. We appraise politicians by the amount of money they can raise; often politicians appraise themselves by the amount of money they can make on the side. I have gained recognition, not because of my philosophy or my philanthropy, but because of my success in making money. The prevailing bias in favor of money and wealth is a good example of what I mean by fallibility.

To translate the concept of fallibility into operational terms and to sharpen the point, I will assert that all our mental constructs, with a few exceptions, are actually or potentially flawed. They may contain an element of truth, but that element is likely to be exaggerated to a point where it distorts reality.

One of the ways in which we cope with our imperfect understanding is by carrying whatever knowledge, experience, or insight we have gained to areas that it does not cover. This is true in visual perception, where we cover our blind spot without any difficulty, as well as in the most complex constructs.

What do you mean by mental constructs?

I mean the products of our thinking, whether they stay inside the recesses of our mind or find expression in the outside world in the form of language or institutions, such as the financial markets or the various exchange rate regimes, or the United Nations, or the nation states, or the legal structure. The mental constructs that stay within the confines of our mind can range all the way from simple sensory perceptions to elaborate belief systems that may or may not relate to the world in which we live. Those that find expression constitute a large part of the world in which we live.

And you say all these mental constructs are flawed.

The best way to explain what I mean by flawed mental constructs is to examine the exceptions—mental constructs that are not flawed. We are capable of making statements that are either true or false. Such statements are not flawed. To the extent that we can rely on true statements, we are capable of attaining knowledge. It is only when they go beyond such "well-formed" statements that our mental constructs are flawed.

So we need to examine what kind of true statements we can make. There are singular statements that correspond to specific facts and there are rules by which the truth of some statements can be derived from other statements, notably in mathematics and logic. Our greatest achievement is science, where we combine singular statements with universally applicable generalizations to form explanations and predictions. But, as Karl Popper has shown, such generalizations cannot be verified, only falsified. They remain hypothetical in character, always subject to falsification.

The common feature of all these forms of knowledge is that there are facts or rules that would serve as reliable criteria for judging their truth or validity if only we knew how to apply them. What makes the criteria reliable is that they are independent of the statements to which they are applied and of the people who apply them.

If you consider our position as human beings trying to understand the world in which we live, you will find that we cannot confine our thinking to subjects that are independent of our thinking. We must make decisions about our lives and in order to do so we must hold views that do not qualify as knowledge, whether we recognize this or not. We must have recourse to beliefs. That is the human condition.

Recognizing the human condition does not quite qualify as knowledge—it would be self-contradictory if it did—but it provides a set of beliefs that is more appropriate to the human condition than any other. At least, that is what I believe when I assert my own fallibility. When I assert my own fallibility, I am articulating a belief—a reasoned belief, to be sure, which is appropriate to a philosophy, but still a belief. I cannot prove it, the way Descartes claimed to prove his own existence. I have tried and it has eluded me. There is something self-contradictory in being able to prove one's own fallibility. Equally, it is self-consistent that one should be unable to do so. So I am happy to assert the truth of my statement as a belief.

This has an important implication. It implies that we need to have some beliefs to guide us through life. We cannot rely on reason alone. Rationality has its uses, but it also has its limitations. If we insist on staying within the limits of reason, we cannot cope with the world in which we live. By contrast, a belief in our own fallibility can take us much further. It can guide us through life.

So you are offering us a philosophy of life.

Yes. Philosophy has deteriorated into an academic profession, but it ought to play a more central role. We cannot live without a set of reasoned beliefs. The question is, can we have a set of beliefs based on the recognition that our beliefs are inherently flawed? I believe we can and, in my own life, I have been guided by my own fallibility. I have been less successful in communicating my ideas and getting them generally accepted. That is why I consider myself a failed philosopher.

How did you arrive at your philosophy?

It was a long journey. As you know, I was greatly influenced by Karl Popper—not only by his *Open Society*, but even more by his philosophy of science. I accepted his idea that our understanding of the world in which we live is inherently imperfect. I attributed this imperfection to the fact that we are part of the world we are trying to understand and we participate in making it what it is.

As a student of economics, I found it strange that classical economic theory, particularly the theory of perfect competition, should assume perfect knowledge. I was also rather weak in mathematics, so I preferred to question the assumptions rather than to study the equations based on them. I cogitated and concluded that economics theory is based on false premises. That is how I developed my theory of reflexivity, which recognizes a two-way interaction between thinking and reality.

My investigation took me from the logical problem of self-reference and the paradox of the liar through Bertrand Russell's theory of types and logical positivism to my theory of reflexivity.

Can you explain the paradox of the liar?

Epimenides, an ancient Cretan philosopher, said, "Cretans always lie." If the statement was true, Cretans did not always lie; therefore the statement was false. The paradox arose from the fact that Epimenides made a self-referential statement. I tried to derive my concept of reflexivity from the idea of self-reference, which gives rise to a logical uncertainty. I argued that the logical uncertainty is linked with a causal uncertainty because participants operating with imperfect knowledge shape the course of events. I am not so sure any more that I need to get involved with self-reference in order to justify the concept of reflexivity. I lost three years of my life—from 1963 to 1966—doing just that.

What is so difficult about it?

There is something paradoxical about trying to prove that our understanding is inherently imperfect. At times, I felt I came quite close to it, but I always got caught in a web of my own weaving. I don't know whether it was because I attempted an impossible task or because I was an impossible philosopher—possibly both. Perhaps you need to spend three years spinning your wheels to develop a belief in your own fallibility. But if you think about it, you may accept that a thinking participant cannot base his decisions on knowledge without spending three years on it.

Knowledge relates to facts and the participants' decisions do not relate to facts. They relate to something in the future, which, by the time it is converted into facts, will incorporate the participants' decisions. Once you accept this, you must realize that the participants' thinking and the actual state of affairs cannot be identical, but they cannot be independent of each other, either. The relationship is more complicated. On the one hand, reality is reflected in people's thinking—I call this the cognitive function; on the other hand, reality is affected by people's decisions—I call this the participating function. You may note that the two functions work in opposite directions. In a narrow band, they overlap: people think about events that are affected by their decisions. These events have a different structure from the events studied by natural science; they need to be thought about differently. I call these events reflexive.

What's the difference?

Natural science deals with events that occur independently of what anybody thinks about them; therefore, it can treat events as a succession of facts. When events have thinking participants, the chain of causation does not lead directly from one set of facts to the next; insofar as the participants' thinking plays a role, it leads from facts to perceptions, from perceptions to decisions and from decisions to the next set of facts. There is also the direct link between one set of facts and the next which is characteristic of all natural phenomena. But the more circuitous link cannot be left out of account without introducing a distortion. The distortion is negligible when people's thinking is close to reality; it becomes significant when perception and reality are far apart.

214

Why should they be far apart?

Because the cognitive and participating functions can interfere with each other. When they do, they introduce an element of uncertainty both into the participants' thinking and the actual state of affairs. It is amazing how far they can be out of sync.

This is too abstract for me. Can you give an example?

Take a simple case: falling in love. The other person's feelings toward you are greatly influenced by your own feelings and actions, except in those rare cases, like Dante and Beatrice, where one person's feelings do not reach the other. Does she love me; does she not? There is an element of uncertainty here that would be absent if it were a question of knowledge. But this is a question of interactions and the interplay of emotions can produce a wide range of outcomes, some of which are sustainable, others not. When you fall in love, strange things happen. It would be quite inappropriate to treat love as a matter of fact, which is independent of the participants' beliefs.

That much is certain.

The reflexive nature of human relations is so obvious that the question I would like to ask is, why has reflexivity not been properly recognized? Why, for instance, did economic theory deliberately ignore it?

And what is the answer?

Because it cannot be reconciled with the goals of analytical science, which is to provide determinate predictions and explanations. Reflexivity throws a monkey-wrench into the works by introducing an element of uncertainty.

Please explain.

That will take some doing. I have to invoke Popper's beautifully elegant model of analytical science. The model is composed of three kinds of statements: specific initial conditions, specific final conditions, and generalizations of universal applicability. These three kinds of statements can be combined in three different ways: generalizations combined with initial conditions yield *predictions;* combined with final conditions, they provide *explanations;* and the combination of specific initial conditions with specific final conditions provides a *test* of the generalizations. To make testing possible, the generalizations must be timeless.

I love the simplicity of the model. Popper used it to resolve the problems of induction, that is, progressing from the particular to the general. He showed that scientific method does not need inductive logic: it can rely on testing instead. Only theories that can be tested qualify as scientific.

I want to use the model to show that reflexivity plays havoc with it. If a reflexive interaction can change both the participants' thinking and the actual state of affairs, timeless generalizations cannot be tested. What happened once does not necessarily recur when you repeat the experiment and the whole beautiful structure collapses. No wonder! Underlying the model is the unspoken assumption of a deterministic universe. If phenomena did not obey timelessly valid universal laws, how could those laws be used to produce predictions and explanations?

How does your theory of reflexivity relate to Heisenberg's Uncertainty Principle in quantum physics? Some critics hold that your theory is nothing more than an adaptation of that principle.

The uncertainty I am talking about is different. It affects not only the subject matter, but also the theories that relate to them. Heisenberg established the Uncertainty Principle and, based on that principle, quantum physics has been able to produce statistical generalizations that have significant predictive and explanatory powers. The Uncertainty Principle asserts that the observation of quantum phenomena affects their behavior. But the Uncertainty Principle itself, or any other theory propounded by quantum physics, does *not* affect the behavior of quantum phenomena; therefore those phenomena provide a reliable criterion for judging the validity of the theories.

Suppose now that I proposed a theory that predicted the behavior of the stock market; surely it would affect the behavior of the stock market. This creates a different kind of uncertainty than the one that confronts quantum physics. It affects the criterion by which the truth of statements or the validity of theories is judged.

Are you saying that in the stock market a true theory may be false and a false theory may be true?

I am saying more than that. I assert that our generally accepted notion of truth needs to be revised. It seems that we need to recognize more than two categories—true and false. The logical positivists claimed that statements which are not true or false are meaningless. I thoroughly disagree. Theories that can affect the subject matter to which they refer are the opposite of meaningless. They can change the world. They exemplify the active role that thinking can play in shaping reality. We need to adjust our concept of truth to account for them.

I propose that we need three categories—true, false, and reflexive. The truth value of reflexive statements is indeterminate. It is possible to find other statements with an indeterminate truth value, but we can live without them. We cannot live without reflexive statements. I hardly need to emphasize the profound significance of this proposition. Nothing is more fundamental to our thinking than our concept of truth.

That is quite a strong statement.

I have never put it quite so strongly. I wonder whether it will stand up to critical examination.

Suppose it does; then what?

Then we need to revise thoroughly our view of the world. Let me give you a small example. There is now a widespread belief that markets are perfect, which is based on the recognition that government regulations fail to fulfill their objective. If you introduce a third category of truth, the reflexive, it becomes apparent that the failure of regulation does not mean that free markets are perfect and vice versa. Both arrangements are flawed and the choice between them is reflexive.

Reflexive statements lack an independent criterion for judging their truth. Their truth value is uncertain. Yet they are the opposite of meaningless. We cannot do without them in coping with the world in which we live, and they are not just passive reflections of what is; they actively construct our world. To be sure, there is a reality outside our thinking, a reality that we cannot bend to our will. Our thinking, our statements, are inside that reality, they form part of that reality. Somehow we have come to imagine that the world and our view of the world constitute separate but similar universes, and it is possible to establish a correspondence between them where the statements mirror the facts. This picture is false and misleading. It is appropriate to scientific method and to axiomatic systems like mathematics and logic, but not to us, living and thinking human beings.

Where does that leave the social sciences like economics?

Popper maintained that the same methods and criteria apply to both social and natural science. He called this the doctrine of the unity of method. I have some doubts about this doctrine. I expressed them in the title of my book, *The Alchemy of Finance.* I argued that the expression "social science" is a false metaphor and reflexive events cannot be explained and predicted by universally applicable laws.

I now believe that I carried my arguments too far. It is possible to apply the methods and criteria of natural science to social phenomena and they may produce worthwhile results within their terms of reference. But we must remember that the terms of reference exclude reflexivity. Economic theory, for instance, is valid as a hypothetical construct in which reflexivity is assumed away. When we apply the conclusions of economic theory to the real world, they may give us a distorted picture. This is particularly noticeable in financial markets, where reflexivity plays an important role. The theory of rational expectations and efficient markets is highly misleading.

Economics theory tried to imitate physics. Classical economists took Newton as their model—forgeting that Newton lost a fortune in the South Sea Bubble. The only way they could imitate physics was by eliminating reflexivity from their subject. Hence the assumption of perfect knowledge, which was later amended to perfect information. Finally, Lionel Robbins, my professor at the London School of Economics, found the perfect subterfuge. He said that economics is concerned neither with the means nor with the ends, but only with the relationship between means and ends. In other words, both means and ends have to be taken as given. It was a methodological device to rule out even the possibility of studying reflexive interactions.

Popper attacked Marxism and Freudian psychoanalysis on the grounds that these theories, among others, claimed to be scientific but they could not be falsified by testing; therefore, their claim was false. I agree, but I would go even further. I think that the argument he used against Marxism also applies to highly respectable theories like the theory of perfect competition, which claims that under certain assumptions, the unrestrained pursuit of self-interest leads to the most efficient allocation of resources. I am not knocking economics; I think it is a very elegant theoretical construct. I do question its applicability to the real world; and I question whether it survives testing in the financial markets. I believe that the performance of Quantum Fund alone falsifies the random walk theory.

What do you propose putting in its place?

I think that the social sciences have done violence to their subject matter in their ambition to imitate the natural sciences. It is high time to liberate social phenomena from the straitjacket of natural science, especially as natural science itself is undergoing a radical change. Analytical science is superseded in certain fields by the study of complexity. The analytical sciences are confined to closed systems; that is why they can produce determinate results. The science of complexity studies open, evolutionary systems; it does not expect to produce deterministic predictions of explanations. All it seeks to do is to build models or run simulations—this has been made possible by the development of computer technology—or produce vague, philosophic generalizations without the predictive power of Popper's model.

I believe this approach is more relevant to the study of social phenomena than analytical science. But even here I find that the difference between social and natural phenomena is not sufficiently recognized. Most computer programs deal with the evolution of populations. To study the interaction between thinking and reality, we need a model of model-builders whose models, in turn, must contain model-builders whose models, in turn, must contain model-builders, ad infinitum. To the best of my knowledge, this has not yet been done by any computer simulation. The infinite nesting of models must be brought to closure somewhere if the models are to serve any practical use. As a result, the models cannot reflect reality in its full complexity. That is another way to arrive at the conclusion that the participants' understanding is inherently imperfect.

Suppose I accept all your arguments. How does your theory of reflexivity explain and predict the course of events?

It doesn't. It doesn't even pretend to be a scientific theory. Heisenberg's Uncertainty Principle is concerned with statistical probability.

It cannot determine the behavior of specific particles, but it has produced remarkably reliable estimates of the probability of certain kinds of behavior. By contrast, my interest is in the course of specific events. As an investor, I find statistical probability of limited value; what matters is what happens in a particular case. The same applies with even greater force to historic events. I cannot make reliable predictions about them; all I can do is formulate scenarios. I can then compare the actual course of events with the hypothetical ones. Such hypotheses have no scientific validity, but they have considerable practical utility. They provide a basis for real-life decisions. I am not able to predict the course of events in accordance with universally valid generalizations, but I can devise a general framework that helps me to anticipate and adjust my expectations in the light of experience.

In other words, Heisenberg formulated a scientific theory about uncertainty, while my framework helps to deal with uncertainty in an unscientific way. That is an important distinction. Judged by scientific standards, my theory is worthless. It does not produce predictions and explanations of either the deterministic or the probabilistic kind. Heisenberg was a scientist studying physical phenomena and his theory is a scientific one. I am a thinking participant trying to make sense of the human condition and my theory is a nonscientific one. This is as it should be because I recognize that the situation of the thinking participant is essentially different from that of the scientific observer.

Is that why you called your book the *Alchemy of Finance?* Because you regard your theory as alchemy, and not science?

Yes. The alchemists made a big mistake trying to turn base metals into gold by incantation. With chemical elements, alchemy doesn't work. But it does work in the financial markets, because incantations can influence the decisions of the people who shape the course of events.

Alchemy implies some kind of intervention, manipulation, alteration of substances.

Exactly. In financial markets, theories can alter the substance to which they relate. For instance, the efficient market theory has given rise to the widespread use of derivatives and derivatives may, on occasion, cause markets to crash. I happen to be addicted to the truth and therefore I insist that social science is a form of alchemy, not a science. Science has a great reputation and it is therefore appealing to say you are doing science. It is a word to conjure with, and social scientists may conjure with the word.

I don't want to overstate my case. Social scientists are just as interested in the pursuit of truth as natural scientists, but they have an opportunity to conjure that is largely denied to the natural scientists. The best way to guard against abuse is by recognizing the possibility. That is what I hoped to achieve by claiming that social science is a false metaphor and insisting that my own approach is more like alchemy than science.

If your theory doesn't provide any generalizations that can be used for predictions or explanations, what good is it?

It opens up a whole wide field for investigation: the relationship between thinking and reality. I have hardly scratched the surface and I have already gained some interesting insights. I find the distinction between near-equilibrium and far-from-equilibrium conditions particularly promising. There are situations where perceptions and reality are not too far apart and there are forces at work that tend to bring them closer together. I call this a state of near-equilibrium. There are other situations where perceptions and reality are quite far removed without any tendency to converge. I call these far-from-equilibrium conditions. There are two kinds of disequilibrium: static disequilibrium, where both the prevailing dogma and the prevailing social conditions are rigidly fixed but quite far removed from each other; and dynamic disequilibrium, where both the real world and the participants' views are changing so rapidly that they cannot help but be far apart.

This brings us back to the $64,000 question that you did not quite answer earlier. Where do you draw the line between the various conditions?

As I said before, I don't yet have a clear answer. One thing I know for sure: The boundary line has to do with the values that guide people in their actions. I draw an analogy with water: Whether it turns into ice or steam is a question of pressure and temperature; here, it is a question of values. The trouble is, values cannot be quantified like temperature; so we must look for a qualitative difference. That is where I become tentative.

It is remarkable how little I know about values. I have studied economics, but economic theory takes values as given. I have studied philosophy, but I have concentrated on epistemology and neglected ethics. Still, I have a pretty good sense of where the demarcation line lies, but I am not sure I can articulate it.

Give it a try.

Looking at the boundary line between static disequilibrium and near-equilibrium, I would say that in a near-equilibrium situation people are aware of the difference between thinking and reality and recognize that the two do not always coincide. They are willing to learn from experience and they exert themselves to realize their aspirations. These efforts prevent their thinking from straying too far from reality. By contrast, in static disequilibrium, people fail to distinguish between the subjective and the objective, or accept a dogma as the ultimate truth. We may use the animism of primitive peoples or the communist dogma of the erstwhile Soviet Union as cases in point.

It is when we come to the boundary line with dynamic disequilibrium that I have some difficulty in formulating my thoughts properly. The separation between thinking and reality becomes blurred, but this time it is because reality has become too unstable. It ceases to command the respect it enjoys in near-equilibrium conditions; it becomes more threatening and more malleable at the same time. This does not happen by itself: The participants' value systems are also unhinged. There is a mutual self-reinforcing interaction between the values that guide people and the course of events. We are on familiar ground: We are talking about boom/bust processes.

The question is, what distinguishes boom/bust processes that get out of hand from those that abort. The question is more easily answered in the financial markets than in a purely abstract form. If you recall the various examples I have used, you will find that in all cases where the process gets out of hand, there is a flaw in the prevailing values. The usual flaw is that what people believe to be fundamental values turns out to be reflexive. This was the case in the conglomerate boom: People believed that earnings per share was something independent of the market value of the shares. It was the case in the international lending boom: Bankers believed that the debt ratios they used to determine the borrowing capacity of debtor countries were independent of their own lending activity. And so on. But there is another source of instability, which I haven't mentioned. When people operate without fundamental values, when they recognize that markets are reflexive and "the trend is your friend," markets do, in fact, become unstable. That is what happens in currency markets. As I showed in *The Alchemy of Finance*, trend-following speculation renders a freely fluctuating exchange rate system unstable and the instability is cumulative: the longer it lasts, the more unstable it becomes.

Going from financial markets to historical processes in general, I would say that in order to stay near equilibrium, people must agree on some fundamental values; they must have a shared sense of right and wrong. If they lose that sense and allow themselves to be guided purely by what is expedient, the situation becomes unstable. I think that this source of instability is particularly relevant at the present moment. You can see it in the stock market, where the bulk of the players are institutional investors who are not concerned with fundamental values, but only with relative performance. And then you have everybody chasing everybody else in the performance game. It encourages trend-following behavior.

It's even more relevant, I think, in the political system, where politicians are guided by only one consideration—how to get elected. That undermines the very foundations of democracy as it was envisioned by our founding fathers. Representative democracy is based on the idea that candidates stand up and announce what their views are and voters then chose among them. But when the people who are standing for election first study what the electorate's views are and then say what they think will appeal to the electorate, a short-circuit is created, and the process becomes unstable. The situation is exacerbated by the pervasive use of television advertising.

So you believe the present condition of the stock market and the election process are both good examples of reflexive behavior?

They are both increasingly unstable and in danger of breaking down and for the same reason: They suffer from a lack of fundamental values. But the problem is more profound than it appears at first sight. The theory of reflexivity holds that all our fundamental values are flawed and, in certain circumstances, those flaws become apparent. Yet fundamental values are needed to preserve near-equilibrium conditions. If we recognize that values are reflexive in nature and abandon all fundamental values, we make the situation more unstable. So there is something self-contradictory in the near-equilibrium position. But, if you come to think of it, that is quite consistent with my theory of reflexivity. If the near-equilibrium position were stable, there would be no room for far-from-equilibrium conditions. Near-equilibrium has to be a precarious condition.

225

You have really lost me here. What do you mean?

As far as financial markets are concerned, if the theory of reflexivity becomes widely accepted, markets will become more reflexive. I don't subscribe to the relative performance concept. I manage my funds strictly on the basis of absolute performance and I think that is the correct yardstick. I think that financial markets would be more stable if people used absolute performance measures rather than relative ones. But one has to recognize that the purpose of investing is performance; therefore, what matters is whether a stock goes up or down, not what the fundamental value of the stock is. And if everybody discards fundamental values and begins to chase relative performance, the market becomes unstable and one must play it accordingly.

Taking a broader view, I see a systemic problem. In order to have a stable system, you need some fundamental values to sustain it.

That is true of the market, and it is even more true of politics. What happens when the fundamental values are flawed or, even worse, people come to the conclusion that all fundamental values are flawed? The system becomes unstable, it enters into a state of dynamic disequilibrium. The trouble is that, in accordance with my theory of reflexivity, all fundamental beliefs are indeed flawed, as all human constructs are flawed. In certain circumstances, the deficiency is liable to become apparent and, if my theory of reflexivity becomes generally accepted, the potential deficiency of *all* fundamental values becomes apparent. How can you rely on values that you know may be deficient? Here is the rub. I consider stability, near-equilibrium conditions, highly desirable, yet my theory of reflexivity undermines the belief in fundamental values.

So your theory of reflexivity is itself reflexive. It's like a self-defeating prophecy.

That's exactly right. It raises the problem: How can you hold beliefs if you know them to be flawed?

Is there an answer?

Yes. If we accept that out understanding is inherently imperfect, we can build a value system on that insight. That is what I have done with my belief in my own fallibility.

This is too abstract for me. Can you be more specific?

Yes, but only if I introduce the concepts of open and closed society. Open society is based on the recognition of our own fallibility; closed society on its denial. If we are, in fact, fallible, open society is preferable to a closed society in which there is no freedom to think and to choose. The trouble is that this point of view is shared only by those who have personally experienced the oppression of a closed society or have strong feelings about it. It doesn't come naturally to people who enjoy the benefits of open society as their birthright.

I had an interesting experience recently when I discussed this subject with an intelligent audience in England. Somebody said, "I never realized that I live in an open society." That is a grave deficiency in an open society. Freedom is like the air: One takes it for granted. But in another way, it is quite unlike the air. If you don't cherish it, if you don't protect it, you are liable to lose it.

But that is happening with clean air, also.

You are right. The analogy is closer than I thought. Anyway, the concept of open society rests on the recognition of one's own fallibility. How to turn that into a fundamental value in its own right is the problem. I have solved it to my own satisfaction, but I am not sure I am able to communicate it. It is a tough assignment. It is easy to believe that whatever you stand for represents the ultimate truth. It is less easy to stand for a form of social organization that is based on the recognition that one may be wrong. One has to show that the ultimate truth is not attainable. That takes time, a lot of time, because one needs to go through the arguments I have presented here. Time is liable to run out, especially if one is arguing with someone who happens to have a gun in his hands.

Popper told me a story, when we met in Prague last summer, just before he died, about how, many years ago, he had tried to argue this point with a man at a lakeside in Austria. The man said, "I don't argue; I shoot." And when he got dressed, he put on an SS uniform.[1]

In a strange way, that is still the main dilemma confronting the world today. If we want an open society, we must be prepared to defend it. We must believe in it as the common good to which the interests of the individual must be subordinated. But very few people who claim to be devoted to democracy and free markets would subscribe to this view.

It is too abstract.

That is true; but there is an abstract concept that seems to command widespread allegiance at present: the idea of free competition. It has become almost like mother's milk: Allow people to pursue their self-interest and the market mechanism will take care of the rest. Underlying this argument is the assumption that markets are always right. As you know, I take the opposite position. All human constructs are inherently flawed, and the fact that government controls don't work *does not* guarantee that the absence of government controls will work any better. The market mechanism is better than other arrangements only because it provides feedback and allows mistakes to be corrected. This is the equivalent of Churchill's dictum about democracy: It is the worst system, except all the others.

I believe in free markets and democracy. But I differ with the proponents of laissez-faire on one point: it is not enough to pursue self-interest. You must put the common interest of free markets,

---

[1] cf. Popper, *The Myth of the Framework*. Obviously, this was a seminal event in Popper's life.

democracy, open society above self-interest, otherwise the system will not survive.

Financial markets have a deficiency: they are inherently unstable. They need some supervision by an authority that has been explicitly charged with preserving or reestablishing stability. History has shown that unregulated markets are liable to break down. The development of central banking was the result of a series of banking crises.

But here we find another quandary: Regulators are no more perfect than the market—indeed, they are even less perfect—so regulation always has unintended consequences. Controls are usually introduced when there is a breakdown in the functioning of the market mechanism, but regulations, in turn, introduce distortions and eventually controls become unworkable and they break down, too. We then experience a swing from laissez-faire to the other extreme of excessive control. I think such swings are inevitable. The important question is, how far do these swings go? Are they are contained within tolerable bounds, or do they go beyond the bounds of tolerance? In a well-functioning financial system or a well-functioning political system, the controls are so subtle that they are not even noticed, but when the system breaks down and you have a crash or a depression, then subsequently controls may also become excessive. If open societies were not subject to breakdowns, there would be no room for closed societies.

So you see history as a grand pattern in which closed societies alternate with open societies.

Not at all. That would be the case only if history followed a predetermined pattern. The whole thrust of my approach is that the course of events is indeterminate. Open society could last forever if people took the trouble to preserve it—its duration is up to them. Closed societies sometimes have seemed to last forever and, even when they didn't, they tried to lay claim to eternity. If you stop to think about it, the pattern you mention of open and closed societies alternating doesn't belong to history—it is introduced into history by us when we distinguish between open and closed societies. If that is the only distinction we draw, that is the only pattern we can observe.

I should point out that open and closed societies are not really historical concepts. History is time-bound while these concepts are timeless. They happen to be relevant to the present moment in history, and they are particularly illuminating as far as the revolution of 1989 is concerned. But there have been many periods in history when other distinctions have been more relevant.

If open society is not a historical concept, what is it?

A strictly theoretical concept, based on the discrepancy between thinking and reality. There are two different ways of dealing with that discrepancy. Open society recognizes that there is a discrepancy; closed society denies it. These are abstract models that may be approximated by actual conditions, but never quite attained, otherwise there would be no discrepancy between thinking and reality.

How does your framework of open and closed societies relate to your distinction between near- and far-from-equilibrium conditions?

Open society corresponds to near-equilibrium conditions and closed society to static disequilibrium. That is not surprising because both dichotomies are based on the same premise, namely that participants act on the basis of imperfect understanding.

Where does dynamic disequilibrium fit into the scheme? Near-equilibrium can be equated with open society, extreme rigidity with closed society, but what about extreme changeability?

Well, that is a regime change, not a regime. It is a process that is condensed in time rather than a state of affairs that has some degree of persistence. Like the quanta in Heisenberg's theory that can be alternately viewed as particles or waves.

The distinction between near- and far-from-equilibrium and the distinction between open and closed societies fuse together into the study of regime change. I am particularly interested in regime change, but I should like to emphasize that open and closed societies are not the only regimes that can be observed in history. Indeed, they can't really be observed in history because they are theoretical constructs. There are many different kinds of regimes that can be observed: political regimes; economic regimes; regimes prevailing in particular firms, industries, or institutions; even regimes in individual lives as in the case of being married to different spouses; schools of thought; styles; and so on. My theory of regime change ought to apply to them, too.

I have been involved with regime change throughout my life, both in theory and in practice. I have not been able to make much headway on the theoretical side because I have not been able to define what constitutes a regime. It is some kind of a mental construct, but what kind?

In real life you are unlikely to find regimes functioning in isolation. Even in financial markets, boom/bust sequences are often punctuated by external shocks. For instance, the boom/bust sequence of international investing has been punctuated by the Mexican crisis. I have said very little about what constitutes a regime and how regimes collide with each other.

But I have gained a lot of practical experience starting quite early in life, as a Jewish boy of 14 under Nazi occupation in Hungary and then under Soviet occupation. When I became active in financial markets, I specialized in boom/bust sequences. When I set up a foundation, I got caught up in a revolution.

How does your concept of open and closed society relate to your boom/bust theory?

It is difficult to study boom/bust processes and other forms of regime change in isolation because regimes are not isolated. Moreover, the relationship between various regimes is quite untidy. They do not nest neatly, smaller regimes within larger ones. They form and dissolve and overlap in a haphazard fashion. That is why there is so much talk of external shocks.

Open and closed societies are quite special in this respect. They are comprehensive; they extend their sway to all aspects of existence. They contain all other regimes. This makes them particularly suitable for the study of regime change. It is quite exceptional to be able to study the rise and fall of a closed society that is as all-encompassing as the Soviet system.

Open and closed societies are also quite special in another way. They constitute ideals to which people may aspire. I have a strong commitment to open society as a desirable form of social organization, and so do many others, especially if they have experienced living in a closed society.

But open society as an ideal is not without warts. Instability, deficiency in values, are not attractive features. That is why open society is so feeble as an ideal. The vision offered by closed societies is much more alluring. But in closed societies, the vision is far removed from reality; in open societies, it is quite close. You need to appreciate the discrepancy between thinking and reality in order to opt for open society.

What qualifies an open society as an ideal in the first place?

It is based on the recognition that our understanding is inherently flawed. That sounds like a negative quality, but it can be turned around: What is imperfect can be improved. Accepting the uncertainties connected with our fallibility opens up the vista for infinite improvement.

Science is the best example. Science is the crowning glory of the human intellect, and it is firmly based on a belief in its own fallibility. If scientific theories embodied the ultimate truth, there would be no point in testing them and scientific advance would come to a halt. Science is something of a special case because it has a reliable criterion at its disposal, namely, the facts. Other spheres of human endeavor—philosophy, the arts, politics, the economy—are less well-situated as far as the critical process is concerned. Still, it is true to say that once you abandon the impossible requirement of perfection, you open the way to progress. When you look at the evidence, you can see that open societies are usually associated with progress and prosperity.

But open society suffers from a fatal flaw. People living in open societies do not accept the concept of open society as an ideal worth fighting for. It can be seen why this should be so. Open society provides freedom of choice. If it is denied, it is worth fighting for it; but if it is available, it does not suffice—the choices still need to be made. You can't be just a democrat; you must be a social democrat, a liberal democrat, a Christian democrat, or whatever. That is why democrats always fight among themselves, whereas those who advocate a closed society can remain disciplined and united.

Does that mean that open societies are doomed to fail?

Not at all. As long as open society is accepted as a shared value, democrats can fight among themselves and still resist the enemies of open society. The trouble is that open society is its own worst enemy because open society is not accepted as a shared value. That is the point Karl Popper failed to make. As I have said before, people may be willing to die for king and country—although that is becoming exceedingly rare also—but they are certainly not willing to die for the concept of open society.

Why should people in this country die for open society in another country?

Good question. The answer is that open society is a universal concept. Fallibility is the human condition. It applies to all of us. The

233

Declaration of Independence proclaimed that all men are created equal. In the form in which it is stated, it is far from self-evident, but as a statement of the human condition it can be justified. In respect to our fallibility (and our mortality), we are indeed created equal. This can serve as the basis of universal values.

It is still not clear to me how your belief in your own fallibility leads to your idea of open society as the basis of universal values.

It is not obvious. I can show it to my own satisfaction. Indeed, I have done it, but I cannot expect others to share my point of view. Indeed, I must recognize that I am in some ways exceptional. Forget intellect; there are few people who have more money than they need. That sets me apart from others. It is as if I were exempt from the law of gravity; I can indulge my flights of fancy and my fancy is to promote the idea of open society. But here I encounter my own fallibility—a constraint I cannot escape.

To bring about an open society it is not enough for me to believe in it; society must share that belief. And that is where I have been sadly deceived. I found people living under communist regimes who passionately believed in the idea of open society although they might not call it by that name. It did not need to be spelled out: We shared the same values. I could reinforce them, empower them through my foundations. I also knew from my theoretical framework that open societies suffer from a deficiency of values. In particular, I felt that Europe needed an idea to inspire it because treaties by themselves were not sufficient to make it united and I thought that Eastern Europe, with its passionate devotion to the idea of open society, could provide that inspiration. Don't laugh; I really believed that.

But events took a different turn; the West failed to rise to the occasion and the flame of revolution has died down. By now it is very hard to speak of a passionate devotion to the idea of open society in the formerly communist countries. I have a network of foundations and they do keep the flame alive. But I must ask myself: Am I pursuing an impossible dream? Those who work with the foundations do, on the whole, believe in open society. In that sense, I am not alone. But I have exempted them from the constraints that afflict others by providing money through the foundations. In that sense, we indulge in a common fantasy. To turn our dream into reality, society at large must come to share the values of open society. But here I see an insuperable difficulty. It is not a pressing one, because the concept of open society is receding. But suppose that these countries succeeded in making the transition to open societies; they would become like the open societies of the West, pursuing their self-interest without any concern for open society as an ideal. I can already see it happening in the Czech Republic.

This has turned my attention to the open societies of the West. They must be persuaded of the need to treat open society as a common good, a shared value. But I am at a loss how to go about it. Usually one can extrapolate from one's own beliefs. I have read somewhere in Aristotle that men create gods in their own image. But in my case, that would be a folly. I must regard myself as an exceptional case. And I must remember that I used to be pretty singlemindedly engaged in making money before I became so wholeheartedly devoted to the idea of open society. I cannot set myself up as an example. I must find another way to make my case. But I am stymied. I realize that I am going against the prevailing trend. As an investor, I would beat a retreat. But there is too much at stake. I can clearly see that the prevailing trend threatens the survival of our civilization. Even a losing battle is worth fighting.

Let me help you a little. Let us take it step by step. First, show me how your belief in fallibility leads to your concept of open society, because that is still not clear to me.

Very well. I thought I had done it, but I'll do it again. If no-one is in possession of the ultimate truth, we need a form of social organization that ensures people's right to choose.

But if no-one is in possession of the ultimate truth, what gives you the right to impose your form of social organization on others?

It is enshrined in the American Constitution and it also underlies the unwritten British constitution.

But I still need an argument that would lead me to fight for open society in another country.

That is where the problem lies. There is a need for a world order that promotes and protects the principles of open society, but the need is not recognized. We have never had a world order; why should we have one now? Relations between states have always been ruled by power; peace and stability have always depended on a balance of power. But the remarkably stable balance of power that prevailed during the Cold War has broken down and no new balance is in sight. We need to find some common ground, some universal concept that would enable us to resist the attempts to create nationalist or fundamentalist dictatorships through conflict. I believe that the concept of open society could provide that common ground, but my belief is not shared. Without some shared beliefs and stable power relations, our civilization is heading for the rocks. That is the point I have been trying to get across; that is where I have failed so far, both as a philosopher and as an activist.

10

THE POWER AND THE MYTH

A lot has happened in your life in the 25 years we've known each other, but probably the most significant change is that you've come to have a great deal of personal power. How has it changed your life?

For the better. It has some negative aspects, but on the whole it amounts to a wish fulfilled. I had always wanted to get a hearing for my ideas, and for most of my life I didn't succeed. It is only after the sterling crisis that I became a public figure and it really changed my position in the world. My main concern now is whether my ideas measure up to the hearing they get.

I remember talking with you in early 1990 about the fact that you couldn't get the Treasury Department and the IMF to listen to some of your ideas concerning Eastern Europe. I told you that Washington viewed you as just another person who had made a lot of money on Wall Street and wanted to be important. At that point, we discussed the idea of your getting more visibility, more press attention because that was a way to get a hearing. You embarked on a major

personal publicity campaign to achieve the power that you now have. It wasn't your style before that, but it served you very well.

That is not quite correct; I did not engage in a publicity campaign. I merely didn't avoid the press as I had done prior to 1989. I know the exact turning point. It came in October or November 1989 when I wanted to reach President Bush to talk to him about a new approach toward what was then still the Soviet Union and I was unable to establish contact with him. I got as far as Larry Eagleburger, who was Assistant Secretary of State, but no further. That is when I decided to write a book. But even earlier, I tried to meet Prime Minister Thatcher because I wanted her to sponsor a Thatcher plan for the Soviet Union. I felt that she was the only person who could lead the world in the right direction because she would have credibility in the United States as well as Europe. I was unable to get to her. I could get some memos to her, but I couldn't meet with her. It was only when she left office that she called me. She wanted advice on setting up a foundation. I couldn't meet with Gorbachev either. He avoided me because he was afraid to discuss economics. So even though I was quite active and influential, I didn't have the access I wanted. It is ironic that it was not because of my philanthropy or my philosophy that I gained recognition, but because of my ability to make money. It was my killing on sterling that gave me a high profile. I think that's a commentary on the values that prevail in our society.

The combination of your success with sterling plus your access to the press really enabled you to build your public image, and as a result, develop your power.

I have a problem with that concept of power. Everybody says that I have a lot of power. But what does that power consist of? Can I move markets? Perhaps, but only if I guess correctly the direction in which markets want to move. If I guess wrong, I'll have my head handed to me. Can I influence governments? I am beginning to be able to, but only because of the reputation I have built up.

Your power came from your fame, not the other way around, but the fame came from the press.

However, I did not court the press. All I did was give a TV interview to Adam Smith's *Money World* on the sterling crisis. That, together with a British TV program established me as "The Man Who Broke the Bank of England." Had I been more accessible, I think the press would have started trying to destroy me much sooner than they did. It was exactly because I did not chase after the press that they were interested in what I had to say. However, I couldn't choose the topic. They sought me out on financial matters and most of the time I wouldn't respond. But I can tell you that until 1992, I had difficulty getting an Op-Ed piece on Eastern Europe published in *The Wall Street Journal* or *The New York Times*.

You've mentioned that recently the press started turning against you.

I basically have had excellent press in most Western countries for longer than one could hope for. It's only when it became boring to hear about all of my wonderful deeds that people started picking holes. So I shouldn't feel too bad about it. But there's something that I find much more disturbing. Because of my exaggerated power, I have become a prime target for the current version of the anti-Semitic conspiracy theory. If there was ever a man who would fit the stereotype of the Judoplutocratic Bolshevik Zionist world conspirator, it is me. And that is, in fact, how I am increasingly depicted in Eastern Europe and also to some extent in Western Europe, but not so much in America. This is a prime example of how good deeds don't go unpunished. My original purpose in setting up the Open Society Foundation was to create a society where this kind of conspiracy theory wouldn't flourish; but in the process of advocating an open society, I amassed a sort of mystic power that actually fostered the conspiracy theory. Don't you see the irony?

I wonder whether this is anything more than what happens when you attain a certain level of celebrity? In the beginning, you become

a news curiosity and the press wants to write about you because you're successful. But after everybody knows everything about you, the only thing that is interesting is to find a reason to attack you. So I think this just comes with the territory. I don't think it's anything deeper than that.

That is because you are an American and you are not attuned to the kind of myths that prevail in Europe, particularly in the Eastern part. Anti-Semitism has very deep roots. It predates Hitler. It goes back to the pogroms of the late last century and even further. It subsists in the dark recesses of people's minds and it breaks out into the open in times of trouble, turbulence, and confusion.

Has your Jewish origin influenced the development of your ideas?

Tremendously. Put yourself in my place. I was facing extermination at the age of 14 because I was Jewish. Wouldn't that make an impression on you? That was when the problem came to the forefront of my consciousness, but it had lurked in the background since I was born. It took the better part of my life to come to terms with it.

Is your Jewishness responsible for your devotion to the concept of open society?

Undoubtedly there is a connection. When you look at the way Jews react to persecution, you'll find that they tend to follow one of two main escape routes. Either they transcend their problem by turning to something universal or they identify with their oppressors and try to become like them. I came from an assimilationist family and I have chosen the first route. The other alternative is Zionism, the founding of a nation where the Jews are in the majority.

Are you opposed to Zionism?

It just doesn't appeal to me. I am interested in the universal human condition. But I never opposed it actively. I felt that as a Jew I had no right to oppose the state of Israel unless I actually became a citizen. I am convinced that, had I moved there, I would have been in opposition most of the time, like so many Israelis. As it is, I simply abstained. Perhaps it was a cop-out.

Recently, I visited Israel and I found myself fully in support of the reconciliation that the Rabin-Peres government is trying to accomplish. The only difficulty is that they are dealing with the wrong party. Arafat has largely lost the support of the Arab population; that is why he was willing to make a deal. I suspect that Hamas will have to be brought into the peace process before it can be fully successful. I told Peres about a meeting I had had with Jaruzelski before the reconciliation that brought Solidarity to power in Poland. Jaruzelski told me that he was willing to deal with anyone except Solidarity because the Solidarity people were traitors. I told him that he was making a big mistake because the leaders of Solidarity were patriots who were anxious to make a settlement even though it would undermine their own power base; their power base was in the heavy industry that would be destroyed by economic reform. As I heard afterwards, my argument made an impression on Jaruzelski. I can't say the same for Peres, but then, Solidarity was a much better bunch than Hamas.

Is it your Jewish identity that makes you so suspicious of all forms of national feeling?

I am not opposed to all forms of national feeling. I am opposed only to the kind of nationalism that holds, "it is my country, right or wrong." Incidentally, that attitude is more characteristic of the diaspora than of the people in the countries concerned. The diaspora creates a lot of mischief in places like Ireland or Greece or the Baltic states, not to mention

Israel. For the rest, I regard a feeling of national or ethnic identity as a valuable aspect of open societies, a welcome source of diversity.

How do you see your own Jewish identity?

I am proud of being a Jew—although I must admit it took me practically a lifetime to get there. I have suffered from the low self-esteem that is the bane of the assimilationist Jew. This is a heavy load that I could shed only when I recognized my success. I identify being a Jew with being in a minority. I believe that there is such a thing as a Jewish genius; one need only look at the Jewish achievements in science, in economic life, or in the arts. These were the results of Jews' efforts to transcend their minority status, and to achieve something universal. Jews have learned to consider every question from many different viewpoints, even the most contradictory ones. Being in the minority, they are practically forced into critical thinking. If there is anything of this Jewish genius in me, it is simply the ability to think critically. To that extent, Jewishness is an essential element of my personality and, as I said, I am very proud of that.

I am also aware that there is a certain amount of Jewish utopianism in my thinking. With my foundations, I am part of that tradition. That is why the concept of the European Union excites me so much. There, every nation is in a minority and that is what makes the concept so appealing.

One always tends to project from the personal to the universal. Most people arrive at their principles out of their personal experiences, and I am no exception. Therefore, I have to answer your initial question about whether my views have to do with my Jewish heritage with a definite yes. But what's wrong with that?

In Eastern Europe, it would definitely be held against you.

That is true. But I believe the concept of open society has to stand or fall on its own merit. Jews are not the only people in the minority. In most societies, the minority opinions would be in the majority if only people would stand up for their opinions when they are in the minority.

How do you respond to anti-Semitic attacks from Eastern Europe?

You cannot combat anti-Semitism directly; you cannot make it disappear by prohibiting it; you merely push it underground. The best way to deal with it is through education. Anti-Semitism is the solace of the ignorant. If you can bring it out in the open, expose it to daylight, it withers. As Justice Brandeis said, "Sunlight is the best disinfectant." That is what happened in Hungary. There was an extreme right-wing group that attacked, among other things, my foundation, and me personally for spreading "un-Hungarian" ideas. But they made the mistake of spelling out their ideas. Public opinion judged them and found them wanting: They did not make it into Parliament.

Didn't the attacks offend you?

Not at all. I didn't take them personally. I was delighted to be confronted with them and to be able to counter them. It was a form of exorcism; at any rate, that is how I looked at it.

It is in that context that I find so disturbing the mystique that surrounds me in the financial markets. The ways of the financial markets are indeed mysterious and even I don't fully understand them. I now realize that I used to be unaware of my influence. I will give you an example. We made a bid for a bankrupt Italian hotel chain, CIGA, but we were outbid by Sheraton. They didn't get control either, because the shareholders subscribed to new shares on the theory that if I wanted the company, they wanted it, too. I think that our reputation has faded since then. The point that I want to make is that my influence in the financial market is not wholly imaginary; rather, it is alchemical. And alchemy feeds right into the mindset that creates conspiracy theories.

You have no idea of the crazy concoctions that East European journalists are capable of. They are used to dealing in innuendoes. It is practically impossible to confront them with facts. And some of the Western press is not that much better.

The press is probably suspicious of your motives. They just can't believe that you're doing what you're doing for altruistic reasons alone. It's almost unique in human experience. Usually everyone has a hidden agenda somewhere and the press is anxious to find out what yours is.

I don't blame them. I would be suspicious, too. I find myself in a very curious situation. The fact is, I have acquired a great deal of authority, particularly in some of the countries where I have foundations. It is only recently that I discovered why that is, in a conversation with Branko Cervenkovski, the Prime Minister of Macedonia. It has been said that states have only interests, no principles; and the same can be said about statesmen. But, as a stateless statesman, I occupy the opposite position: I have only principles, no interests. That is what gives me my authority. It is a strange position for a stock market speculator to be in, but it is very gratifying. I wouldn't want to give it up for the world. So, even if I had a hidden agenda, I couldn't afford to indulge in it. But I can't expect the press to understand that; I didn't understand it myself until recently.

I don't want to parade as an altruist. I don't believe it is possible to act without a personal motivation. I happen to be in a very privileged position because I have made more money than I need. If I didn't have a surplus, I wouldn't be a philanthropist. I want to remind you that I did not start until I was rich. It's the old magic of compound interest—if you keep on making 30 to 40 percent per annum for 25 years, you make an awful lot of money even if you start with very little. So the amount of money I have amassed is truly awesome. And I would say that the main difference between me and other people who have amassed this kind of money is that I am primarily interested in ideas,

244

and I don't have much personal use for money. But I hate to think what would have happened if I hadn't made money: My ideas would not have gotten much play.

Everybody has focused on your foundations. Are there other philanthropies that you support in addition to your own foundations? Do you support arts organizations? Do you give to causes in which you're not directly involved?

Very little. My foundations support other foundations that pursue similar goals, but I confine my support to my own foundations. Actually, I'm quite hard-headed about it because if I started making exceptions there would be no end to it. For instance I refuse to endow university chairs; I don't support the opera or symphony orchestras.

Material things have never given you significant pleasure. You don't collect anything.

No. I find collecting totally alien to my nature because I have an abstract mind and collecting is the most concrete thing you can possibly do. It's not just a matter of buying a certain number of paintings or having a certain number of wine bottles in your cellar, but you've also got to remember their names. I find that very tiresome.

The way you think about money is fascinating. You once said to me that I was smart enough to get rich, but I did not seem to want to make a lot of money. What did you mean?

Business isn't that complicated. A lot of people of average intelligence make a good living. Really smart people can accumulate a fortune if they are truly committed. Your problem is that you like to do interesting work. Someone who wants to get rich doesn't care what he does. He only focuses on the bottom line. All day long he thinks about how he can make more money. If that means setting up more shoe shine stands, that's what he does.

Well then, what does bring you joy?

As a student, I read a book called *The Adventure of Ideas.* I think it was Alfred North Whitehead who wrote it. I would say that it's the adventure of ideas that attracts me. Basically, thinking is the most important aspect of my existence. I'm quite contemplative. I like to understand. I used to do a lot of philosophical speculation as a young man. I wasted a large part of my youth regurgitating certain ideas. Then I discovered that one can learn a great deal more through action than through contemplation. So I became an active thinker where my thinking played an important role in deciding what actions to take and my actions play an important role in improving my thinking. This two-way interaction between thinking and action became the hallmark of my philosophy and the hallmark of my life.

What material benefits have you derived from being a billionaire?

Probably the most tangible benefit is that I get a very good tennis game. There are some other advantages as well. Certainly the ability to meet interesting people ranks very high although now that I am invited everywhere I don't have time to go anywhere. But I do get involved in some interesting situations. You might call me a history junkie because I really do want to influence history. Interestingly, I am beginning to be cured of my addiction. In the early days, I would do practically anything to have an impact, to feel important. But as I begin to make an impact I become much more reserved and much less eager to make my influence felt. I think this is making me more effective because I no longer rush in where angels fear to tread. I keep a certain distance. I don't push my ideas, but wait for people to ask for my opinion rather than try to inflict it on them. There is no doubt that being an actor on the stage of history has great fascination for me, but I don't need to feel important any more.

How do you see your place in history?

Very questionable. True, I have carved myself a place on Mount Rushmore as a money manager and I am unlikely to lose it, whatever happens. It may just erode a little. I have also made a real impact through the foundations in the countries where they operate. But can I make a mark with my ideas? Can I formulate them and communicate them properly? Are they valid? That is what matters to me most and that is where I feel most insecure. The same set of ideas has served me for making money and for giving it away. It has worked for me, but that does not mean that it has universal validity. On the contrary, in some ways, I am an exception. Having made more money than I need, I have been liberated from the law of gravity: I can afford to stand up for abstract principles. But I cannot expect others to do the same. I didn't do it myself until I became rich—and if I had stood up for those principles earlier, I might not have become rich. That is what worries me about open society as a policy goal. Can people afford to stand up for it?

You can. You are in a unique position. That can be your role in history.

That's exactly how I see it. And I feel very good about it. The difficulty I have is going from the personal to the universal. Abstractions mean a lot to me; there is a lot of emotion and personal experience packed into them. Can they carry the same meaning for others? I wonder. But if people generally do not recognize open society as a goal worth striving for, how will our global system survive? That is the problem that confronts the world and I don't know the answer. That is where I am stuck. That is where I believe we are all stuck.

Has the complexity of world problems discouraged you somewhat?

Definitely. You see, our human capacity is limited. For the first 60 years of my life, I was mainly confronted with external obstacles. But as I gained some power and influence, I became increasingly aware of my internal limitations. There are limits to the extent to which I can become emotionally involved. As I am confronted with some of the more horrendous problems of humanity—Bosnia, Chechnya—I become somewhat inured to them. I don't like to admit it, but it is happening. And I am increasingly aware of my intellectual limitations as well. I used to think that I had a positive contribution to make in solving the world's problems. I always knew that many problems didn't have solutions, but I thought I could bring a new insight. I still think so, but I find some situations baffling. I find the problems of the world, the question of the world order, and the reform of the United Nations practically insoluble.

As you've become more focused on geopolitical issues, don't you feel you sometimes lose your awareness of detail?

Not really, but then I don't remember things as well as I used to. That's one of the blessings of growing older. Most people are very concerned about losing their memory. It causes them anguish. I am not bothered by it. First, I have associates around to remember things for me. Second, people assume that I have more important things on my mind than remembering names and other pieces of information. Losing your memory is only a problem if you worry about it. My mind remains clear on current concepts and their historical reference points, however.

Well, George, you've been on an incredible odyssey. I wonder if you ever had any inkling of how far you would go?

As an adolescent, I certainly had some superhuman fantasies. I have spoken about my godlike and messianic impulses from time to time. The closer I have come to actually fulfilling them, the more I've become aware of my own humanity. But with all these great ambitions, I am sometimes still amazed at my actual accomplishments. This is particularly true in my philanthropy. As I travel around and see the results, I find them quite awesome and very gratifying.

How do you view your public persona, the way others view you?

It isn't me. I'm aware of the position that I occupy and try to live up to it, but it doesn't correspond to my own picture of myself. I don't know the real me any better than anybody else, but I know one thing: Even though I realize that the public persona is not me—it's outside me— it does affect me. I am different because of it. There is a two-way, re-flexive interaction between the personal me and the public persona. Obviously, I have a role in shaping that persona, but the persona also shapes me. I can see how it has affected me. And I must say that, on the whole, the effect has been very beneficial. The real me has become a happier, better, more harmonious, more contented person than be-fore. In other words, I really like my persona. It is my creation and I'm proud of it. That is a big change from the way I used to feel about my-self during the most productive period of my business career. For some reason, I used to be ashamed of myself, and I've simply grown out of that. I also used to be very isolated; now I am very involved. So, when all is said and done, having that public persona has made me a happier private person.

This notion of the private person intrigues me because it seems to me that a lot of the things that give you pleasure are things you experience by yourself. Do you derive any pleasure through other people—your family and friends?

Yes. But I must admit that I am my own most severe critic. And my own estimation of myself is more important to me than other people's opinion. I find gratitude and adulation downright embarrassing. Still, I have a good enough opinion of myself by now that I can accept when other people have a good opinion of me and sometimes I derive a great deal of satisfaction from other people's positive feelings about me. And having so amply fulfilled my own aspirations, I now have some time left over for family and friends.

249

Sports are also important to you—skiing, tennis. Do you wish you had more time for them?

No. I think I have as much time as I want. My capacity for sports is now somewhat limited. I play tennis regularly. I used to be very keen on skiing, but now I find it quite exhausting. So I think I do as much sport as I am capable of. I'm not sure I want to answer these personal questions any further.

There has been too much attention paid to me as a person. The subject interests me and I could go on about it forever because I am fascinated how the conflict between my father and my mother—which obviously made a deep impression on me as a child—continues to unfold inside me long after they are dead. But this preoccupation with myself is beginning to have some harmful side effects. I became a public personality in order to promote certain ideas. Now the question arises, among my collaborators and also in my own mind, whether the foundation network and everything else I do is not just for the purpose of self-aggrandizement. This is a serious issue. I am not immune from the accusation of building a personality cult just because it is me doing it. I think I have reached a point where I must suppress my yearning for self-revelation. This book should be the last occasion when I delve into my personality the way I am doing now. I hope I shall have the strength to keep this resolution.

Selected Writings
by
George Soros

Open and Closed Societies

The following chapter was excerpted from the author's unpublished manuscript, "The Burden of Consciousness" written in 1962 and published in his 1990 book Underwriting Democracy. *It is included here because it expands on the concept of open society. The distinctions between open and closed society are further articulated and the benefits of open society versus closed society are elaborated.*

In this chapter I shall present the framework of open and closed societies as I originally conceived it—that is to say, as a choice that confronts humanity at the present moment in history.

The constructs, being reflexive, have two aspects. One depicts the way people think, and the other, the way things really are. The two aspects interact in a reflexive fashion: the mode of thinking influences the actual state of affairs, and vice versa, without ever reaching a correspondence between the two.

I must point out a flaw in the construction of the models, as distinct from the distortions in the situations they depict. They are theoretical constructs and not historical ones, but the situations they describe are not timeless but evolutionary. There is a process of learning (and forgetting) involved, and it is not adequately dealt with. The solution I chose was to distinguish between changelessness in its original form (organic society and the traditional mode of thinking) and change-lessness imposed later on in the evolutionary process (closed society and the dogmatic mode of thinking).

Change is an abstraction. It does not exist by itself but is always combined with a substance that is changing or is subject to change. Of course, the substance in question is also an abstraction, without independent existence. The only thing that really exists is substance-cum-change, which is separated into substance and change by the human mind in its quest to introduce some sense into a confusing universe. Here we are concerned not with changes as they occur in reality, but with change as a concept.

The important point about change as a concept is that it requires abstract thinking. Awareness of change is associated with a mode of thinking characterized by the use of abstractions; lack of awareness reflects the lack of abstractions. We can construct two distinct modes of thinking along these lines.

In the absence of change the mind has to deal only with one set of circumstances: that which exists at the present time. What has gone before and what will come in the future is identical with what exists now. Past, present, and future form a unity, and the whole range of possibilities is reduced to one concrete case: things are as they are because they could not be any other way. This principle tremendously simplifies the task of thinking; the mind needs to operate only with concrete information, and all the complications arising out of the use of abstractions can be avoided. I shall call this the traditional mode of thinking.

Now let us consider a changing world. Man must learn to think of things not only as they are but also as they have been and as they could be. There is then not only the present to consider but an infinite range of possibilities. How can they be reduced to manageable proportions? Only by introducing generalizations, dichotomies, and other abstractions. Once it comes to generalizations, the more general they are, the more they simplify matters. The world is best conceived as a general equation in which the present is represented by one particular set of constants. Change the constants and the same equation will apply to all past and future situations. Working with general equations of this kind, one must be prepared to accept any set of constants that conforms to them. In other words, everything is to be considered possible, unless it has proved to be impossible. I shall call this the critical mode of thinking.

The traditional and the critical modes of thinking are based on two diametrically opposed principles, yet each presents an internally consistent view of reality. How is that possible? Only by presenting a distorted view. But the distortion need not be as great as it would be if it applied to the identical set of circumstances, because, in accordance with the theory of reflexivity, the circumstances are bound to be influenced by the prevailing mode of thinking. The traditional mode of thinking is associated with what I shall call organic society, the critical mode with "open" society. This provides the starting point for the theoretical models I seek to establish.

The Traditional Mode of Thinking

Things are as they have always been—therefore they could not be any other way. This may be taken as the central tenet of the traditional mode of thinking. Its logic is less than perfect; indeed, it contains the built-in flaw we expect to find in our models. The fact that its central tenet is neither true nor logical reveals an important feature of the traditional mode of thinking: it is neither so critical nor so logical as we have learned to be. It does not need to be. Logic and other forms of argument are useful only when one has to choose between alternatives.

Changeless society is characterized by the absence of alternatives. There is only one set of circumstances the human mind has to deal with: the way things are. While alternatives can be imagined, they appear like fairy tales, because the path that would lead to them is missing.

In such circumstances, the proper attitude is to accept things as they seem to be. The scope for speculation and criticism is limited: the primary task of thinking is not to argue but to come to terms with a given situation—a task that can be performed without any but the most pedestrian kind of generalizations. This saves people a great deal of trouble. At the same time, it deprives them of the more elaborate tools of thinking. Their view of the world is bound to be primitive and distorted.

Both the advantages and the drawbacks become apparent when we consider the problems of epistemology. The relationship of thoughts to reality does not arise as a problem. There is no world of ideas separate from the world of facts. Even more important, there seems to be nothing subjective or personal about thinking; it is firmly rooted in the tradition handed down by generations. Its validity is beyond question. Prevailing ideas are accepted as reality itself, or, to be more precise, the distinction between ideas and reality is simply not drawn.

This may be demonstrated by looking at the way language is used. Naming something is like attaching a label to it.* When we think in concrete terms, there is always a "thing" to which a name corresponds, and we can use the name and the thing interchangeably: thinking and reality are co-extensive. Only if we think in abstract terms do we begin giving names to things that do not exist independently of our naming them. We may be under the impression that we are still attaching labels to "things," yet these "things" have come into existence through our labeling them; the labels are attached to something that was created in our mind. This is the point at which thinking and reality become separated.

By confining itself to concrete terms, the traditional mode of thinking avoids the separation. But it has to pay heavily for this supreme simplicity. If no distinction is made between thinking and reality, how can one distinguish between true and false? The only statement that can be rejected is one that does not conform to the

---

* Ludwig Wittgenstein, *Philosophical Investigations*, I.15.

prevailing tradition. Traditional views must be accepted automatically because there is no criterion for rejecting them. The way things appear is the way things are: the traditional mode of thinking cannot probe any deeper. It cannot establish causal relationships between various occurrences, because these could prove to be either true or false; if they were false there would be a reality apart from our thinking, and the very foundations of the traditional mode of thinking would be undermined. Yet if thinking and reality are to be regarded as identical, an explanation must be provided for everything. The existence of a question without an answer would destroy the unity of thinking and reality just as surely as would the existence of a right and a wrong answer.

Fortunately it is possible to explain the world without recourse to causal laws. Everything behaves according to its nature. Since there is no distinction between natural and supernatural, all questions can be put to rest by endowing objects with a spirit whose influence explains any occurrence whatsoever and eliminates the possibility of internal contradictions. Most objects will seem to be under the command of such a force, because in the absence of causal laws most behavior has an arbitrary quality about it.

When the distinction between thoughts and reality is missing, an explanation carries the same conviction whether it is based on observation or on irrational belief. The spirit of a tree enjoys the same kind of existence as its body, provided we believe in it. Nor do we have any reason to doubt our beliefs: our forefathers believed in the same thing. In this way the traditional mode of thinking with its simple epistemology may easily lead to beliefs that are completely divorced from reality.

To believe in spirits and their magic is equivalent to accepting our surroundings as being beyond our control. This attitude is profoundly appropriate to a changeless society. Since people are powerless to change the world in which they live, their task is to acquiesce in their fate. By humbly accepting the authority of the spirits who rule the world, they may propitiate them; but to probe into the secrets of the universe will not do any good at all. Even if people did discover the causes of certain phenomena, the knowledge would bring no practical advantages unless they believed that they could change the conditions of their existence, which is unthinkable. The only motive for inquiry that remains is idle curiosity; and whatever inclination they may have to indulge in it, the danger of angering the spirits will effectively discourage it. Thus the search for causal explanations is likely to be absent from people's thoughts.

In a changeless society social conditions are indistinguishable from natural phenomena. They are determined by tradition, and it is just as much beyond the power of people to change them as it is to change the rest of their surroundings. The distinction between social and natural laws is one that the traditional mode of thinking is incapable of recognizing. Hence the same attitude of humble submissiveness is required toward society as toward nature.

We have seen that the traditional mode of thinking fails to distinguish between thoughts and reality, truth and falsehood, social and natural laws. If we searched further, other omissions could be found. For instance, the traditional mode of thinking is very vague on the question of time: past, present, and future tend to melt into each other. Such categories are indispensable to us. Judging the traditional mode of thinking from our vantage point, we find it quite inadequate. It is not so, however, in the conditions in which it prevails. In a society that lives by oral tradition, for instance, it can fulfill its function perfectly: it contains all necessary concrete information while avoiding unnecessary complications. It represents the simplest possible way of dealing with the simplest possible world. Its main weakness is not its lack of subtlety but the fact that the concrete information it contains is inferior to that which can be attained by a different approach. This is obvious to us, blessed as we are with superior knowledge. It need not disturb those who have no knowledge other than tradition, but it does make the whole structure extremely vulnerable to outside influences. A rival system of thought can destroy the monopolistic position of existing beliefs and force them to be subjected to critical examination. This would mean the end of the traditional mode of thinking and the beginning of the critical mode.

Take the case of medicine. The tribal medicine man has a completely false picture of the workings of the human body. Long experience has taught him the usefulness of certain treatments, but he is liable to do the right things for the wrong reasons. Nevertheless he is regarded with awe by the tribe; his failures are attributed to the work of evil spirits with whom he is on familiar terms but for whose actions he is not responsible. Only when modern medical science comes into direct competition with primitive medicine does the superiority of correct therapies over mistaken ones become manifest. However grudgingly and suspiciously, the tribe is eventually forced to accept the white man's medicine because it works better.

The traditional mode of thinking may also come up against difficulties of its own making. As we have seen, at least part of the prevailing body of beliefs is bound to be false. Even in a simple and unchanging society, some unusual events occur that must be accounted for. The new explanation may contradict the established one, and the struggle between them might tear apart the wonderfully simple structure of the traditional world. Yet the traditional mode of thinking need not break down every time there is a change in the conditions of existence. Tradition is extremely flexible as long as it is not threatened by alternatives. It encompasses all prevailing explanations by definition. As soon as a new explanation prevails, it automatically becomes the traditional one and, with the distinction between past and present blurred, it will seem to have prevailed since timeless times. In this way, even a changing world may appear to be changeless within fairly wide limits. For instance, the primitive tribes of New Guinea have been able to accommodate themselves to the advent of civilization by adopting the cargo cult.

Traditional beliefs may be able to retain their supremacy even in competition with modern ideas, especially if they are supported by the requisite amount of coercion. Under these circumstances, however, the mode of thinking can no longer be regarded as traditional. It is not the same to declare the principle that things must be as they have always been as to believe in it implicitly. In order to uphold such

259

a principle, one view must be declared correct and all others eliminated. Tradition may serve as the touchstone of what is eligible and what is not, but it can no longer be what it was for the traditional mode of thinking, the sole source of knowledge. To distinguish the pseudo-traditional from the original, I refer to it as the "dogmatic mode of thinking." I shall discuss it separately.

Organic Society

As we have seen, the traditional mode of thinking does not recognize the distinction between social and natural laws: the social framework is considered just as unalterable as the rest of man's environment. Hence the starting point in a changeless society is always the social Whole and not the individuals who constitute it. While society fully determines the existence of its members, the members have no say in determining the nature of the society in which they live. That has been fixed for them by tradition. This does not mean that there is a conflict of interest between the individual and the Whole in which the individual must always lose out. In a changeless society the individual as such does not exist at all; moreover, the social Whole is not an abstract idea that stands in contrast to the idea of the individual but a concrete unity that embraces all members. The dichotomy between the social Whole and the individual, like so many others, is the result of our habit of using abstract terms. In order to understand the unity that characterizes a changeless society, we must discard some of our ingrained habits of thought, especially our concept of the individual.

The individual is an abstract concept and as such has no place in a changeless society. Society has members, each of whom is capable of thinking and feeling; but, instead of being fundamentally similar, they are fundamentally different according to their station in life.

Just as the individual as an abstraction has no existence, so the social Whole exists not as an abstraction but as a concrete fact. The unity of a changeless society is comparable to the unity of an organism.

Members of a changeless society are like organs of a living body. They cannot live outside society, and within it there is only one position available to them: that which they occupy. The functions they fulfill determine their rights and duties. A peasant differs from a priest as greatly as the stomach from the brain. It is true that people have the ability to think and feel, but as their position in society is fixed, the net effect is not very different from what it would be if they had no consciousness at all.

The term "organic society" applies only to a society in which the analogy would never be thought of, and it becomes false the moment it is used. The fact that Menenius Agrippa found it necessary to propose it indicates that the established order was in trouble.

The unity of an organic society is anathema to another kind of unity, that of mankind. Since the traditional mode of thinking employs no abstract concepts, every relationship is concrete and particular. The fundamental similarity of one man to another and the inalienable rights of man are ideas of another age. The mere fact of being human has no rights attached to it: a slave is no different from another chattel in the eyes of the law. Privileges belong more to a position than to a person. For instance, in a feudal society the land is more important than the landlord; the latter derives his privileges only by virtue of the land he holds.

Rights and titles may be hereditary, but this does not turn them into private property. We may be inclined to consider private property as something very concrete; actually it is the opposite. To separate a relationship into rights and duties is already an abstraction; in its concrete form it implies both. The concept of private property goes even further; it implies absolute possession without any obligations. As such, it is diametrically opposed to the principle of organic society, in which every possession carries corresponding obligations. Indeed, private ownership of productive assets cannot be reconciled with organic society, because it would permit the accumulation of capital and introduce a potent source of change. Common ownership, by contrast, ensures that the property will be left unimproved, because every time a person invests his time and energy he bears all the costs but derives only a small part of the benefits. No wonder that the enclosure of common lands marks the beginning of modern agriculture.

Nor does organic society recognize justice as an abstract principle. Justice exists only as a collection of concrete rights and obligations. Nevertheless, the administration of law involves a certain kind of generalization. Except in a society that is so changeless as to be dead, each case differs in some detail from the previous one, and it is necessary to adapt the precedent in order to make it applicable. Without abstract principles to guide him, it depends upon the judge how he performs this task. There is at least a chance that the new decision will be in conflict with the precedent. Fortunately this need not cause any difficulties since the new ruling itself immediately becomes a precedent that can guide later decisions.

What emerges from such a process is common law, as opposed to legislative statutes. It is based on the unspoken assumption that the decisions of the past continue to apply indefinitely. The assumption is strictly speaking false, but it is so useful that it may continue to prevail long after society has ceased to be organic. The effective administration of justice requires that the rules be known in advance. In view of man's imperfect knowledge, legislation cannot foresee all contingencies, and precedents are necessary to supplement the statutes. Common law can function side by side with statute law because, in spite of the underlying assumption of changelessness, it can imperceptible adjust itself to changing circumstances. By the same token organic society could not survive the codification of its laws, because it would lose its flexibility. Once laws are codified the appearance of changelessness cannot be maintained and organic society disintegrates. Fortunately, the need to codify laws, draw up contracts, or record tradition in any permanent way is not very pressing as long as tradition is not threatened by alternatives.

The unity of organic society means that its members have no choice but to belong to it. It goes even further. It implies that they have no desire but to belong to it, for their interests and those of society are the same: they identify themselves with society. Unity is not a principle proclaimed by the authorities but a fact accepted by all participants. No great sacrifice is involved. One's place in society may be onerous or undignified, but it is the only one available; without it, one has no place in the world.

Nevertheless, there are bound to be people who do not abide by the prevailing mode of thinking. How society deals with such people is the supreme test of its adaptability. Repression is bound to be counterproductive because it provokes conflict and may encourage the evolution of alternative ways of thinking. Tolerance mixed with disbelief is probably the most effective answer. Craziness and madness in all its variety can be particularly useful in dealing with people who think differently, and primitive societies are noted for their tolerance of the mentally afflicted.

It is only when traditional ties are sufficiently loosened to enable people to change their relative positions within society by their own efforts that they come to dissociate their own interests from those of the Whole. When this happens, the unity of organic society falls apart, and everyone seeks to pursue his self-interest. Traditional relationships may be preserved in such circumstances, too, but only by coercion. That is no longer a truly organic society but one that is kept artificially changeless, like the Soviet system. The distinction is the same as that between the traditional and dogmatic modes of thinking, and to emphasize it I shall refer to this state of affairs as Closed Society.

The Critical Mode of Thinking

Abstractions

As long as people believe that the world is changeless, they can rest happily with the conviction that their view of the world is the only conceivable one. Tradition, however far removed from reality, provides guidance, and thinking need never move beyond the consideration of concrete situations.

In a changing world, however, the present does not slavishly repeat the past. Instead of a course fixed by tradition, people are confronted by an infinite range of possibilities. To introduce some order into an otherwise confusing universe they are obliged to resort to simplifications, generalizations, abstractions, causal laws, and all kinds of other mental aids.

Thought processes not only help to solve problems; they create their own. Abstractions open reality to different interpretations. Since they are only aspects of reality, one interpretation does not exclude all others: every situation has as many aspects as the mind discovers in it. If this feature of abstract thinking were fully understood, abstractions would create fewer problems. People would realize that they are dealing with a simplified image of the situation and not the situation itself. But even if everyone were fully versed in the intricacies of modern linguistic philosophy, the problems would not disappear, because abstractions play a dual role. In relation to the things they describe they represent aspects of reality without having a concrete existence themselves. For instance, the law of gravity does not make apples fall to the ground but merely explains the forces that do. In relation to the people who employ them, however, abstractions are very much a part of reality: by influencing attitudes and actions they have a major impact on events. For instance, the discovery of the law of gravity changed people's behavior. Insofar as people think about their own situation, both roles come into play simultaneously, and the situation becomes reflexive. Instead of a clear-cut separation between thoughts and reality, the infinite variety of a changing world is compounded by the infinite variety of interpretations that abstract thinking can produce.

Abstract thinking tends to create categories which contrast opposite aspects of the real world against each other. Time and Space; Society and the Individual; Material and Ideal are typical dichotomies of this kind. Needless to say, the models I am constructing here also belong to the collection. These categories are no more real than the abstractions that gave rise to them. That is to say, they represent a simplification or distortion of reality in the first place but, through their influence on people's thinking, may also introduce divisions and conflicts into the real world. They contribute to making reality more complex and abstractions more necessary. In this way the process of abstraction feeds on itself: the complexities of a changing world are, to a large extent, of man's own making.

In view of the complications, why do people employ abstract concepts at all? The answer is that they avoid them as much as possible. As long as the world can be regarded as changeless, they use no abstractions at all. Even when abstractions become indispensable, they prefer to treat them as part of reality rather than as the product of their own thinking. Only bitter experience will teach them to distinguish between their own thoughts and reality. The tendency to neglect the complications connected with the use of abstractions must be regarded as a weakness of the critical mode of thinking, because abstractions are indispensable to it, and the less they are understood, the greater confusion they create.

Despite their drawbacks, abstractions serve us well. It is true that they create new problems, but the mind responds to these with renewed efforts until thinking reaches degrees of intricacy and refinement that would be unimaginable in the traditional mode. A changing world does not lend itself to the kind of certainty that would be readily available if society were changeless, but in its less than perfect way thinking can provide much valuable knowledge. Abstractions generate an infinite variety of views; as long as a fairly effective method is available for choosing between them, the critical mode should be able to come much closer to reality than the traditional mode, which has only one interpretation at its disposal.

The Critical Process

Choosing between alternatives may then be regarded as the key function of the critical mode of thinking. How is this task performed?

First, since there is a divergence between thinking and reality, one set of explanations will fit a given situation better than another. All outcomes are not equally favorable; all explanations are not equally valid. Reality provides an inducement to choose and a criterion by which the choice may be judged. Second, since our understanding of reality is imperfect, the criterion by which choices may be judged is not fully within our grasp. As a result, people will not necessarily make the correct choice and, even if they do, not everybody will accept it as such. Moreover, the correct choice represents merely the better of the available alternatives, not the best of all possible solutions. New ideas and interpretations may emerge at any time. These are also bound to be flawed and may have to be discarded when the flaws become apparent. There is no final answer, only the possibility of a gradual approximation to it. It follows that the choice between alternatives involves a continuous process of critical examination rather than the mechanical application of fixed rules.

It is to emphasize these points that I speak of "the critical mode of thinking." The expression should not be taken to suggest that in a changing world everyone maintains an open mind. People may still commit themselves unreservedly to a particular view; but they cannot do so without at least being aware of alternatives. The traditional mode of thinking accepts explanations uncritically, but, in a changing society, no one can say "this is how things are, therefore they cannot be any other way." People must support their views with arguments. Otherwise they will convince no one but themselves, and to believe unconditionally in an idea rejected by everyone else is a form of madness. Even those who believe they have the final answer must take into account possible objections and defend themselves against criticism.

The critical mode of thinking is more than an attitude: it is a prevailing condition. It denotes a situation in which there are a large number of divergent interpretations; their proponents seek to gain acceptance for the ideas in which they believe. If the traditional mode of thinking represents an intellectual monopoly, the critical mode can be described as intellectual competition. This competition prevails regardless of the attitude of particular individuals or schools of thought. Some of the competing ideas are tentative and invite criticism; others are dogmatic and defy opposition. One could expect all thinking to embody a critical attitude only if people were completely rational—a contradiction of our basic premise.

Critical Attitude

It can be argued that a critical attitude is more appropriate to the circumstances of a changing world than a dogmatic one. Tentative opinions are not necessarily correct, and dogmatic ones need not be completely false. But a dogmatic approach can only lose some of its persuasive force when conflicting views are available: criticism is a danger, not a help. By contrast, a critical attitude can and does benefit from the criticism offered; the view held will be modified until no further valid objection can be raised. Whatever emerges from this rigorous treatment is likely to fulfill its purpose more effectively than the original proposition.

Criticism is basically unpleasant and hard to take. It will be accepted, if at all, only because it is effective. It follows that people's attitude greatly depends on how well the critical process functions; conversely, the functioning of the critical process depends on people's attitude. This circular, reflexive relationship is responsible for giving the critical mode of thinking its dynamic character, as opposed to the static permanence of the traditional mode.

What makes the critical process effective? To answer this question, we must recall the demarcation line between near-equilibrium and far-from-equilibrium conditions introduced previously. If there is a clear separation between thinking and reality, people have a reliable criterion for recognizing and correcting bias before it becomes too influential. But when the participating function is actively at work, bias and trend become hard to disentangle. Thus, the effectiveness of the critical process varies according to the subject matter and purpose of thinking. But even in those areas where the separation is not given by nature, it can be introduced by thinking.

Scientific Method

The critical process functions most effectively in natural science. Scientific method has been to develop its own rules and conventions on which all participants are tacitly agreed. These rules recognize that no individual, however gifted and honest, is capable of perfect understanding; theories must be submitted to critical examination by the scientific community. Whatever emerges from this interpersonal process will have reached a degree of objectivity of which no individual thinker would be capable.

Scientists adopt a thoroughly critical attitude not because they are more rational or tolerant than ordinary human beings but because scientific criticism is less easily disregarded than other forms: their attitude is more a result of the critical process than a cause of it. The effectiveness of scientific criticism is the result of a combination of factors. On the one hand, nature provides easily available and reliable criteria by which the validity of theories can be judged; on the other hand, there is a strong inducement to recognize and abide by these criteria: nature operates independently of our wishes, and we cannot utilize it to our benefit without first understanding how it works. Scientific knowledge not only serves to establish the truth; it also helps us in the business of living. People might have continued to live quite happily believing that the Earth was flat, despite Galileo's experiments. What rendered his arguments irresistible was the gold and silver found in America. The practical results were not foreseen: indeed, they would not have been achieved if scientific research had been confined to purely practical objectives. Yet they provided the supreme proof for scientific method: only because there is a reality, and because man's knowledge of it is imperfect, was it possible for science to uncover certain facets of reality whose existence people had not even imagined.

Outside the realm of natural phenomena the critical process is less effective. In metaphysics, philosophy, and religion the criteria are missing; in social science the inducement to abide by them is not so strong. Nature operates independently of our wishes; society, however, can be influenced by the theories that relate to it. In natural science theories must be true to be effective; not so in the social sciences. There is a shortcut: people can be swayed by theories. The urge to abide by the conventions of science is less compelling, and the interpersonal process suffers as a result. Theories seeking to change society may take on a scientific guise in order to exploit the reputation science has gained without abiding by its conventions. The critical process offers little protection, because the agreement on purpose is not as genuine as in the case of natural science. There are two criteria by which theories can be judged—truth and effectiveness—and they no longer coincide.

The remedy proposed by most champions of scientific method is to enforce the rules developed by natural science with redoubled vigor. Karl Popper has proposed the doctrine of the unity of science: the same methods and criteria apply in the study of both natural and social phenomena. As I have argued in *The Alchemy of Finance*, I consider the doctrine misguided. There is a fundamental difference between the two pursuits: the subject matter of the social sciences is reflexive in character, and reflexivity destroys the separation between statement and fact which has made the critical process so effective in the natural sciences. The very expression "social science" is a false metaphor; it would seem more appropriate to describe the study of social phenomena as alchemy, because the phenomena can be molded to the will of the experimenter in a way that natural substances cannot. Calling the social sciences alchemy would preserve the critical process better than the doctrine of the unity of science. It would acknowledge that the criteria of truth and effectiveness do not coincide, and it would prevent social theories from exploiting the reputation of natural science. It would open avenues of investigation that are currently blocked: differences in the subject matter would justify differences in approach. The social sciences have suffered immeasurably from trying to imitate the natural sciences too slavishly.

Democracy

Having abandoned the convention of objectivity, how are social theories to be judged? The artificial distinction between scientific theories, which purport to describe society as it is, and political ones, which seek to decide how it should be, disappears, leaving ample room for differences of opinion. The various views divide into two broad classes: one contains those that propose a fixed formula; the other makes the organization of society dependent on the decisions of its members. As we are not dealing with scientific theories, there is no objective way of deciding which approach is correct. It can be shown, however, that the latter represents a critical attitude, while the former does not.

Definitive social schemes assume that society is subject to laws other than those enacted by its members; moreover, they claim to know what those laws are. This makes them impervious to any positive contributions from the critical process. On the contrary, they must actively seek to suppress alternative views because they can command universal acceptance only by forbidding criticism and preventing new ideas from emerging—in short, by destroying the critical mode of thinking and arresting change. If, by contrast, people are allowed to decide questions of social organization for themselves, solutions need not be final: they can be reversed by the same process by which they were reached. Everyone is at liberty to express his or her views, and, if the critical process is working effectively, the view that eventually prevails may come close to representing the best interests of the participants. This is the principle of democracy.

For democracy to function properly, certain conditions must be met. They may be compared to those which have made scientific method so successful: in the first place there must be a criterion by which conflicting ideas can be judged, and in the second there must be a general willingness to abide by that criterion. The first prerequisite is provided by the majority vote as defined by the constitution, and the second by a belief in democracy as a way of life. A variety of opinions is not enough to create democracy; if separate factions adopt opposing dogmas the result is not democracy but civil war. People must believe in democracy as an idea; they must consider it more important that decisions be reached by constitutional means than to see their view prevail. This condition will be satisfied only if democracy does in fact produce a better social organization than a dictatorship would.

There is a circular relationship here: democracy can serve as an ideal only if it is effective, and it can be effective only if it is generally accepted as an ideal. This relationship has to evolve through a reflexive process in which the achievements of democracy reinforce democracy as an ideal and vice versa. Democracy cannot be imposed by edict.

The similarity with science is striking. The convention of objectivity and the effectiveness of scientific method are also mutually dependent on one another. Science relies on its discoveries to break the vicious circle: they speak more eloquently in its favor than any argument. Democracy, too, requires positive accomplishments to ensure its existence: an expanding economy, intellectual and spiritual stimulation, a political system that satisfies man's aspirations better than rival forms of government.

Democracy is capable of such achievements. It gives free rein to what may be called the positive aspect of imperfect knowledge, namely creativity. There is no way of knowing what that will produce; the unforeseen results may provide the best justification for democracy, just as they do for science. But progress is not assured. The positive contributions can come only from the participants. The results of their thinking cannot be predicted; they may or may not continue to make democracy a success. Belief in democracy as an ideal is a necessary but not a sufficient condition of its existence. This makes democracy as an ideal very tricky indeed. It cannot be enforced by eliminating rival views; its success cannot be guaranteed even by gaining universal acceptance for the ideal. Democracy simply cannot be assured, because it remains conditional on the creative energies of those who participate in it. Yet it must be regarded as an ideal if it is to prevail. Those who believe in it must put their faith in the positive aspect of imperfect knowledge and hope that it will produce the desired results.

The Quest for Certainty

Democracy as an ideal leaves something to be desired. It does not provide a definite program, a clear-cut goal, except in those cases where people have been deprived of it. Once people are free to pursue alternative goals, they are confronted by the necessity of deciding what their goals are. And that is where a critical attitude is less than totally satisfactory. It is generally assumed that people will seek to maximize their material well-being. That is true as far as it goes, but it does not go far enough. People have aspirations beyond material well-being. These may surface only after the material needs have been satisfied; but often they take precedence over narrow self-interest. One such aspiration is the creative urge. It is likely that material wealth is being pursued in modern Western society long after material needs have been filled exactly because the pursuit gratifies the creative urge. In other societies, wealth has ranked much lower in the hierarchy of values and the creative urge has found other means of expression. For instance, people in Eastern Europe care much more about poetry and philosophy than do people in the West.

There is another set of aspirations that the critical attitude is singularly ill-equipped to satisfy: the quest for certainty. Natural science can produce firm conclusions because it has an objective criterion at its disposal. Social science is on far shakier grounds, because reflexivity interferes with objectivity; when it comes to creating a dependable value system, a critical attitude is not much use at all. It is very difficult to base a value system on the individual. For one thing, individuals are subject to the ultimate in uncertainty, death. For another, they are part of the situation they have to cope with. Truly independent thought is an illusion. External influences, be it family, peer group, or merely the spirit of the age, are much more potent than one would care to admit.

Yet we need an independent set of values if the perils of disequilibrium are to be avoided.

The traditional mode of thinking meets the quest for certainty much more effectively than the critical mode. It draws no distinction between belief and reality: religion, or its primitive equivalent, animism, embraces the entire sphere of thought and commands unquestioning allegiance. No wonder people hanker after the lost paradise of primeval bliss! Dogmatic ideologies promise to satisfy that craving. The trouble is that they can do so only if they eliminate conflicting beliefs. This makes them almost as dangerous to democracy as the existence of alternative explanations is to the traditional mode of thinking.

The success of the critical mode of thinking in other areas may help to minimize the importance attached to dogmatic beliefs. There is an area of vital interest, namely, the material conditions of life, where positive improvement is possible. The mind tends to concentrate its efforts where they can produce results, neglecting questions of a less promising nature. That is why business takes precedence over poetry in Western society. As long as material progress can be maintained—and continues to be enjoyed—the influence of dogma can be contained.

Open Society

Perfect Competition

A perfectly changeable society seems difficult to imagine. Surely, society must have a permanent structure and institutions that ensure its stability. Otherwise, how could it support the intricate relationships of a civilization? Yet not only can the perfectly changeable society be postulated, but it has already been extensively studied in the theory of perfect competition. Perfect competition provides economic units with alternative situations that are only marginally inferior to the one they actually occupy. Should there be the slightest change in circumstances, they are ready to move; in the meantime their dependence on present

273

relationships is kept at a minimum. The result is a perfectly change-able society that may not be changing at all.

I am in fundamental disagreement with the theory of perfect com-petition, but I shall use it as my starting point, because it is relevant to the concept of a perfectly changeable society.

The theory assumes that there is a large number of units, each with perfect knowledge and mobility. Each unit has its own scale of preferences and is faced with a given scale of opportunities. Even a cursory examination shows that these assumptions are completely unrealistic. The lack of perfect knowledge is one of the starting points of this study, and of scientific method in general. Perfect mo-bility would negate fixed assets and specialized skills, both of which are indispensable to the capitalistic mode of production. The reason economists have tolerated such unacceptable assumptions for so long is that doing so produced results that were considered desirable in more ways than one. First, it established economics as a science com-parable in status with physics. The resemblance between the static equilibrium of perfect competition and Newtonian thermodynamics is no coincidence. Second, it proved the point that perfect competi-tion maximizes welfare.

In reality, conditions approximate those of perfect competition only when new ideas, new products, new methods, and new preferences keep people and capital on the move. Mobility is not perfect: it is not without cost to move. But people are on the move nevertheless, at-tracted by better opportunities or dislocated by changing circum-stances, and once they start moving they tend toward the more attractive opportunities. They do not have perfect knowledge but, being on the move, are aware of a larger number of alternatives than if they occupied the same position all their lives. They will object to other people taking their places, but, with so many opportunities com-ing up, their attachment to the existing situation is less strenuous, and they will be less able to align support from others who are actually or potentially in the same situation. As people move more often, they de-velop a certain facility in adjusting, which reduces the importance of any specialized skills they may have acquired. What we may call "effective mobility" replaces the unreal concept of perfect mobility, and the critical mode of thinking takes the place of perfect knowledge. The result is not perfect competition as defined in economics but a condition I shall call "effective competition." What sets is apart from perfect competition is that values and opportunities, far from being fixed, are constantly changing.

Should equilibrium ever be reached, the conditions of effective competition would cease to apply. Every unit would occupy a specific position, which would be less easily available to others for the simple reason that he would fight to defend it. Having developed special skills, moving would involve him in a loss.

He would resist any encroachment. If necessary, he would rather take a cut in remuneration than make a move, especially as he would then have to fight someone else's vested interest. In view of his entrenched position and the sacrifices he would be willing to make to defend it, an outsider would find it difficult to compete. Instead of almost unlimited opportunities, each unit would then be more or less tied to the existing arrangement. And, not being endowed with perfect knowledge, they might not even realize the opportunities they are missing. A far cry from perfect competition!

Instability

The differences with the classical analysis of perfect competition are worth pursuing. To some extent I have already done so in *The Alchemy of Finance,* but I did not present my argument as strongly there as I could have. I did not insist that there is a flaw in the very foundations of economic theory: it assumes that the demand and supply curves are independently given, and that is not necessarily the case. The shape of the demand curve may be altered by advertising or, even worse, may be influenced by price movements. That happens particularly in financial markets, where trend-following speculation is rampant. People are buying futures contracts not because they want to own the underlying commodity but because they want to make a profit on them. The same may be true of stocks, bonds, currencies, real estate, or even art. The prospects for profit depend not on the intrinsic value of the underlying objects but on the intentions of other people to buy and sell as expressed by the movement in prices.

According to economic theory, prices are determined by demand and supply. What happens to prices when the demand and supply curves are themselves influenced by price movements? The answer is that they are not determined at all. The situation is unstable, and in an unstable situation trend-following speculation is often the best strategy. Moreover, the more people adopt it, the more rewarding it becomes, because the trend in prices acts as an ever more important factor in determining the trend in prices. Price movements feed on themselves until prices become totally unrelated to intrinsic values. Eventually, the trend becomes unsustainable and a crash ensues. The history of financial markets is littered with such boom and bust sequences. This is far-from-equilibrium territory where the distinction between fundamentals and valuations is blurred, and instability reigns.

Clearly the contention that independently given supply and demand curves determine prices is not based on fact. On closer examination, it turns out to be a partially self-validating illusion, because its widespread acceptance can be helpful in fostering stability. Once it is recognized as an illusion, the task of maintaining stability in financial markets can get awfully complicated.

It can be seen that instability is an endemic problem in a market economy. Instead of equilibrium, the free play of market forces produces a never ending process of change in which excesses of one kind yield to those of another. Under certain conditions, particularly where credit is involved, the disequilibrium may become cumulative until a breaking point is reached.

This conclusion opens a Pandora's box. Classical analysis is based entirely on self-interest; but if the pursuit of self-interest does *not* lead to a stable system, the question arises whether individual self-interest is sufficient to ensure the survival of the system. The answer is a resounding "no." The stability of financial markets can be preserved only by some form of regulation. And once we make stability a policy objective, other worthy causes follow. Surely, in conditions of stability, competition must also be preserved. Public policy aimed at preserving stability and competition and who knows what else is at loggerheads with the principle of laissez faire. One of them must be wrong.

The nineteenth century can be invoked as an age in which laissez faire was the generally accepted and actually prevailing economic order in a large part of the world. Clearly, it was not characterized by the equilibrium claimed by economic theory. It was a period of rapid economic advance during which new methods of production were invented, new forms of economic organization were evolving, and the frontiers of economic activity were expanding in every direction. The old framework of economic controls had broken down; progress was so rapid that there was no time for planning it; developments were so novel that there was no known method of controlling them. The mechanism of the state was quite inadequate for taking on additional tasks; it was hardly in a position to maintain law and order in the swollen cities and on the expanding frontiers.

As soon as the rate of growth slowed down, the mechanisms of state regulation began to catch up with the requirements made on it. Statistics were collected, taxes were gathered, and some of the more blatant anomalies and abuses of free competition were corrected. As new countries embarked on a course of industrialization, they had the example of others before them. For the first time the state was in a position to exercise effective control over industrial development, and people were given a real choice between laissez faire and planning. As it happened, this marked the end of the gold age of laissez faire: protectionism came first, and other forms of state control followed later.

By the beginning of the twentieth century the state was in a position to set the rules by which the game was played. And when the instability of the financial markets led to a general breakdown of the banking system, causing the Great Depression of the 1930s, the state was ready to step into the breach.

The principle of laissez faire has enjoyed a strong revival in recent years. President Reagan invoked the magic of the marketplace, and Margaret Thatcher encouraged the survival of the fittest. Again, we are living in a period of rapid change, innovation, and instability. But the principle of laissez faire is just as flawed as it was in the nineteenth century.

The fact is that every social system, every human construct is flawed, and discovering the drawbacks of one arrangement ought not to be used to justify its opposite. Doing so is a common fault. One of the major lessons to be learned from recent experience is that narrow self-interest does not provide an adequate set of values for dealing with the policy issues confronting us today. We need to invoke broader values that relate to the survival of the system and not merely to the prosperity of the individual participant. This is a point to which I shall return when I consider the question of values.

Freedom

Effective competition does not produce equilibrium, but it does maximize the freedom of the individual by reducing his dependence on existing relationships. Freedom is generally regarded as a right or a series of rights—freedom of speech, of movement, of worship—enforced by law or the Constitution. This is too narrow a view. I prefer to give the word a wider meaning. I regard freedom as the availability of alternatives. If the alternatives to one's current situation are greatly inferior, or if moving involves great effort and sacrifice, people remain dependent on existing arrangements and are exposed to all kinds of restraints, insults, and exploitation. If they have alternatives at their disposal that are only marginally inferior, they are free from these pressures. Should pressure be applied, they merely move on. Freedom is then a function of people's ability to detach themselves from their existing positions. When the alternatives are only marginally inferior, freedom is maximized.

This is very different from the way people usually look at freedom, but then freedom is generally regarded as an ideal and not as a fact. As an ideal, freedom is generally associated with sacrifice. As a fact, it consists of being able to do what one wants without having to make sacrifices for it.

People who believe in freedom as an ideal may fight for it passionately, but they do not necessarily understand it. Since it serves them as an ideal, they tend to regard it as an unmitigated blessing. As a matter of fact, freedom is not devoid of undesirable aspects. When the sacrifices have borne fruit and freedom is accomplished, this may become more apparent than it was when freedom was only an ideal. The aura of heroism is dispelled, the solidarity based on a common ideal dissipated. What is left is a multitude of individuals, each pursuing his own self-interest as he perceives it. It may or may not coincide with the public interest. This is freedom as it is to be found in an open society, and it may seem disappointing to those who have fought for it.

Private Property

Freedom, as defined here, extends not only to human beings but to all other means of production. Land and capital can also be "free" in the sense that they are not tied to particular uses but are provided with marginally graduated alternatives. This is a prerequisite of the institution of private property.

Factors of production are always employed in conjunction with other factors, so that any change in the employment of one must have an influence on the others. As a consequence, wealth is never truly private; it impinges on the interests of others. Effective competition reduces the dependence of one factor upon another, and under the unreal assumptions of perfect competition the dependence disappears altogether. This relieves the owners of any responsibility toward other participants and provides a theoretical justification for regarding private property as a fundamental right.

It can be seen that the concept of private property needs the theory of perfect competition to justify it. In the absence of the unreal assumptions of perfect mobility and perfect knowledge, property carries with it not only rights but also obligations toward the community.

279

Effective competition also favors private ownership, but in a more qualified manner. The social consequences of individual decisions are diffuse, and adverse effects are cushioned by the ability of the affected factors to turn to alternatives. The social obligations associated with wealth are correspondingly vague and generalized, and there is much to be said for property being privately owned and managed, especially as the alternative of public ownership has worse drawbacks. But, in contrast to classical analysis, private ownership rights cannot be regarded as absolute, because competition is not perfect.

Social Contract

When freedom is a fact, the character of society is determined entirely by the decisions of its members. Just as in an organic society the position of the members could be understood only in relation to the Whole, now the Whole is meaningless by itself and can be understood only in terms of the individuals' decisions. It is to underscore this contrast that I use the term "open society." A society of this kind is likely to be open also in the more usual sense that people are able to enter and leave at will, but that is incidental to my meaning.

In a civilized society people are involved in many relationships and associations. While in organic society these are determined by tradition, in open society they are shaped by the decisions of the individuals concerned: they are regulated by written and unwritten contract. Contractual ties take the place of traditional ones.

Traditional relationships are closed in the sense that their terms and conditions are beyond the control of the interested parties. For instance, the inheritance of land is predetermined; so is the relationship between serf and landlord. Relationships are closed also in the sense that they apply only to those who are directly involved and do not concern anyone else. Contractual relationships are open in the sense that the terms are negotiated by the interested parties and can be altered by mutual agreement. They are also open in the sense that the contracting parties can be replaced by others. Contracts are often publicly known, and flagrant discrepancies between arrangements covering similar situations are corrected by competition.

In a sense, the difference between traditional and contractual relationships corresponds to that between concrete and abstract thought. While a traditional relationship applies only to those who are directly involved, the terms of a contract may be considered to have universal validity.

If relationships are determined by the participants, then membership in the various institutions that constitute civilized society ought also to be the subject of a contract. It is this line of reasoning that has led to the concept of a social contract. As originally expounded by Rousseau, the concept has neither theoretical nor historical validity. To define society in terms of a contract freely entered into by completely independent individuals would be misleading; and to attribute the historical genesis of civilized society to such a contract would be an anachronism. Nevertheless, Rousseau's concept pinpoints the essence of open society as clearly as Menenius Agrippa's allegory defined organic society.

Open society may be regarded as a theoretical model in which all relations are contractual in character. The existence of institutions with compulsory or limited membership does not interfere with this interpretation. Individual freedom is assured as long as there are several different institutions of roughly equal standing open to each individual so that he can choose which one to belong to. This holds true even if some of those institutions, such as the state, carry compulsory powers, and others, such as social clubs, limit their membership. The state cannot oppress individuals, because they can contract out by emigrating; social clubs cannot ostracize them, because they can contract in elsewhere.

Open society does not ensure equal opportunities to all. On the contrary, if a capitalistic mode of production is coupled with private property, there are bound to be great inequalities which, left to themselves, tend to increase rather than diminish. Open society is not necessarily classless; in fact, it is difficult—although not impossible—to imagine it as such. How can the existence of classes be reconciled with the idea of open society? The answer is simple. In open society classes are merely generalizations about social strata. Given the high level of social mobility, there can be no class consciousness of the kind Marx spoke about. His concept applies only to a closed society, and I shall discuss it more fully under that heading.

Brave New World

Let me try to carry the concept of an open society to its logical conclusion and describe what a perfectly changeable society would look like. Alternatives would be available in all aspects of existence: in personal relations, opinions and ideas, productive processes and materials, social and economic organization, and so on. In these circumstances, the individual would occupy a paramount position. Members of an organic society possess no independence at all; in a less than perfectly changeable society, established values and relationships still circumscribe people's behavior; but in a perfectly open society none of the existing ties are final, and people's relation to nation, family, and their fellows depends entirely on their own decisions. Looking at the reverse side of the coin, this means that the permanence of social relationships has disappeared; the organic structure of society has disintegrated to the point where its atoms, the individuals, float around without any roots.

How the individual chooses among the alternatives available to him or her is the subject matter of economics. Economic analysis therefore provides a convenient starting point. All that is necessary is to extend it. In a world in which every action is a matter of choice, economic behavior characterizes all fields of activity. That does not necessarily mean that people pay more attention to the possession of goods than to spiritual, artistic, or moral values, but merely that all values can be reduced to monetary terms. This renders the principles of the market mechanism relevant to such far-ranging areas as art, politics, social life, sex, and religion. Not everything that has value is subject to buying and

282

selling, because there are some values that are purely personal and therefore cannot be exchanged (e.g., maternal love), others that lose their value in the process of exchange (e.g,. reputation), and still others that it would be physically impossible or illegal to trade (e.g., the weather or political appointments). Still, in a perfectly changeable society the scope of the market mechanism would be extended to its utmost limit. Even where the operation of market forces is regulated by legislation, legislation itself would be the result of a process of haggling akin to economic behavior.

Choices arise that would not even have been imagined in an earlier age. Euthanasia, genetic engineering, and brainwashing become practical possibilities. The most complex human functions, such as thinking, may be broken down into their elements and artificially reproduced. Everything appears possible until it has been proved impossible.

Perhaps the most striking characteristic of a perfectly changeable society is the decline in personal relationships. What makes a relationship personal is that it is tied to a specific person. Friends, neighbors, husbands and wives would become, if not interchangeable, at least readily replaceable by only marginally inferior (or superior) substitutes; they would be subject to choice under competitive conditions. Parents and children would presumably remain fixed, but the ties that connect them may become less influential. Personal contact may altogether decline in importance as more efficient means of communication reduce the need for physical presence.

The picture that emerges is less than pleasing. As an accomplished fact, open society may prove to be far less desirable than it seems to those who regard it as an ideal. To put things in perspective, it should be remembered that any social system becomes absurd and intolerable if it is carried to its logical conclusion, be it More's *Utopia,* Defoe's imaginary countries, Huxley's *Brave New World,* or Orwell's *1984.*

The Question of Values

The great boon of open society, and the accomplishment that qualifies it to serve as an ideal, is the freedom of the individual. The most obvious attraction of freedom is a negative one: the absence of restraint. But freedom has a positive aspect, too, which is even more important. It allows people to learn to think for themselves, to decide what they want and to translate their dreams into reality. They can explore the limits of their capabilities and reach intellectual, organizational, artistic, and practical achievements that otherwise they might not have even suspected were attainable. That can be an intensely exciting and satisfying experience.

On the debit side, the paramount position enjoyed by individuals imposes a burden on them that at times may become unbearable. Where can they find the values they need to make all the choices that confront them? It is a contradiction in terms to expect an unattached individual to operate with a fixed set of values. Values are just as much a matter of choice as everything else. The choice may be conscious and the result of much heart-searching and reflection; it is more likely to be impulsive or based on family background, advice, advertising, or some other external influence. When values are changeable, changing them is bound to be an important part of business activities. Individuals have to choose their values under great external pressures.

If it were only a matter of choices about consumption there would be no great difficulty. When it comes to deciding which brand of cigarette to choose, the sensation of pleasure may provide adequate guidance—although even that is doubtful in light of the amounts spent on cigarette advertising. But a society cannot be built on the pleasure principle alone. Life includes pain, risks, dangers, and ultimately the prospect of death. If pleasure were the only standard, capital could not be accumulated, and many of the associations and institutions that go to make up society could not survive, nor could many of the discoveries, artistic and technical creations that form a civilization, be accomplished.

Deficiency of Purpose

When we go outside those choices that provide immediate satisfaction we find that open society suffers from what may be termed a "deficiency of purpose." By this I do not mean that no purpose can be found, but merely that it has to be sought and found by each individual for and in themselves.

It is this obligation that creates the burden I referred to. People may try to identify themselves with a larger purpose by joining a group or devoting themselves to an ideal. But voluntary associations do not have the same reassuringly inevitable quality as organic society. One does not belong as a matter of course but as a result of conscious choice, and it is difficult to commit oneself wholeheartedly to one particular group when there are so many to choose from. Even if one does, the group is not committed in return: there is constant danger of being rejected or left out.

The same applies to ideals. Religious and social ideals compete with each other so that they lack the inevitability that would enable people to accept them unreservedly. Allegiance to an ideal becomes as much a matter of choice as allegiance to a group. The individual remains separate; his adherence does not signify identity but a conscious decision. The consciousness of this act stands between the individual and the ideal adopted.

The need to find a purpose for and in themselves places individuals in a quandary. The individual is the weakest among all the units that go to make up society and has a shorter life span than most of the institutions that depend on him. On their own, individuals provide a very uncertain foundation on which to base a system of values sufficient to sustain a structure that will outlast them and which must represent a greater value in their eyes than their own life and welfare. Yet such a value system is needed to sustain open society.

The inadequacy of the individual as a source of values may find expression in different ways. Loneliness or feelings of inferiority, guilt, and futility may be directly related to a deficiency in purpose. Such psychic disturbances are exacerbated by people's tendency to hold themselves personally responsible for these feelings instead of putting their personal difficulties into a social context. Psychoanalysis is no help in this regard: whatever its therapeutic value, its excessive preoccupation with the individual tends to aggravate the problems it seeks to cure.

The problems of the burden individual consciousness become greater the more wealth and power he or she possesses. Someone who can hardly make ends meet cannot afford to stop and ask about the purpose of life. But what I have called the "positive aspect of imperfect knowledge" can be relied on to make open society affluent, so that the quandary is likely to present itself in full force. A point may be reached where even the pleasure principle is endangered: people may not be able to derive enough satisfaction from the results of their labor to justify the effort that goes into reaching them. The creation of wealth may provide its own justification as a form of creative activity; it is when it comes to the enjoyment of the fruits that signs of congestion tend to appear.

Those who are unable to find a purpose in themselves may be driven to a dogma that provides the individual with a ready-made set of values and a secure place in the universe. One way to remove the deficiency of purpose is to abandon open society. If freedom becomes an unbearable burden, closed society may appear as the salvation.

The Dogmatic Mode of Thinking

We have seen that the critical mode of thinking puts the burden of deciding what is right or wrong, true or untrue, squarely on the individual. Given the individual's imperfect understanding, there are a number of vital questions—notably those that concern the individuals' relation to the universe and his place in society—to which he or she cannot provide a final answer. Uncertainty is hard to bear, and the human mind is likely to go to great lengths to escape from it.

There is such an escape: the dogmatic mode of thinking. It consists in establishing as paramount a doctrine that is believed to originate from a source other than the individual. The source may be tradition or an ideology that has succeeded in gaining supremacy in competition with other ideologies. In either case, it is declared as the supreme arbiter over conflicting views. Those who conform are accepted, and those who are in conflict are rejected. There is no need to weigh alternatives: every choice is ready made. No question is left unanswered. The fearful specter of uncertainty is removed.

The dogmatic mode of thinking has much in common with the traditional mode. By postulating an authority that is the source of all knowledge, it attempts to retain or recreate the wonderful simplicity of a world in which the prevailing view is not subject to doubt or questioning. But it is exactly the lack of simplicity that differentiates it from the traditional mode. In the traditional mode, changelessness is a universally accepted fact; in the dogmatic mode, it is a postulate. Instead of a single universally accepted view, there are many possible interpretations but only one that is in accord with the postulate. The others must be rejected. What makes matters complicated is that the dogmatic mode cannot admit that it is making a postulate, because that would undermine the unquestionable authority that it seeks to establish. To overcome this difficulty, incredible mental contortions may be necessary. Try as it may, the dogmatic mode of thinking cannot recreate the conditions of simplicity which characterized the traditional mode. The essential point of difference is this: a genuinely changeless world can have no history. Once there is an awareness of conflicts past and present, precepts lose their inevitable character. This means that the traditional mode of thinking is restricted to the earliest stages of man's development. Only if people could forget their earlier history would a return to the traditional mode be possible.

A direct transition from the critical to the traditional mode can thus be ruled out altogether. If a dogmatic mode of thinking prevailed for an indefinite period, history might fade out gradually, but at the present juncture this does not deserve to be regarded as a practical possibility. The choice is only between the critical and the dogmatic modes.

The dogmatic mode of thinking tends to resort to a superhuman authority such as God or History, which reveals itself to mankind in one way or another. The revelation is the only and ultimate source of truth. While men, with their imperfect intellect, argue endlessly about the applications and implications of the doctrine, the doctrine itself continues to shine in its august purity. While observation records a constant flow of changes, the rule of the superhuman power remains undisturbed. This device maintains the illusion of a well-defined permanent world order in the face of much evidence that would otherwise discredit it. The illusion is reinforced by the fact that the dogmatic mode of thinking, if successful, tends to keep social conditions unchanging. Yet even at its most successful, the dogmatic mode does not possess the simplicity that was the redeeming feature of the traditional mode.

The traditional mode of thinking dealt entirely with concrete situations. The dogmatic mode relies on a doctrine that is applicable to all conceivable conditions. Its tenets are abstractions which exist beyond, and often in spite of, direct observation. The use of abstractions brings with it all the complications from which the traditional mode was exempt. Far from being simple, the dogmatic mode of thinking can become even more complex than the critical mode. This is hardly surprising. To maintain the assumption of changelessness without admitting that an assumption has been made, is a distortion of reality. One must go through complicated contortions to achieve a semblance of credibility, and must pay heavy penalties in terms of mental effort and strain. Indeed, it would be difficult to believe that the human mind is capable of such self-deception if history did not provide examples. It appears that the mind is an instrument that can resolve any self-generated contradiction by creating new contradictions somewhere else. This tendency is given free rein in the dogmatic mode of thinking, because, as we have seen, its tenets are exposed to minimum contact with observable phenomena.

With all efforts devoted to resolving internal contradictions, the dogmatic mode of thinking offers little scope for improving the available body of knowledge. It cannot admit direct observation as evidence because in case of a conflict the authority of dogma would be undermined. It must confine itself to applying the doctrine. This leads to arguments about the meaning of words, especially those of the original revelation—sophistic, talmudic, theological, ideological discussions, which tend to create new problems for every one they resolve. Since thinking has little or no contact with reality, speculation tends to become more convoluted and unreal the further it proceeds. How many angels can dance on the head of a needle?

What the actual contents of a doctrine are depends on historical circumstances and cannot be made the subject of generalizations. Tradition may provide part of the material, but in order to do so it must undergo a radical transformation. The dogmatic mode of thinking requires universally applicable statements, which tradition was originally couched in concrete terms. It must now be generalized in order to make it relevant to a wider range of events than it was destined for. How this can be accomplished is clearly demonstrated by the growth of languages. One of the ways in which a language adjusts itself to changing circumstances is by using in a figurative sense words that originally had only a concrete connotation. The figurative meaning retains only one characteristic aspect of the concrete case and may then be applied to other concrete cases which share that characteristic. The same method is used by preachers who take as their text a piece of narrative from the Bible.

A doctrine may also incorporate ideas originating in an open society. Every philosophical and religious theory offering a comprehensive explanation for the problems of existence has the makings of a doctrine; all it needs is unconditional acceptance and universal enforcement. The originator of a comprehensive philosophy may not have intended to put forth a doctrine that is to be unconditionally accepted and universally enforced, but personal inclinations have little influence on the development of ideas. Once a theory becomes the sole source of knowledge, it assumes certain characteristics which prevail irrespective of its original intention.

Since the critical mode of thinking is more powerful than the traditional mode, ideologies developed by critical thinking are more likely to serve as the basis of dogma than tradition itself. Once established, they may take on a traditional appearance. If language is flexible enough to permit the figurative use of concrete statements, it can also lend itself to the reverse process, and abstract ideas can be personified. The Old Testament God is a case in point, and Frazer's *Golden Bough* offers many other examples. We may find in practice that what we call tradition incorporates many products of critical thinking translated into concrete terms.

The primary requirement of dogma is to be all-embracing. It must provide a yardstick by which every thought and action can be measured. If one could not evaluate everything in its light, one would have to cast around for other methods of distinguishing between right and wrong; such a search would destroy the dogmatic mode of thinking. Even if the validity of the dogma were not attacked directly, the application of other criteria would tend to undermine its authority. If a doctrine is to fulfill its function as the foundation of all knowledge, its supremacy must be asserted in every field. It may not be necessary to refer to it all the time: the land can be cultivated, pictures painted, wars fought, rockets launched, each in its own fashion. But whenever an idea or action comes into conflict with a doctrine, the doctrine must be given precedence. In this way, even larger areas of human activity may come under its control.

The other main characteristic of dogma is its rigidity. The traditional mode of thinking is extremely flexible. As tradition is timeless, any alteration is immediately accepted not only in the present but as something that has existed since time immemorial. Not so the dogmatic mode. Its doctrines provide a yardstick by which thoughts and actions are to be judged. Hence they must be permanently fixed, and no amount of transgression can justify a change. If there is a departure from the norm, it must be corrected at once. The dogma itself must remain inviolate.

In the light of our inherently imperfect understanding, it is clear that new developments may clash with established doctrines or create internal contradictions in unforeseen ways. Any change represents a potential threat. To minimize the danger, the dogmatic mode of thinking tends to inhibit new departures both in thinking and in action. It does so not only by eliminating unregulated change from its own view of the universe but also by actively suppressing unregulated thoughts and actions. How far it will go in this direction depends on the extent to which it is attacked.

In contrast with the traditional mode of thinking, the dogmatic mode is inseparably linked with some form of compulsion. Compulsion is necessary to ensure the supremacy of dogma over actual and potential alternatives. Every doctrine is liable to raise questions that do not resolve themselves by mere contemplation; in the absence of an authority that defines the doctrine and defends its purity, the unity of the dogmatic view is bound to break up into conflicting interpretations. The most effective way to deal with this problem is to charge a human authority with interpreting the will of the superhuman power from which the validity of doctrines is derived. Its interpretations may evolve with time and, if the authority operates efficiently, prevailing doctrines can keep pace with changes occurring in reality to a considerable extent. But no innovation not sanctioned by the authority can be tolerated, and the authority must have sufficient power to eliminate conflicting views.

There may be circumstances in which the authority need have little recourse to force. As long as the prevailing dogma fulfills its function of providing an all-embracing explanation, people will tend to accept it without question. After all, the dogma enjoys monopoly: while there may be various views available on particular issues, when it comes to reality as a whole there is only one view in existence. People are brought up under its aegis and are trained to think in its terms: it is more natural for them to accept than to question it.

Yet when internal contradictions develop into ever more unrealistic debates, or when new events occur that do not fit in with established explanations, people may begin to question the foundations. When this happens, the dogmatic mode of thinking can be sustained only by force. The use of force is bound to have a profound influence on the evolution of ideas. Thinking no longer develops along its own lines

291

but becomes intricately interwoven with power politics. Particular thoughts are associated with particular interests, and the victory of an interpretation depends more on the relative political strength of its proponents than on the validity of the arguments marshaled in its support. The human mind becomes a battlefield of political forces, and, conversely, doctrines become weapons in the hands of warring factions.

The supremacy of a doctrine can thus be prolonged by means that have little to do with the validity of arguments. The greater the coercion employed to maintain a dogma in force, the less likely it is to satisfy the needs of the human mind. When finally the hegemony of a dogma is broken, people are likely to feel that they have been liberated from terrible oppression. Wide new vistas are opened, and the abundance of opportunities engenders hope, enthusiasm, and tremendous intellectual activity.

It can be seen that the dogmatic mode of thinking fails to recreate any of the qualities that made the traditional mode so attractive. It turns out to be convoluted, rigid, and oppressive. True, it eliminates the uncertainties that plague the critical mode, but only at the cost of creating conditions that the human mind would find intolerable if it were aware of any alternatives. Just as a doctrine based on a superhuman authority may provide an avenue of escape from the shortcomings of the critical mode, the critical mode itself may appear as the salvation to those who suffer from the oppression of a dogma.

Closed Society

Organic society presents some very attractive features to the observer: a concrete social unity, an unquestioned belonging, an identification of each member with the collective. Members of an organic society would hardly consider this an advantage, ignorant as they are that the relationship could be any different; only those who are aware of a conflict between the individual and the social Whole in their own society are likely to regard organic unity as a desirable goal. In other words, the attractions of organic society are best appreciated when the conditions required for its existence no longer prevail.

It is hardly surprising that throughout history mankind should have shown a yearning to return to its original state of innocence and bliss. The expulsion from the Garden of Eden is a recurrent theme. But innocence, once lost, cannot be regained—except perhaps by forgetting every experience. In any attempt to recreate artificially the conditions of an organic society, it is precisely the unquestioning and unquestionable identification of all members with the society to which they belong that is the most difficult to achieve. In order to re-establish organic unity it is necessary to proclaim the supremacy of the collective. The result, however, will differ from organic society in one vital respect: individual interests, instead of being identical with those of the collective, become subordinated to them.

The distinction between personal and public interest raises a disturbing question as to what the public interest really is. The common interest must be defined, interpreted, and, if necessary, enforced over conflicting personal interests. This task is best performed by a living ruler, because he or she can adjust his or her policies to the circumstances. If it is entrusted to an institution, it is likely to be performed in a cumbersome, inflexible, and ultimately ineffective manner. The institution will seek to prevent changes, but in the long run it cannot succeed.

However the common interest is defined in theory, in practice it is likely to reflect the interest of the rulers. It is they who proclaim the supremacy of the Whole, and it is they who impose its will on recalcitrant individuals. Unless one assumes that they are totally selfless, it is also they who benefit from it. The rulers are not necessarily furthering their selfish ends as individuals, but they do benefit from the existing system as a class: by definition, they are the class that rules. Since the membership of classes is clearly defined, the subordination of the individual to the social Whole amounts to the subordination of one class to another. Closed society may therefore be described as a society based on class exploitation. Exploitation may occur in open society as well, but, since the position of the individual is not fixed, it does not operate on a class basis. Class exploitation in Marx's sense can exist only in a closed society. Marx made a valuable contribution when he established the concept, just as Menenius Agrippa did when he compared society with an organism. Both of them, however, applied it to the wrong kind of society.

If the avowed aim of a closed society is to ensure the supremacy of one class (or race or nationality) over another, it may fulfill its purpose effectively. But if its aim is to bring back the idyllic conditions of an organic society, it is bound to fail. There is a gap between the ideal of social unity and the reality of class exploitation. To bridge the gap, an elaborate set of explanations is needed, which is, by definition, at variance with the facts.

Getting the ideology universally accepted is the prime task of the ruling authority and the criterion of its success. The more widely an ideology is accepted, the smaller the conflict between the collective interest and the policies actually pursued, and vice versa. At its best, an authoritarian system can go a long way toward re-establishing the calm and harmony of organic society. More commonly, some degree of coercion has to be employed, and then this fact must be explained away by tortuous arguments, which render the ideology less convincing, requiring the use of further force until, at its worst, the system is based on compulsion and its ideology bears no resemblance to reality.

I have some reservations about the distinction that Jeane Kirkpatrick has drawn between authoritarian and totalitarian regimes, because she used it to distinguish between America's friends and enemies, but there is a point to it. An authoritarian regime devoted to maintaining itself in power can admit more or less openly what it is about. It may limit the freedom of its subjects in various ways, it may be aggressive and brutal, but it need not extend its influence over every aspect of existence in order to preserve its hegemony. On the other hand, a system that claims to serve some ideal of social justice needs to cover up the reality of class exploitation. This requires control over the thoughts of its subjects, not merely their actions, and renders its constraining influence much more pervasive.

The Soviet system is the prime example of a closed society based on a universal idea. But a closed society need not embody a universal idea; it may be confined to a particular group or nation. In a way, a more narrow definition is closer to the spirit of an organic society than a dogma that applies to all of humanity. After all, a tribe is concerned only with its members. Now that communism is dead, those who hanker after the security and solidarity of an organic society are more likely to look for it in an ethnic or religious community. As I have explained earlier, those who reject communism oppose it either because it is closed or because it is universal; the alternatives are either open society or fundamentalism of one kind or another. Fundamental beliefs are less easy to justify by rational argument, but they may have greater emotional appeal exactly because they are more primitive.

When we speak of fundamentalism, Islamic fundamentalism springs to mind, but we can observe the reawakening of fundamentalist tendencies throughout the erstwhile communist bloc. They combine national and religious elements. They do not have fully developed ideologies—indeed, they are not fully articulate—but draw their inspiration from a nebulous past. The struggle between the concepts of open and closed society has not come to an end with the collapse of communism. It is merely taking a different form. The mode of thinking currently associated with the concept of a closed society is probably better described as traditional than dogmatic, although, if the concept of a closed society prevails, the formulation of the appropriate dogmas will probably not lag far behind. In the case of Islamic fundamentalism it is already fully formed. In the case of Russian fundamentalism the groundwork has also been laid.*

---

* See Alexander Yanov, *The Russian Challenge* (Oxford: Basil Blackwell, 1987).

Prospect for
European Disintegration

The following is the transcript of a speech delivered at the invitation of the Aspen Institute of Berlin on September 29, 1993.

T he European Community is a highly desirable form of organization. Indeed, in some ways it is the ideal of an open society, because it has a very interesting feature: all the participating states are in a minority. Respect for the minority is the basis of its construction, and that is also a basis of an open society. The unresolved question is: How much power should be delegated to the majority? How far should Europe be integrated?

The way Europe evolves will have a profound influence on what happens to the east of Europe. The societies devastated by communism cannot make the transition to an open society on their own. They need a Europe that is open and receptive and supportive of their effort. East Germany got too much help, the rest of Eastern Europe is getting too little. I am deeply engaged in helping the rest of Eastern Europe. As you may know, I have set up a network of foundations devoted to this cause, and that is the bias that I bring to the subject of Europe.

I have made a particular study of what I call the "boom/bust sequence," which can be observed from time to time in financial markets; and I think it is also applicable to the integration and disintegration of the European Community. Since the revolution of 1989 and the re-unification of Germany, Europe has been in a condition of dynamic disequilibrium. Therefore it presents a very interesting case study for my theory of history.

I am myself a participant in this process of dynamic disequilibrium because I am an international investor. I used to call myself a speculator and I used to joke that an investment is a speculation that has gone wrong but, in view of the campaign against speculators, I am no longer amused. International investors did play an important role in the breakdown of the exchange rate mechanism, but it is impossible to have a common market without international capital movements. To blame speculators is like shooting the messenger.

I shall deal here with the subject of Europe's disequilibrium on the basis of my theory of history. The fact that I am also a participant does not interfere with my ability to apply the theory. On the contrary, it has allowed me to test the theory in practice. Nor does it matter that I bring a particular bias to the subject because it is part of my theory that participants in a historical process always act on the basis of a bias. And, of course, the same rule applies to the proponents of theories.

But I must confess that my particular bias—namely, that I want to see a united, prosperous, and open Europe—does interfere with my activities as a participant in financial markets. I had no problem as long as I was an anonymous participant. Sterling would have left the ERM whether or not I speculated against it. But, after sterling left the ERM, I received a lot of publicity and I ceased to be an anonymous participant. I became a guru. I could actually influence the behavior of markets, and it would be dishonest of me to pretend otherwise. This has created opportunities and imposed responsibilities. Given my bias, I did not want to be responsible for the French franc being pushed out of the exchange rate mechanism. I decided to abstain from speculating against the franc in order to be able to put forward a constructive solution; but nobody thanked me for it. Indeed, my public utterances seemed to annoy the monetary authorities even more than my activities in the financial markets, so I can't say I am doing well in my newfound role of guru. Nevertheless, given my bias, I must say what I am going to say, even if it is inconvenient for me as a participant.

In commenting on the boom/bust process of European integration, I shall pay particular attention to the exchange rate mechanism which is playing such a crucial role in the process. It had worked perfectly well in near-equilibrium conditions, until the reunification of Germany. But the reunification has created conditions of dynamic disequilibrium. Since that time, the course of events has been shaped by mistakes and misunderstandings. The most tangible result is the disintegration of the exchange rate mechanism which, in turn, is an important factor in the possible disintegration of the European Community.

Let me start at the point where near-equilibrium conditions were replaced by a condition of dynamic disequilibrium. This point can be fixed in time with great precision: it was the fall of the Berlin Wall. This opened the way to German reunification. Chancellor Kohl rose to the historic occasion. He decided that reunification must be complete, immediate, and achieved in a European context. Actually, he had no choice in the matter, since the German constitution gave East Germans citizenship of Germany and Germany was a member of the European Community. But it makes all the difference whether you take charge of events or merely react to them. Chancellor Kohl exhibited real leadership. He went to President Mitterand and said to him, in effect, "I need your support and the support of Europe to achieve immediate and complete reunification." The French replied, in effect, "Let's create a stronger Europe in which the reunified Germany can be fully embedded." This gave a tremendous impulse toward integration. It set into motion the "boom" part of the boom/bust process. The British were opposed to the creation of a strong central authority; you will recall Margaret Thatcher's speech at Bruges. Tough negotiations ensued, but there was a sense of urgency, a self-imposed deadline. The result was the Treaty of Maastricht, whose two main goals were to establish a common currency and a common foreign policy. It had a number of other provisions, but they were less important and, when the British objected, they were allowed to opt out of some of them. All in all, the Treaty was a giant step forward toward integration, a valiant attempt to create a Europe strong enough to cope with the revolutionary changes resulting from the collapse of the Soviet empire. It went, perhaps, further and faster than public opinion was prepared for; but that was a chance that the leaders took in order to cope with the revolutionary situation. Rightly so, in my opinion, because that is what leadership entails.

The trouble lay elsewhere. I shall not dwell on a side deal in which Germany got the agreement of the European Community to recognize Croatia and Slovenia as independent states. It was little discussed and little noticed at the time, but it had horrendous consequences. I want to focus on the internal disequilibrium in Germany which was generated by the reunification because it was that disequilibrium which has turned the boom into a bust.

The German government seriously underestimated the cost of reunification and was, in any case, unwilling to pay the full cost through higher taxation or a reduction of other government expenditures. This created tensions between the Bundesbank and the government on two levels: one was that the government acted against the express advice of the Bundesbank; the other was that a very loose fiscal policy—that is to say, a huge budget deficit—required a very tight monetary policy in order to reestablish monetary equilibrium. The injection of purchasing power through the exchange of East German currency at par created an inflationary boom, and the fiscal deficit added fuel to the fire. The Bundesbank was charged, by law, with the mission of maintaining the value of the Deutschemark and it acted with alacrity. It raised the repo rate to 9.70 percent. But that policy was very harmful to the other member countries of the European monetary system. In other words, the monetary policy which was designed to reestablish equilibrium at home created a disequilibrium within the European monetary system. It took some time for the disequilibrium to develop but, with the passage of time, the tight monetary policy imposed by the Bundesbank pushed all of Europe into the deepest recession it has experienced since the Second World War. The Bundesbank plays a dual role: it is the guardian of sound money at home and it is the anchor of the European monetary system. It acted as the transmission mechanism for turning the internal disequilibrium of the German economy into a force for the disintegration of the European monetary system.

There was also a third and deeper level of conflict between the Bundesbank and the German government. Chancellor Kohl, in order to obtain French support for German reunification, entered into the Treaty of Maastricht. That Treaty posed a profound threat to the institutional dominance, indeed, institutional survival, of the Bundesbank as the arbiter of European monetary policy. In the European monetary system, the German mark serves as the anchor. But, under the Maastricht Treaty, the role of the Bundesbank was to be replaced by a European Central Bank in which the Bundesbank would only have one vote out of twelve. Admittedly, the European Central Bank was based on the German model; but it makes all the difference in the world whether you serve as the model or whether you are actually in charge. The Bundesbank never openly acknowledged that it was opposed to this institutional change, and it remains unclear to what extent its actions were designed to prevent it. All I can tell you is that, as a market participant, I acted on the hypothesis that it was the Bundesbank's underlying motivation. I cannot prove to you that my hypothesis was correct; all I can say is that it worked.

For instance, I listened to Helmut Schlesinger, President of the Bundesbank, warn that the markets are mistaken when they think that the ECU consists of a *fixed* basket of currencies. I asked him what he thought of the ECU as the future common currency of Europe. He said he would like it better if it were called the mark. I was guided accordingly. Shortly thereafter, the lira was forced out of the ERM.

I don't want to get into a blow-by-blow account of what happened because I want to establish a broad historical perspective. From that perspective, the salient features are that the Maastricht referendum was defeated in Denmark; it passed with a very narrow margin in

France; and it barely squeaked through Parliament in Britain. The European exchange rate mechanism has, for all intents and purposes, broken down and it has done so in several installments, of which the last one, namely, the broadening of the band in August, was the most far-reaching because it loosened the strongest tie within the European Community, the one which ties Germany and France together. What is in the long run even more important, Europe is in the midst of a deep recession from which there is no immediate prospect of recovery. Unemployment is a serious and still-growing problem which continues to be aggravated by monetary policies which are far too restrictive for this stage of the cycle. From these observations I conclude that the trend toward the integration of Europe has passed its peak and has now been reversed.

The exact moment of reversal can be identified as the defeat in the Danish referendum. It could have brought forth a groundswell of support for the Maastricht Treaty; in that case, there would have been no reversal. Instead, it generated the breakdown of the exchange rate mechanism. Europe is now in a process of disintegration. Since we are dealing with a boom/bust process, it is impossible to say how far it will go. But it may go much further than people are currently willing or able to envisage because a boom/bust process is self-reinforcing in both directions.

I can identify at least five elements which are mutually self-reinforcing. First and foremost is the recession; 11.7 percent unemployment in France, 14.1 percent in Belgium, and 22.25 percent in Spain, are simply not acceptable. They generate social and political unrest which is easily channelled in an anti-European direction. Second, there is the progressive disintegration of the exchange rate mechanism. This is very dangerous because in the medium to long term the Common Market cannot survive without stability in exchange rates.

The ERM functioned perfectly well in near-equilibrium conditions for more than a decade. But the reunification of Germany has revealed a fundamental flaw in the mechanism, namely, that the Bundesbank plays a dual role: guardian of domestic monetary stability and anchor of the European monetary system. As long as the two roles are in harmony, there is no problem. But when there was a conflict, the Bundesbank gave precedence to domestic considerations, to the detriment of its international obligations. This was clearly demonstrated, for instance, on Thursday, July 29, when it refused to lower the discount rate in order to relieve the pressure on the French franc. It can be argued that the Bundesbank has no choice in the matter: it is obliged by law, the Grundgesetz, to give absolute priority to the preservation of the value of the German currency. In that case, there is an irreconcilable conflict between the ERM and the Grundgesetz.

This episode revealed another fundamental flaw in the ERM, namely, that there is an asymmetry between the obligations of the anchor currency and the currency which is under pressure. All the obligations fall on the weak currency. It will be recalled that, at the time of the Bretton Woods agreement, John Maynard Keynes emphasized the need for symmetry between the strong and the weak. He based his arguments on the experiences of the interwar period. The current situation is increasingly reminiscent of that period and sometimes it seems as if Keynes had not lived.

This brings me to the third element, namely, mistaken economic and monetary policies. Here it is not so much the Bundesbank that is to blame but those who have opposed it, like the German government, or those who have been the victims of its policy, like the United Kingdom and France. The German government is, of course, responsible for creating the internal disequilibrium in the first place. The British committed an egregious error in joining the exchange rate mechanism on October 8, 1990, after the reunification of Germany. They did so on the basis of arguments which had been developed in 1985, but were strenuously resisted by Margaret Thatcher. When her position weakened she finally gave in but, by that time, the arguments which had been valid in 1985 were no longer applicable. So the British made two mistakes—one in 1985 and one in 1990.

They were particularly hard hit by the high interest rate regime imposed on them by the Bundesbank because they were already in a recession when they went into the ERM. Being pushed out of the ERM brought them much-needed relief. They ought to have welcomed it, but they were too dazed to react. They did the right thing eventually and lowered interest rates, but they failed to seize the initiative. This has made it harder to build up confidence and it will make it much harder to reassert control over wages when the economy does pick up.

One would have thought the French would learn from the British experience. But they are proving even more inflexible. One could sympathize with their efforts to defend the franc fort policy because they fought so long and so hard to establish it, and they were on the verge of reaping the benefits in the form of improved competitiveness vis-à-vis Germany when the reward was snatched from their hands by recurrent attacks on the franc. But, once the franc fort policy proved untenable, they ought to have adjusted their approach to the new situation. Instead, they are sticking voluntarily with a regime which proved so disastrous when it was imposed on them by the ERM. I think I understand their motivation: they are concerned with rebuilding their reserves and repaying the debt that the Banque de France incurred with the Bundesbank in defending the parity. But they got their priorities wrong. France is in a serious recession and it needs to lower interest rates. That is what brought on the August crisis. To try and keep the French franc close to the Deutschemark by keeping interest rates high is self-defeating. The only way to have a strong franc is to have a strong economy.

The Bundesbank itself has been remarkably consistent in the pursuit of its objectives, especially if we include institutional self-preservation among those objectives, and amazingly successful. It found itself in an impossible situation after the reunification of Germany: a sudden increase in the stock of money, an enormous budget deficit, and a threat to its institutional survival. Yet it came out victorious. Whether it was worth the cost—a Europe—wide recession and the breakdown of the ERM—is another question. A few months ago I was convinced that the Bundesbank was following the wrong monetary policy, even for domestic purposes, because Germany was in a recession and monetary policy ought to be countercyclical. The Bundesbank stuck to its medium-term monetary targets, but I thought that M3—which had worked well as a target in near-equilibrium conditions—had been rendered irrelevant in today's far-from-equilibrium conditions; and I thought that the Bundesbank had overstayed its course in following a tight monetary policy.

But that was before the widening of the bands in the ERM. Since then, the Deutschemark has rallied, the German long bonds have strengthened, and, on top of it all, the German economy is showing some signs of strength. I must now admit that I may have been wrong and the Bundesbank may have been successful in its pursuit of its domestic policy goals. But, if anything, that strengthens my argument that there is a conflict of interest between the domestic responsibilities of the Bundesbank and its role as the anchor of the European monetary system. The events of the last two months have clearly demonstrated that the needs of Germany and the rest of Europe are very different. Germany needs low interest rates on *long* bonds because it borrows at the long end, whereas the rest of Europe needs lower interest rates at the *short* end because the liquidity of the banking system needs to be rebuilt and lower short-term rates are needed to stimulate economic activity. Germany got what it needs, but the rest of Europe did not.

The fact that I may have been wrong on the Deutschemark brings me to the fourth factor. It is not only the authorities who make mistakes, but also market participants. Markets are often wrong. Specifically, they were wrong when they assumed that the path to a common currency would follow a straight line. International investors, particularly managers of international bond funds, went for the highest yields, ignoring exchange rate risks. Helmut Schlesinger was right in warning that the ECU does not consist of a fixed basket of currencies. There had been large capital movements into weak-currency countries like Italy, Spain and Portugal. The movement was initially self-reinforcing but eventually self-defeating. It created excessive rigidity in exchange rates in the first place, and excessive instability in the second. The errors of the market compounded the errors of the authorities in creating dynamic disequilibrium.

Finally, there is a fifth factor that contributes to the disequilibrium. It has to do with attitudes. Events of the last year have administered a number of shocks to a number of countries and it is engendering an atmosphere of recrimination and resentment. There would be good reason for the French to draw closer together with the British and the Spanish and the Italians; but the events of the last year have driven them further apart. The commitment to the Franco-German alliance is still the cornerstone of French policy and it is deeply felt in France; but it is under tremendous strain, and the strain is likely to increase even further if economic conditions continue to deteriorate.

I am less familiar with conditions in Germany, but I can foresee a generational change coming. The present generation is still obsessed with the guilt of its fathers and is determined to be good Europeans. I was very impressed, in 1990, when Egon Bahr said at a conference here in Berlin, in all seriousness, that Germany has no foreign policy other than a European foreign policy. How much conditions have changed since then! It would be only natural if the new generation rejected the guilt feelings of its fathers and became more unabashed in its pursuit of the national interest. In this context, it should be noted that a strong Deutschemark has become a prime symbol of German national identity.

The British have always been rather suspicious of Germany. I used to tell them that the Germans are much better Europeans than the British, but now they can point to the recognition of Croatia and Slovenia and to the actions of the Bundesbank and argue that they were right in the first place.

There is also a sixth element which needs to be considered; namely, the instability of Eastern Europe and particularly of the former Yugoslavia. I believe that this factor is working in the opposite direction. The threat of instability and the influx of refugees are good reasons for banding together and building a "Fortress Europe." At the same time, the lack of unity in the European Community has the effect of reinforcing the political instability and economic decline in Eastern Europe. The outcome is going to be a European Community which is a far cry from the open society to which the people whom I support in Eastern Europe aspire.

All this is truly disturbing and depressing. I realize that I sound more like a prophet of gloom and doom than a guru. But let me remind you that there is nothing determinate about the boom/bust sequence; that the direction of the process can be reversed practically at any time. Indeed, a reversal of direction is an essential part of a boom/bust sequence. What I am trying to say is that events are now going in the wrong direction and they will continue to go in that direction until we recognize that there is something fundamentally wrong and we take resolute action to correct it.

There can be no doubt that there is something fundamentally wrong with the European monetary system as it is currently constituted. First, the domestic obligations of the Bundesbank have proven to be irreconcilable with its role as the anchor currency; indeed, one could argue that the Bundesbank has exploited its role as the anchor currency in order to solve its domestic problems. Second, there is an asymmetry between the obligations of the strong and the weak currencies. And most importantly, there is asymmetry between the risks and rewards of international investors, that is to say, speculators. These structural faults were there from the beginning but they only became apparent in the course of the last year. Once they became known, it is impossible to return to the conditions which prevailed previously. The best way to eliminate the faults of the ERM is to have no exchange rate mechanism at all. But freely floating exchange rates would destroy the Common Market. Hence the necessity for a common currency. That means implementing the Maastricht Treaty. At the time the treaty was negotiated, the path leading to the common currency was envisaged as a gradual, near-equilibrium path. But the gradual path has run into unexpected obstacles. To continue on a gradual path will now lead in the opposite direction because there has been a trend reversal and we are now in a process of disintegration. Therefore we must find a different path. If we can't get there gradually, it is better to get there all at once than not to get there at all.

At the emergency meeting on August 1, an official from Portugal reportedly proposed that the introduction of a common currency should be speeded up. A German participant reportedly reacted by saying, "Surely, you must be joking!" If my line of argument is correct, it is time to take the suggestion seriously. This may sound a little too facile, and it is. My argument will be taken seriously only if I can show a path that would lead to a common currency. Since we are in dynamic disequilibrium, the path has to be a disequilibrium one. At present, the first priority of the French monetary authorities is to rebuild their reserves. In order to do so, they are trying to keep the French franc strong. That is wrong. The first priority ought to be to stimulate the French economy, and the maturity of the French debt to the Bundesbank ought to be extended for, say, two years so that France could lower interest rates *now*. When I say lower interest rates, I mean 3 percent. The rate reduction ought to be coordinated with the other members of the European monetary system, excluding Germany and Holland. The Deutschemark would undoubtedly appreciate. The overvaluation of the Deutschemark would have a negative effect on the German economy, hastening the decline in German interest rates. As the German economy weakened and the rest of Europe picked up, the trend in exchange rates would be reversed and they may eventually settle down not very far from where they were before the bands were widened. The main difference would be in economic activity. The rest of Europe would recover, first at the expense of Germany; but eventually Germany would also join the recovery. When that happened, the dynamic disequilibrium would have been corrected, and the march toward a common currency could be resumed in near-equilibrium conditions. The whole process would not take more than two years. After that, you could move to a common currency directly, without reinstituting the narrow bands. But you cannot get there in a straight line. Right now, you are caught in a vicious circle; you need to turn it around and make it a virtuous circle. This has already happened, up to a point, in Italy. It could be done in the rest of Europe.

I have not dealt with issues of foreign policy, the future of NATO, and the fate of Eastern Europe, but I have covered too much ground already. In any case, those issues are intricately interlinked with monetary policy. European monetary policy is wrong and it can be corrected.

Hedge Funds and Dynamic Hedging

The following is an edited transcript of testimony given to the United States House of Representatives Committee on Banking, Finance, and Urban Affairs, on April 13, 1994.

I welcome this opportunity to testify before your distinguished committee. I believe that the committee is right to be concerned about the stability of financial markets because financial markets have the potential to become unstable and require constant and diligent supervision to prevent serious dislocations. Recent price volatility, particularly in the market for interest rate instruments, suggests that it is appropriate to take a close look at the way markets operate.

A Different View of Markets

I must state at the outset that I am in fundamental disagreement with the prevailing wisdom. The generally accepted theory is that financial markets tend toward equilibrium and, on the whole, discount the future correctly. I operate using a different theory, according to which financial markets cannot possibly discount the future correctly because they do not merely discount the future; they help to shape it. In certain circumstances, financial markets can affect the so-called fundamentals

311

which they are supposed to reflect. When that happens, markets enter into a state of dynamic disequilibrium and behave quite differently from what would be considered normal by the theory of efficient markets. Such boom/bust sequences do not arise very often, but when they do, they can be very disruptive, exactly because they affect the fundamentals of the economy.

The time is not sufficient to elaborate on my theory. I have done so in my book, *The Alchemy of Finance*. The only theoretical point I want to make here is that a boom/bust sequence can develop only if the market is dominated by trend-following behavior. By trend-following behavior, I mean people buying in response to a rise in prices and selling in response to a fall in prices in a self-reinforcing manner. Lopsided trend-following behavior is necessary to produce a violent market crash, but is not sufficient to bring one about.

The key question you need to ask, then, is: What generates trend-following behavior? Hedge funds may be a factor and you are justified in taking a look at them, although, as far as my hedge funds are concerned, you are looking in the wrong place. There are at least two other factors which I consider much more relevant and deserving of closer scrutiny. One is the role of institutional investors in general and of mutual funds in particular; the second is the role of derivative instruments.

Institutional Investors

The trouble with institutional investors is that their performance is usually measured relative to their peer group and not by an absolute yardstick. This makes them trend followers by definition. In the case of mutual funds, this tendency is reinforced by the fact that they are open-ended. When money is pouring in, they tend to maintain less-than-normal cash balances because they anticipate further inflows. When money is pouring out, they need to raise cash to take care of redemptions. There is nothing new about this, but mutual funds have grown tremendously, even more than hedge funds, and they have many new and inexperienced shareholders who have never invested in the stock market before.

Derivatives

The trouble with derivative instruments is that those who issue them usually protect themselves against losses by engaging in so-called delta, or dynamic, hedging. Dynamic hedging means, in effect, that if the market moves against the issuer, the issuer is forced to move in the same direction as the market, and thereby amplify the initial price disturbance. As long as price changes are continuous, no great harm is done, except perhaps to create higher volatility, which in turn increases the demand for derivative instruments. But if there is an overwhelming amount of dynamic hedging done in the same direction, price movements may become discontinuous. This raises the specter of financial dislocation. Those who need to engage in dynamic hedging, but cannot execute their orders, may suffer catastrophic losses.

That is what happened in the stock market crash of 1987. The main culprit was the excessive use of portfolio insurance. Portfolio insurance was nothing but a method of dynamic hedging. The authorities have since introduced regulations, so-called "circuit breakers," which render portfolio insurance impractical, but other instruments which rely on dynamic hedging have mushroomed. They play a much bigger role in the interest rate market than in the stock market, and it is the interest rate market which has been most turbulent in recent weeks.

Dynamic hedging has the effect of transferring risk from customers to the market makers and when market makers all want to delta hedge in the same direction at the same time, there are no takers on the other side and the market breaks down.

The explosive growth in derivative instruments holds other dangers. There are so many of them, and some of them are so esoteric, that the risks involved may not be properly understood even by the most

313

sophisticated of investors. Some of these instruments appear to be specifically designed to enable institutional investors to take gambles which they would otherwise not be permitted to take. For example, some bond funds have invested in synthetic bond issues which carry a 10 or 20-fold multiple of the normal risk within defined limits. And some other instruments offer exceptional returns because they carry the seeds of a total wipeout. It was instruments of this sort which forced the liquidation of a $600 million fund specializing in so-called "toxic waste," or the residue of Collateralized Mortgage Obligations that generated a selling climax in the United States bond market on April 4th, 1994.

The issuers of many of these derivative instruments are commercial and investment banks. In the case of a meltdown, the regulatory authorities may find themselves obliged to step in to preserve the integrity of the system. It is in that light that the authorities have both a right and an obligation to supervise and regulate derivative instruments.

Generally, hedge funds do not act as issuers or writers of derivative instruments. They are more likely to be customers. Therefore, they constitute less of a risk to the system than the dynamic hedgers at the derivatives desks of financial intermediaries. Please do not confuse dynamic hedging with hedge funds. They have nothing in common except the word "hedge."

What are Hedge Funds?

I am not here to offer a blanket defense for hedge funds. Nowadays, the term is applied so indiscriminately that it covers a wide range of activities. The only thing they have in common is that the managers are compensated on the basis of performance and not as a fixed percentage of assets under management.

Our type of hedge fund invests in a wide range of securities and diversifies its risks by hedging, leveraging, and operating in many

314

different markets. It acts more like a sophisticated private investor than an institution handling other people's money. Since it is rewarded on absolute performance, it provides a healthy antidote to the trend-following behavior of institutional investors.

But the fee structure of hedge funds is not perfect. Usually there is an asymmetry between the upside and the downside. The managers take a share of the profits, but not of the losses; the losses are usually carried forward. As a manager slips into minus territory, he has a financial inducement to increase the risk to get back into positive fee territory, rather than to retrench as he ought to. This feature was the undoing of the hedge fund industry in the late 1960s, just as I entered the business.

The Quantum Group of Funds

I am proud to say that the Quantum Group of Funds, with which I am associated, is exempt from this weakness because the managers have a substantial ownership interest in the funds they manage. That is a key point. Our ownership is a direct and powerful incentive to practice sound money management. At Soros Fund Management, we have an operating history stretching over 25 years during which there was not a single occasion when we could not meet a margin call. We use options and more exotic derivatives sparingly. Our activities are trend bucking rather than trend following. We try to catch new trends early and in later stages we try to catch trend reversals. Therefore, we tend to stabilize rather than destabilize the market. We are not doing this as public service. It is our style of making money.

So I must reject any assertion or implication that our activities are harmful or destabilizing. That leaves, however, one other area of concern: we do use borrowed money and we could cause trouble if we failed to meet a margin call. In our case, the risk is remote, but I cannot speak for all hedge funds.

It has been our experience at Soros Fund Management that banks and securities firms exercise great care in establishing and monitoring our activities. As we mark our portfolios to market daily, and communicate with banks regularly they can easily monitor their credit exposure. I believe that it is a sound and profitable business for them and that our activities are a far sight simpler to monitor than most of their other activities.

Supervision and Regulation

Nevertheless, this is an area that the regulatory authorities need to supervise and, if necessary, to regulate. If regulations are to be introduced, they ought to apply to all market participants equally. It would be wrong to single out hedge funds.

And if it comes to regulations, beware of the unintended consequences! For instance, it may seem advisable to introduce margin regulations on currency or bond transactions, but that may drive market participants to the use of options or other derivatives which may be even more destabilizing. One of the driving forces behind the development of derivatives was a desire to escape regulation.

I should like to draw a distinction between supervision and regulation. I am for maximum supervision and minimum regulation. I should also like to draw a distinction between information gathering and disclosure. I think the authorities need a lot more information than the general public. In fact, information we are legally obliged to disclose has, on occasion, caused unwarranted price movements.

Let me conclude by saying that this is a propitious moment to assess the new risks created by new instruments and other new developments. Financial markets have recently suffered a serious enough correction that an inquiry is unlikely to precipitate the kind of dislocation which it ought to prevent.

I should like to emphasize that I see no imminent danger of a market crash or meltdown. We have just punctured a bit of a bubble that had developed in asset prices. As a result, market conditions are much healthier now than they were at the end of last year. I do not think that investors should be unduly fearful at this time.

This concludes my general remarks. I have answered your questions in writing and shall endeavor to answer any specific questions you may have now. Thank you Mr. Chairman, and members of the committee, for providing me this opportunity to share my perspective with you.

Questions

Q: We are the only country that has the privilege of paying our debts in our own currency. Should the dollar be replaced, then we would have to be paying this huge debt in somebody else's currency. Do you see that as anything that we should be worried about?

A: I think you are right to be concerned about this in a general and theoretical sense. But I don't see any imminent or practical danger. I think that the period of rapidly rising debt and rapid inflation is behind us and, I hope, not about to return.

Q: Top bank assets under management in bank trading accounts have grown over 500 percent over the past four years. In fact, they are considerably larger than the assets of hedge funds. In what ways do hedge funds compete with bank trading accounts?

A: We are basically customers of banks, not competitors. But they do have propriety trading accounts. They are more or less doing the same thing as we are doing, and I think it is an area of legitimate concern, and an area for close supervision, I would say.

Q: Do you have any advice for finance ministries? Should they leave the currency markets free or attempt to defend set values?

A: I am rather reluctant to give any advice. My views don't correspond to the views of most financial experts I believe that freely floating exchange rates are not sustainable in the long run. On the other hand, fixed exchange rate systems are liable to break down. The European monetary system worked very well for about 10 years, then it broke down because a dynamic disequilibrium developed after the reunification of Germany. I think the survival of the European Union depends on having a unified monetary system, but it is going to be difficult to get there.

Q: Many instruments that companies, hedge funds, and investment banks deal in are designed to limit risks of one kind or another. But does systemic risk increase or decrease? Would we be better off with somewhat smaller markets and somewhat less refined products? Or have we built up a quasi-gambling system?

A: The instruments of hedging transfer the risk from the individual to the system. As more of these instruments are used—because manufacturers and traders don't want to take a currency risk—more risk is passed on to the system. So there is a danger that at certain points you may have a discontinuous move. In currencies, you don't call it a crash, but an overshoot, a large move in the value of a currency.

Since the risk has been passed on from the individual to the system, it behooves the people who are in charge of the system to provide stability. When everybody is out for themselves, they can destroy the system. This is the point I'm really trying to bring home. There is this danger.

Q: What do you do about it? Governments don't have near the resources of the private sector actors.

A: I think the people in charge of the monetary system need to coordinate economic policies so that currency fluctuations are not too great; so that you don't have fundamental imbalances.

Q: Do hedge funds move markets?

A: I am sure that they don't because Soros Fund Management represents about 15 percent of the hedge fund industry. And we are probably more active in currencies than the average hedge fund. I'm sure that our average daily trading does not exceed $500 million. Now, that $500 million is a very large amount of money in absolute terms, but in terms of the $1 trillion or more that trades daily, it is something like four-tenths of 1 percent of the total volume. I think that puts it in perspective.

Q: You say that the banks can monitor their loans to hedge funds fairly easily; that they have good information; mark-to-market daily, and so on. And your investors are sophisticated, willing to take market risks and, presumably, could afford to lose their investment if that is what happens. So what's the public policy issue here?

A: We are subject to the same rules and regulations that apply to everyone as far as disclosure is concerned. So, for instance, our portfolio is available to the public the same way as any other large institutional portfolio. We have reporting obligations. If we own more than a certain percentage of a company, we have to report. So as far as markets are concerned, we are actually regulated in exactly the same way as any other institution. Where we are not regulated is in our relationship with our shareholders. In other words, there is no Securities and Exchange Commission protecting the shareholders against the misdeeds of the management. But since I am a large shareholder in the funds that I manage, I think that the shareholders have a protection that is more reliable than any regulation could possibly be—namely, I am putting my own money where I am putting their money. There is no need for shareholder protection in the case of this kind of partnership.

Q: You said in your testimony that you fully support more information sharing and more supervision.

A: I think that the authorities ought to be in a position to assess, let's say, the role of hedge funds in the recent market decline. They ought to be able to put their hands on some kind of information. And we certainly are ready to cooperate with them. I think it would probably be detrimental, however, if we were forced to disclose our positions more or less in real time. That would make it very difficult for us, and I think it would probably cause unwarranted trend-following by other investors, although they ought to know better. So I don't think that more disclosure would be good. But if the authorities feel they don't have enough information, we are certainly at their disposal to provide them with it.

Q: You warned us to beware of unintended consequences in designing regulations. Could you give us an example of where this principle could work to our disadvantage?

A: One of the obvious things one would think of is to introduce margin regulations for bond and currency transactions. There are no such margin regulations at the present time. There is a margin requirement for stock transactions. You have to put up 50 percent in cash. You don't have anything like it in fixed interest—in bonds. And yet bonds can also vary in price. So maybe there should be a margin requirement on bonds, perhaps of 5 percent or 10 percent. But if you establish too onerous a margin, then instead of buying bonds, investors will buy options on bonds, because that is a way to avoid putting up a margin.

Q: Are not derivatives materially changing in terms of their impact on the global and on the domestic market?

A: They are. A lot of new and more esoteric instruments have been brought into existence. There has been a remarkable shift of the terrain as far as derivatives are concerned. It is an appropriate area for investigation. If, for example, you look at recently developed instruments that separate interest from principal, they are very interesting instruments. But I am not quite sure that they are really necessary.

Q: What do you believe to be the regulatory implications of the growth of finance off-shore?

A: I think that any kind of regulation now needs to be international. The main regulation that has been imposed is the Bank of International Settlements' capital requirements, an international agreement. I think the issue that now needs to be addressed is capital requirements with regard to derivative instruments, and I think this needs to be addressed in an international forum.

Q: Is the banking industry sufficiently careful?

A: With every boom, there is a danger of excess, but I am not aware of any current excess of lending. In fact, I think that banks, having been hurt, are still in the comeback stage. Generally speaking, you can't accuse the banks of overlending. The difficulty has been to get them to lend.

Q: What are the lending sources for major hedge funds?

A: The major lenders are the money center banks. Investment banks are also a large source of finance.

Q: Are investment banks now lending more than the banks?

A: They're doing a significant amount of lending right now, but I still think banks are the primary lending institutions.

Q: Are mutual funds withdrawals a source of instability in the markets?

A: That is a point that I made in my testimony which I didn't develop. It concerns mutual funds. There was a very large flow of cash into mutual funds because certificates of deposits were yielding so little for so long. And that did create a bit of a financial bubble. I think that bubble has been broken and I think correction has occurred.

Q: Could you discuss what your fund does?

A: We engage in many different markets. We have a portfolio of stocks, and we also operate in bonds, some fixed interest instruments, and we do it on a worldwide basis. Therefore, we also have significant currency exposure. We use derivative instruments to a much lesser extent than generally believed, very largely because we don't really understand how they work. Since we are using borrowed money, we don't need to leverage through options very much.

INDEX